FAVORITE FOODS: NO-FAT COOKING

FAVORITE FOODS NO-FAT COOKING

BY NORMAN ROSE

A Division of WRS Group, Inc.
Waco, Texas

If you have coronary heart disease, diabetes, other health problems, or suspected health problems, please consult your physician before beginning any weight-loss program or undergoing drastic dietary changes.

This book is intended as a helpful tool, not as a substitute for conventional medical therapy.

First published in the United States of America in 1994 by WRS Publishing,
A Division of WRS Group, Inc., 701 New Road, Waco, Texas 76710.
Book and jacket design by Stephen Ott.

Owing to limitations of space, all acknowledgments for permission to reprint previously published material may be found on page 263.

10 9 8 7 6 5 4 3 2 1

Library of Congress Cataloging-in-Publication Data

Rose, Norman, 1935-
Favorite foods no-fat cooking / Norman Rose.
p. cm.
Includes index.
ISBN 1-56796-039-1
1. Low-fat diet—Recipes. I. Title.
RM237.7.R67 1994
613.2'6—dc20 94-13674
CIP

Dedicated to all those folks who have fought the fight against fat and failed. May you find your solution in the following pages.

"And ye shall eat old store, and bring forth the old because of the new."

—LEV. 26:10

TABLE OF CONTENTS

FOREWORD

One day several years ago, immediately after running in a local 10K race, I went over to a booth where you could get your cholesterol checked. Being a physician, one might think I'd know my cholesterol level, but at that time I didn't have the slightest idea what it was. At any rate, it came out to be almost 300, and I just about dropped through the ground. After a trip to The Cooper Clinic in Dallas and a consultation with Dr. Cooper that proved I did indeed have a genetically-inspired high cholesterol, I launched into a change in lifestyle eating that is still with me today. ❧ I'm often kidded that I eat nothing but hay and berries. In actuality, I don't eat that Spartan-like, but I do eat an essentially vegetarian diet with as low fat as I can manage, considering all the restaurant food I'm forced to eat as I travel. Needless to say, I'm a perfect candidate for Norman Rose's book because I'm always looking for something that tastes a little better without a lot of fat. ❧ As we learn more and more about nutrition, research bears out the suspicion that truly "we are what we eat," and that a large percentage of our present-day ills are diet-related. Coronary heart disease, several types of cancer, diabetes, and many other diseases are the direct result of a diet that contains too much fat and cholesterol. We just can't continue to eat the way most of us have been accustomed and expect to remain healthy. ❧ Norman Rose has based his book on his own tried and true methods of taking the fat and cholesterol out of the foods and recipes that we love. You will be amazed at how easy it is to transform your favorite "regular food" recipes into delicious, healthful ones that look and taste the same as you are used to. Can you imagine buttermilk biscuits that contain just four grams of fat in the whole pan? Or a cheeseburger that contains only six grams of fat? ❧ *We know what we need to do, and now Norman Rose shows us how to do it. You'll be surprised at how much easier it is than you ever thought.*

—WAYMAN R. SPENCE, M.D.
Founder and Chairman, Health Edco

AUTHOR'S NOTE

Writing about and teaching no-fat cooking has proven to be a truly satisfying vocation. I vividly remember the peaceful grin of a Kansas City heart-transplant patient as he eagerly consumed two no-fat chili dogs topped with melted cheese. And I'll never forget the letter from the grandparents of an eleven-year-old Minnesota girl who, after two open-heart surgeries, could not tolerate more than ten grams of fat a day. To these folks this book has proven to be a godsend. ❧ This book is a continuation of my first book. It is intended to make you a great no-fat cook, capable of turning out a full day's supply of wonderful food, while rarely exceeding twenty grams of fat per person, per day. ❧ You will learn to make perfect gravy every time, guaranteed, along with unbelievable nachos. And when the craving for medium-rare prime rib hits, you will have learned how to prepare it in a very healthful manner. ❧ The principles and techniques espoused in my book will result in a diet containing approximately ten percent of calories from fat. I do not tell you what to eat, but show you how to simply take the fat out. If you are one of the five-million-plus cardiac-event people, I know this is of prime importance. If you are too fat it will help you to lose fat. If indigestion is a problem, or you just want to feel better, then I suggest the low-fat approach to food preparation. ❧ To each person who reads this book, I wish a sincere and heartfelt best to you and yours!

Oftentimes, the first symptom of coronary heart disease is instant death.

—UNKNOWN

CHAPTER 1

FAT & OIL

Until you take the excessive fat and oils out of your diet, you are bound to fail in your attempts to control your weight permanently and to become physically fit.

All oils are pure 100 percent fat. All oils contain saturated fat, to some degree. Fat and oils make you fat. Therefore, if you are fat, oils and animal fats should be your number-one and number-two enemies.

Now that we have identified fat people's enemies number one and two, let's look at three fundamental truths that have evolved over the last several decades.

TRUTH NUMBER ONE

Your brain and stomach don't help much in your weight-loss or weight-control efforts.

When you substantially reduce the amount of food you consume each day, your body mistakenly "believes" that it is starving. It takes immediate action by slowing down the fuel-burning process (metabolism). The principles and techniques in this book will show you how to stop such negative communication because the stomach will be full and happy.

TRUTH NUMBER TWO

Most people are going to revert back to their regular, established menus after a diet with unfamiliar foods.

According to Dr. William Castelli, the director of the famous Framingham Heart Study, most Americans eat the same ten meals week in and week out.

Those ten meals, with rare exception, are very high in fat and provide fuel that is easily converted into stored body fat. What follows most diets is almost immediate weight gain, even though food volume may not be as large as it was prior to the diet.

Looking back over a lifetime, it is apparent that food-as-a-response-to-stress is introduced at birth, literally on day one. We cry, and something warm with food in it is stuck into our mouths. It doesn't matter what causes the crying, food is the quick solution. On through early childhood certain foods and menus become mainstays. During adolescence, menus are most certainly self-modified. Then during young adulthood and cohabitation, foods and menus seemingly become "etched in stone," as do eating habits in response to everyday stress.

People who avail themselves of weight-loss clinics, diet centers, and medically assisted programs for weight control are exposed to proper foods and positive directions for a sensible approach to weight control. However, many participants revert back to the old familiar foods once the direct supervision is removed.

If our foods, menus, and eating habits are in fact fixed by young adulthood or sooner then it is very difficult to change them. Where then are we to look for a successful approach to weight control after the diet? Let's look at the next "Truth."

TRUTH NUMBER THREE

When you eat no more than 20 grams of fat each day for women or 30 grams for men, it is difficult to gain weight unless you overdose on sugar and become truly sedentary.

Dr. Dean Ornish, in his landmark book, *Dr. Dean Ornish's Program for Reversing Heart Disease* (Random House), establishes that the average person needs only fourteen grams of fat each day. Unfortunately, the average person eats up to ten times that amount each day, and therein lies the problem.

If the problem is too much fat in the diet, then it follows that part of the solution is to take the fat out of the traditional daily diet.

CHAPTER 2

THE BAD EFFECTS OF EXCESSIVE FAT

Most Americans don't worry about heart disease until after "the big one," as the late Redd Fox would say. Likewise, you probably don't care that 80 percent of those people who have Type II diabetes are overweight, which contributed to the development of their disease. And if I tell you that high dietary fat has been linked to cancer, specifically of the breast, prostate, and colon, your internal response probably is, "but that won't happen to me." Now that I have given due effort to informing you of the really devastating fat-related diseases that can do you in, I ask that you read the next paragraph with a high degree of interest.

This paragraph is specifically directed toward you men who have a big inner tube of fat around your midsection and you women who now wear muumuus, tent-like dresses, and pregnant clothes even though you are not pregnant. *Dietary fat has made you look and act differently than you normally would look and act.* The "look" part is self-explanatory. The "act" part is not so evident to most people.

Too much body fat lowers your quality of life. The first thing to go is stamina, which is defined as "resistance to fatigue, illness, and hardship." Recently an NFL football team, in a dietary experiment, raised the level of fat in the team meals. Players were tested for treadmill performance before and after the high-fat regimen. Peak performance took a real drop after the inclusion of high levels of dietary fat. As soon as the fatty diet was discontinued, performance returned to original levels.

Stamina, as "resistance to illness and disease," has been clearly demonstrated in many research projects, the most notable study being about heart disease. High on the list of probabilities for overweight people are breast cancer in women and prostate cancer in men. Not only should you follow your doctor's directions for preventive measures, you should also follow common-sense prevention in the form of a low-fat diet.

Stamina, as "resistance to hardship," is well understood by most overweight folks. Many people eat when subjected to stress. Usually, the food is high in fat and promptly goes into storage as body fat. More stress, more food, more fat in storage. Pretty soon, all that fat in storage begins to create its own stress. The cycle becomes more treacherous, and a person is creating their own mental and physical hardships. Such hardships are directly linked to excessive dietary fat. A simple way to break this cycle is to lower the dietary fat content to about 10 percent of total calories. You will find it almost impossible to gain weight on a 10-percent–fat diet!

Finally, current research suggests that 75 percent of deaths due to heart disease and cancer could be eliminated by two simple prevention efforts—elimination of tobacco and incorporation of a proper, low-fat, balanced diet.

CHAPTER 3

THE BALANCING ACT

Bad eating habits die hard. Most of us who have poorly balanced diets formed our eating patterns at an early age. After having finished previous diet plans, have you found yourself straying back to the old foods?

Instead of trying in vain to eat new or different foods, why not find ways of preparing the foods you love in ways that are not fattening? This recipe book contains the secrets of preparing satisfying meals that look, taste, and satisfy the same cravings, yet help your body get back in balance.

As adults, we intellectually know that the four basic food groups are...

Protein
Bread
Fruits and Vegetables
Dairy

...but our behaviors insist that the four food groups are:

Cheeseburgers and Pizza
French Fries and Chips
Chocolate
Cakes and Sweets

If this is the way your instincts behave, you face two problems getting your diet balanced. The first is overcoming a lack of variety in the foods you consume. The second, and major problem, is the excessive fat content of your diet. In order to overcome the fat obstacle, you must learn to purchase and prepare fat-free foods that fit into your group of acceptable foods.

Getting back on balance is easier if we don't try to fight our food instincts head on, but gently nudge them in the right direction. This can be done by eating many of the same foods you enjoyed before, but prepared in ways that restrict dietary fat.

Chapter 3

FOUR REQUIREMENTS FOR FAT REDUCTION

The recipes included in this book seek to bring about weight loss by concentrating on four basic requirements. Think of them just as you would the four basic food groups:

Protein
Fat
Carbohydrates
Physical Exercise

Now let's explore these requirements.

PROTEIN

The average adult needs no more than two ounces of protein a day. Protein is required to build muscles, repair damaged tissue, and produce mother's milk.

All protein you consume in excess is converted by the body to fuel. (Unfortunately, protein is a very inefficient fuel.)

Highly publicized high-protein weight-loss programs get quick results, which our impatient, "I want it now" society demands. The problem is that much of the weight loss experienced occurs because of loss of muscle and water. Such diets result in temporary, unsatisfactory weight loss at best and, at worst, teach your body how to gain weight faster.

FAT

Fat is used almost exclusively for fuel to make the muscles work and provide prolonged energy to your body.

Your minimum daily requirement of fat is 14 grams (about one-half ounce); but don't worry about not getting it. In our society, that is practically impossible. With all the oils used in prepared foods, the average person consumes ten times the daily fat requirement without trying. That's why the recipes in this book include no added fat or fatty food ingredients.

Your body's fat reserve is a lot like a bank account that accepts deposits and withdrawals. If you are consuming 150 grams of fat each day and are neither gaining nor losing weight, it is safe to assume that you are using up 150 grams of fat each day. If tomorrow you consume only 20 grams of fat, your body will withdraw 130 grams from reserve to meet its current 150 grams daily "expenditure." This is in fact a fat loss of 130 grams a day, or about 2 pounds of fat loss a week. The recipes in this book will help keep your fat intake as low as possible, encouraging your body to tap into its fat reserve for its energy needs.

CARBOHYDRATES

For steady, prolonged physical activity, fat provides most of the fuel. But for explosive bursts of physical activities, carbohydrates are the principle source of energy. To illustrate, I like to compare the action of carbohydrates on the body to grain in a grain silo. In the Midwest, grain silos occasionally explode with amazing force. Carbohydrates in the form of wheat dust can be as explosive as dynamite when accidentally ignited in a grain storage facility. Your body uses carbohydrates in much the same way.

If you get your two-ounce daily requirement of protein and your fourteen-gram (one-half ounce) daily requirement of fat, then the rest of your energy requirements should come from carbohydrates. Your body readily converts carbohydrates into glucose, which is in turn used as fuel for the muscles and brain.

Good sources of carbohydrates are bread, potatoes, rice, corn, pasta, and beans.

Interestingly, beans, when combined with grains, also form an excellent source of protein. In some countries, beans and rice or bean tacos almost completely replace meat as a source of protein.

PHYSICAL ACTIVITY

The only way that fat is removed from the body is when it is needed as fuel for muscles. Muscles burn fat! In order to become an efficient fat burner, *you must increase your muscle mass*, especially those big muscles located in your calves, thighs, and buttocks. One of the best ways to develop those muscles is by simple, steady walking on a daily basis.

A regular walking routine should be your biggest priority. I don't mean speed walking and I don't mean a leisurely la-dee-da walk, but rather a steady walk. (About the speed you'd use walking to the next gas station after having run out of gas.) Your walk should last for at least twenty minutes at a time, and if possible you should walk five or six days a week.

An important note: Don't count the time you are on your feet in the course of your regular daily routine as exercise. You need to INCREASE the level of your exercise above and beyond what your body receives in a normal day.

If you want to build muscle mass and your fat-burning ability more rapidly, walk longer, not faster. Other activities such as tennis, golf, baseball, and swimming should be considered as fun and games, and NOT part of your minimum physical activity requirement.

Some people's minds are like concrete,

all mixed up and permanently set.

—ANONYMOUS

CHAPTER 4

GOOD CALORIES, BAD CALORIES, FAT AND THE MENU

I personally don't think in terms of calories. I think in terms of how many grams of fat per serving. My basic "fat" rule is: **NO MORE THAN 1 GRAM OF FAT PER SERVING.**

The only exception to this rule is meat, poultry, fish, and meat substitutes. For these items I try to observe the "one gram of fat per ounce" rule. This gives me my choice of:

(a) Breast of chicken
(b) Breast of turkey
(c) Venison
(d) Buffalo
(e) Low-fat fish
(f) Harvest Burgers®

I like beef, so occasionally I do indulge. However, beef sirloin (lean only, broiled) measures in at about 2.4 grams of fat per ounce, which means that a 6-ounce cut would contain about 14.4 grams of fat. As you will see later in this chapter, if you restrict your "filet" choices to chicken, turkey, venison, buffalo, fish, or Harvest Burgers®, then your entire day's consumption of fat is just 14.6 grams.

I like my "fat" rule because it is so simple. When I look at a label, I look for the amount of fat per serving that the product contains. If it says 1 gram or less, then it fits into the plan. If it says 2 grams or more, I put it down quickly and go on about my business. As you can see, all I need to be able to read is the word "fat" and understand the mathematics of the number "1," which is:

Fat = 1 gram = OK
Fat = 2 grams = DON'T BUY

This means I don't buy shortening, lard, cooking oil, butter, margarine, peanut butter, nuts, potato chips, corn chips, and other products that contain more than one gram of fat per serving. When adhering to this rule, I simply can't gain weight, and yet I eat a lot of really great food and I never feel deprived.

For those of you who feel compelled to count calories, you should know that all calories are not created equal, and you should learn the difference between fat calories and carbohydrate or protein calories.

Current research at Cornell University indicates that what you eat (not necessarily how much) is the main factor behind weight control. In the longest controlled human-feeding study ever undertaken, Cornell nutritionists have found that people on low-fat diets lose weight. What's more, people on low-fat diets continue to lose weight for months without suffering hunger pangs, cravings, or becoming depressed.

In the 22-week study, 13 women whose average age was 34 were asked to eat a carefully controlled regular- or low-fat laboratory diet, and their food intake and weight loss were monitored. The scientists found that the women on low-fat diets steadily lost weight—about one-half pound per week.

David Levitsky, professor of nutrition and of psychology at Cornell University, published results of the study in the May 1991 issue of the American Journal of Clinical Nutrition. Coauthors are lecturer Anne Kendall-Casela and senior research associate and adjunct professor of psychology Barbara J. Strupp, both of Cornell.

Previous studies have strongly suggested that when dieters reduce their carbohydrates or substitute artificial sweeteners for sugar they fully compensate for the resulting calorie deficits by eating more from other food groups, Levitsky explained.

"In our studies on low-fat diets, though, there's no evidence that less fat in the diet results in a person feeling more hungry, having food cravings, or compensating for the calorie deficit. Dieters can still eat ice cream, cookies, and pizza—just low-fat versions," said Levitsky.

The Cornell University low-fat diet allowed approximately 40–50 grams of fat per day.

Incidentally, every nutritionist in the world agrees on the issue of a low-fat diet.

The difference between a fat calorie and a carbohydrate or protein calorie is: During digestion the body uses much more energy in converting excess protein or carbohydrates into fat for storage. For example, if you eat 100 calories of carbohydrates that are not needed, then your body burns up about 25 of those calories when converting them to body fat. For each 100 calories of excess fat eaten, 97 are turned into body fat. This is an enormous difference! One gram of fat equals 9 calories, whereas one gram of carbohydrate or protein equals just 4 calories. Fat is a very dense source of energy, and if you subtracted 10 grams of fat at 90 calories from the diet and replaced it with 22.5 grams of carbohydrates at 90 calories, you could eat over twice as much (by weight). This fact makes for a happy stomach when you present the following 1600-calorie "diet" to a husky 200-pound man.

BREAKFAST
3 waffles
1 cup fresh strawberries, sliced
4 tablespoons maple-flavored syrup
coffee or tea

LUNCH
sweet & sour chicken on rice
fresh sliced vegetables
diet cola, coffee, tea, or water

DINNER (SUPPER)
6-ounce, bacon-wrapped filet
baked potato, sour cream, and butter sauce
vegetable/shrimp kabob with butter sauce
2 large, feather-light biscuits

For women looking for a 1300-calorie menu, just remove one waffle, half a baked potato, and one biscuit.

Let's itemize and analyze this menu and understand that purchasing and preparation are keenly important in controlling the amount of fat in any diet. If you buy wrong, you can't possibly eat right.

BREAKFAST	**GRAMS OF FAT**	**CALORIES**
3 waffles (frozen, fat free)	*1*	*240*
4 tablespoons of "lite" butter flavored syrup	*0*	*100*
1 cup of fresh strawberries, sliced	*0*	*45*
coffee/tea, plain or artificial sweetener	*0*	*0*
TOTAL	**1**	***385***
LUNCH		
sweet & sour chicken	*2*	*140*
rice (1 cup)	*0*	*225*
fresh sliced peppers, carrots, and celery	*0*	*30*
diet cola, unsweetened tea, water	*0*	
TOTAL	**2**	***401***
DINNER		
1 baked potato (8 ounces)	*0*	*220*
1 ounce "lite" sour cream	*2*	*30*
1 strip turkey bacon	*2*	*25*
6-ounce mesquite broiled filet	*6.6*	*318*
vegetable/shrimp kabob	*.5*	*40*
butter sauce	*0*	*0*
2 big biscuits	*1.5*	*200*
Total fat	*12.6*	
Minus fat loss during cooking	*-1.0*	
TOTAL	***11.6***	***833***

ANALYSIS

	FAT CONTENT	**TOTAL CALORIES**
BREAKFAST	***1 gram***	***385***
LUNCH	***2 grams***	***401***
DINNER	***11.6 grams***	***833***
TOTAL	***14.6 grams***	***1619***

Calories from fat = 131.4
Percent of calories from fat = 8.1 percent
Grams of saturated fat = 7.55
Percent of calories from saturated fat = 4.1 percent
Total cholesterol (with buffalo filet) = 160.6 mg

Once you get the hang of it, you will find that scrambled eggs (fat-free substitute), bacon, hash browns, and biscuits also fit into your breakfast menu. And sticky buns, Irish soda bread toast and jam, creamy oatmeal and scones, fresh fruit, cold cereals, bagels and cream cheese, along with steak and gravy over feather-lite biscuits. These are just some possible breakfast items. I'm sure whatever your favorite item is, it can probably be purchased and prepared fat free.

The selected lunch menu here was, in fact, left over from the night before. I find it is an easy solution to the problem of what to have for lunch. Just prepare enough the night before so as to allow for the number of lunches you'll need tomorrow. Zap it in the microwave at work. Lunch, you'll discover, could have been a chicken and green chili burrito, cold sandwich, hot sandwich, or any evening entree you've prepared.

The dinner menu has an almost unlimited number of possible combinations. If you are trying to eliminate cholesterol, your filet would be a cholesterol-free Midland Harvest Burger®. You would replace the shrimp with scallops and probably not eat the turkey bacon. If you crave red meat, I know you'll love farm-raised venison or buffalo. I'll tell you later in chapters 9 and 10 where and how to purchase these items that are so low in fat and cholesterol. Of course chicken, turkey, and fish, wrapped in bacon and grilled over a mesquite fire, are always good. When you get to the point where you can afford to eat another 300 calories, just throw in a slab of pie or a slice of cake—just make sure they are *fat free.*

Cooking and preparing this same menu the old-fashioned American way would have resulted in an extra 1,614 calories, bringing the daily total to 3,233. The fat content likewise shoots up like a sky rocket, adding an extra 126.8 grams of fat, for a total fat content of 141.4 grams. The good ol' American way provides 39.3 percent of your daily calories from fat, which puts many people in the intensive coronary care unit of the local hospital.

Any discussion of bad calories would be lacking without the inclusion of alcohol calories.

A good wine with good food can be soul-satisfying. A cold glass of beer on a hot summer day can be a welcome thirst-quencher. The New Testament exhorts us to "use a little wine for the stomach's sake and thine often infirmities..." I Tim. 5:12. If you look for justification for the use of alcohol, I'm sure you can find it; however, you should know a few pertinent facts about alcohol calories.

According to Paolo M. Suter, M.D., ("Ethanol and Fat Storage", Suter, et al, *New England Journal of Medicine,* Vol. 326, No. 14, April 9, 1992) alcohol *significantly slows the burning of fat* in your body. Three ounces of alcohol in a 24-hour period will reduce the amount of fat burned by about 50 grams. This equates to about three-fourths of a pound of fat placed in storage for each seven-day fishing trip with the beer-drinking buddies.

Another way to state the results of this study would be to say that three ounces of alcohol will reduce the number of calories burned by about one-third in a given day.

Apparently the body first burns the alcohol, then carbohydrates and protein, and lastly the body burns some fat and puts the rest in storage.

If you want to be a social drinker, you should attempt to substitute the alcohol calories for fat calories. Although you may be able to control your weight this way, your body-fat content will probably increase and tend to turn you into a jellyfish.

The one word to summarize alcohol consumption is *moderation.*

Chapter 5

SO YOU HAVE HIGH BLOOD CHOLESTEROL*

It has been estimated that *most* deaths due to heart disease and cancer could be eliminated by the mastering of two problems. Those two problems are tobacco and diet.

Anyone can develop high blood cholesterol regardless of age, sex, race, or ethnic background. But, because there are no warning symptoms or signs, you are likely to be surprised at such a diagnosis. Don't be alarmed, but do take it seriously. As with high blood pressure, most people are unaware that their blood cholesterol levels are high until they learn it from their doctor. And, like high blood pressure, it is a very real threat to your health.

If you have high blood cholesterol, there are some important facts you should know to protect your health. First, know how high your level is and what you can do to lower it. Then prepare to make some changes. Although these changes will depend on many factors considered by your doctor, modifying your diet is the preferred way to lower blood cholesterol.

High blood cholesterol is one of the three major risk factors for coronary heart disease (cigarette smoking and high blood pressure are the other two). In other words, high blood cholesterol can significantly increase your risk of developing heart disease. Fortunately, all three risk factors are "modifiable"; that is, you can do something about them. You can take steps to lower your cholesterol level and thus lower your risk for coronary heart disease.

High blood cholesterol occurs when there is too much cholesterol in your blood. Your cholesterol level is determined partly by your genetic makeup and the saturated fat and cholesterol in the foods

**Medical information in this chapter has been provided by the U.S. Department of Health and Human Services, Public Health Service, National Institute of Health.*

you eat. Even if you didn't eat any cholesterol, your body would manufacture enough for its needs.

The risk of developing coronary heart disease increases as your blood cholesterol level rises. This is why it is so important that you have your blood cholesterol level measured. Currently, more than half of all adult Americans have blood cholesterol levels of 200 mg/dl or greater, which places them at an increased risk for coronary heart disease. Approximately 25 percent of the adult population twenty years of age or older has blood cholesterol levels that are considered high, that is, 240 mg/dl greater.

Your doctor will measure your level with a blood sample taken from your finger or your arm and will confirm the result with a second test if it is greater than 200 mg/dl. The table on page 23 can help you see how the results of your total blood cholesterol tests relate to your risk of developing coronary heart disease.

A blood cholesterol level of 240 mg/dl or greater is considered high blood cholesterol. But any level above 200 mg/dl, even in the borderline-high category, increases your risk for heart disease. If your blood cholesterol is 240 mg/dl or greater, you have more than twice the risk of someone whose cholesterol is 200 mg/dl, and you need medical attention and further testing.

When your high blood cholesterol level is combined with another major risk factor (either high blood pressure or cigarette smoking), your risk for coronary heart disease increases even further. For example, if your cholesterol level is in the high category and you have high blood pressure, your risk for coronary heart disease increases six times. If you also smoke, your risk increases more than twentyfold. Other factors that increase your risk include a family history of coronary heart disease before the age of fifty-five, diabetes, vascular (blood vessel) disease, obesity, and being male. Whether your total blood cholesterol is in the borderline-high category or high category, you should make some changes in your diet to lower your level. More specifically, if your level is in the borderline-high category and you have coronary heart disease or two other risk factors for coronary heart disease, or it is in the high category, your physician will prescribe more aggressive treatment and follow your cholesterol levels more closely. If your cholesterol level is desirable, you should have your level checked again in five years and take steps to prevent it from rising.

CHAPTER 5

RISK FACTORS FOR CORONARY HEART DISEASE

- ***High blood cholesterol***
- ***High blood pressure***
- ***Cigarette smoking***
- ***Family history of coronary heart disease before the age of 55***
- ***Diabetes***
- ***Vascular disease***
- ***Obesity***
- ***Being male***

Most coronary heart disease is caused by atherosclerosis, which occurs when cholesterol, fat, and other substances build up in the walls of the arteries that supply blood to the heart. These deposits narrow the arteries and can slow or block the flow of blood. Among other things, blood carries a constant supply of oxygen to the heart. Without oxygen, the heart muscle weakens, resulting in chest pain (angina), a heart attack (myocardial infarction), or even death. Atherosclerosis is a slow, progressive disease that may start very early in life, yet might not produce symptoms for many years.

Lowering your high blood cholesterol level will slow fatty build-up in the walls of the arteries and reduce your risk of a heart attack. In fact, some studies have shown that, in adults with high blood cholesterol levels, for each one-percent reduction in total cholesterol levels, there is a two-percent reduction in the number of heart attacks. In other words, if you reduce your cholesterol level fifteen percent, your risk of coronary heart disease could drop by thirty percent.

DIET

Among the factors you can do something about, diet has the largest effect on your blood cholesterol level. *Saturated fat raises your blood cholesterol level more than anything else you eat.* Dietary cholesterol also increases your blood cholesterol level. If you have high blood cholesterol, changing your diet will be a very important step to lower it.

WEIGHT

Being overweight may also increase your blood cholesterol level. Most overweight patients with high levels of cholesterol can help lower their levels by weight reduction.

PHYSICAL ACTIVITY/EXERCISE

Although it is not clear whether physical activity can prevent atherosclerosis, regular exercise may help you control weight, lower your blood pressure, and increase your level of HDL-cholesterol, the "good" type of blood cholesterol.

GENETIC FACTORS

Genetic factors play a major role in determining your blood cholesterol level and can determine your ability to lower your level by diet. A small number of people have an inherited tendency to have a high blood cholesterol level. If you have a genetic disorder contributing to a high blood cholesterol level, then your parents, children, brothers, and sisters should also have their blood cholesterol levels measured.

SEX/AGE

Coronary heart disease is the leading cause of death and disability for both men and women in the United States. Estimates are that one out of five men and one out of seventeen women will have symptoms of heart disease before the age of sixty. This means that men have two to three times the risk of developing heart disease as women. However, in women as in men, cholesterol levels are predictive of coronary heart disease.

In the United States, blood cholesterol levels in men and women start to rise at about age twenty. Women's blood cholesterol levels prior to menopause (forty-five to sixty years of age) are lower than those of men of the same age. After menopause, however, the cholesterol level of women usually increases to a level higher than that of men. In men, blood cholesterol levels off around age fifty and the average blood cholesterol level declines slightly after age fifty. Since the risk of coronary heart disease is especially high in the latter decades of life, reducing blood cholesterol levels may be important in the elderly.

In addition, oral contraceptives and pregnancy can increase blood cholesterol levels in some women. For pregnant women, blood cholesterol levels should return to normal twenty weeks after delivery.

ALCOHOL

You may have heard that modest amounts of alcohol can improve your cholesterol profile by increasing your HDL-cholesterol level. However, it is not known whether the higher level produced by alcohol protects against coronary heart disease. With this in mind, and because drinking can have serious adverse effects, alcohol is not recommended in the prevention of coronary heart disease.

STRESS

Although stress has been reported to raise blood cholesterol levels, there may be other explanations for this effect. For example, during periods of stress people may eat more foods that are high in saturated fat and cholesterol, which may increase their blood cholesterol levels.

While all of these factors can influence your blood cholesterol level, clearly you can do something about a number of them. In fact, most people are able to lower their blood cholesterol levels with diet alone.

WHAT IS BLOOD CHOLESTEROL?

Cholesterol is an odorless, soft, waxy substance. Your body needs cholesterol to function normally (for example, as a component of cell membranes and for the production of many hormones, vitamin D, and bile acids, which are important for the absorption of fat). Cholesterol is present in all parts of the body, including the brain and nervous system, muscle, skin, liver, intestines, heart, skeleton, etc. The cholesterol level of your blood is affected by:

- ***The cholesterol your body produces***
- ***The saturated fat and cholesterol in your diet***

Cholesterol travels in the blood in packages called lipoproteins. All lipoproteins are formed in the liver and carry cholesterol through the body.

Blood cholesterol packaged in low-density lipoproteins (LDLs) is transported from the liver to other parts of the body, where it can be used. LDLs carry most of the cholesterol in the blood, and if not removed from the blood, cholesterol and fat can build up in the arteries contributing to atherosclerosis. This is why LDL-cholesterol is often called "bad cholesterol."

Cholesterol is also packaged in high-density lipoproteins (HDLs). HDLs carry cholesterol back to the liver for processing or removal from the body. HDLs, therefore, help remove cholesterol from the blood, preventing the accumulation of cholesterol in the walls of the arteries. Thus, they are often referred to as "good cholesterol."

If your total cholesterol level is either in the high category or in the borderline-high category and you have coronary heart disease or two other risk factors for coronary heart disease, your doctor will want a more complete cholesterol profile that includes LDL-cholesterol, HDL-cholesterol levels, and triglyceride levels. A blood test provides this information: You will have to fast for twelve hours prior to the test. (You may notice that your LDL- and HDL-cholesterol levels do not add up to your total blood cholesterol level. LDLs usually carry about 60–70 percent and HDLs about 25 percent of the total cholesterol in your blood. Other lipoproteins carry the rest.)

Some laboratories may calculate your cholesterol ratio. This measurement is actually just your total cholesterol or LDL-cholesterol divided by your HDL-cholesterol. For example, if your LDL-cholesterol level is 140 mg/dl and your HDL-cholesterol level is 35 mg/dl, your cholesterol ratio is 140/35 or 4. However, HDL-, LDL-, and total-cholesterol levels are independent predictors of your risk for coronary heart disease. Because combining these values into a ratio can conceal information useful to you and your physician, it is more important to know each value separately.

Along with your total blood cholesterol level, your LDL and HDL levels provide more information on your risk of developing coronary heart disease. A high LDL-cholesterol level or a low HDL-cholesterol level puts you at increased risk. LDL- and HDL-cholesterol levels more accurately predict your risk for coronary heart disease than a total cholesterol level alone.

If your doctor measured your LDL-cholesterol level, use the chart on the next page to see how your LDL-cholesterol level measures up.

Desirable Blood Cholesterol	Borderline-High Blood Cholesterol	High Blood Cholesterol
Less than 200 mg/dl	200 to 239 mg/dl	240 mg/dl and above

NOTE: These categories apply to anyone 20 years of age or older

If your LDL-cholesterol level is in the desirable category, you are at an acceptable level of risk. If your LDL level is in the borderline-high risk category, you could benefit from lowering your blood cholesterol level by making some dietary changes. If your LDL level is in the borderline-high risk category and you have coronary heart disease or two risk factors for coronary heart disease, you should begin diet treatment under your physician's supervision, as should a person in the high risk category. In general, this means you will be paying closer attention to your cholesterol level and making more dietary changes than a person at lower risk.

HDL-cholesterol will also be measured if your total blood cholesterol puts you in a high-risk category. The lower your HDL-cholesterol level, the greater your risk for coronary heart disease. Any HDL-cholesterol level lower than 35 mg/dl is considered too low. Quitting smoking, losing weight and becoming physically active may help raise your HDL-cholesterol level. Although it is not known for certain that raising HDL levels in this way will reduce the risk of coronary heart disease, these measures are likely to be good for your heart in any case.

HOW TO LOWER YOUR HIGH BLOOD CHOLESTEROL

The primary treatment for high blood cholesterol is a diet that is low in saturated fat and low in cholesterol. This new way of eating is also nutritious, with all the protein, carbohydrates, fat, vitamins, and minerals your body needs. To lower your blood cholesterol, you will:

- ***Eat less high-fat food (especially those high in saturated fat)***
- ***Replace part of the saturated fat in your diet with unsaturated fat***
- ***Eat less high-cholesterol food***
- ***Choose foods high in complex carbohydrates (starch and fiber)***
- ***Reduce your weight, if you are overweight.***

Saturated fats raise your cholesterol level more than anything else in your diet. Dietary cholesterol also raises blood cholesterol levels. Instead of eating foods rich in saturated fat and cholesterol, try more breads, cereals, and other foods high in complex carbohydrates, as well as more fruits and vegetables. Using unsaturated fats in place of saturated fats can also help lower your blood cholesterol.

Fortunately, these dietary changes work together. For example, eating less saturated fat may also help you decrease the amount of cholesterol you eat and may help you lose weight. This is because foods high in saturated fat are often high in cholesterol, as well as high in calories. In fact, all fats have more than twice as many calories as either carbohydrates or protein. And, by losing weight, if you are overweight, you can help lower your LDL-cholesterol level and increase your HDL-cholesterol level.

Saturated fats are found primarily in animal products, particularly fatty meats and many dairy products. Coconut oil, palm kernel oil, and palm oil (sometimes called the tropical oils) are also very saturated. Some of the unsaturated fats in vegetable oils are also made more saturated by a process called hydrogenation. Commercially prepared and processed foods made with these vegetable oils or with saturated fats like butter and lard can be high in saturated fat.

There are two kinds of unsaturated fat: polyunsaturated and monounsaturated. You should substitute both of these for saturated fat in your diet. Polyunsaturated fats are found primarily in plant products including safflower, sunflower, corn, soybean, and cottonseed oils; nuts, seeds, and fatty fish. Major vegetable oil sources of monounsaturated fats are primarily olive oil and canola oil.

Cholesterol is found only in foods of animal origin, both high-fat foods (like hot dogs and cheddar cheese) and low-fat foods (like liver and other organ meats). And the amount of cholesterol in these foods varies. A daily intake of less than 300 mg is recommended. A three-ounce piece of meat, fish, or poultry has 60–90 mg of cholesterol; one egg yolk contains about 270 mg; and a three-ounce serving of liver has about 390 mg of cholesterol.

Again, to reduce your blood cholesterol level, your diet should be low in fat, particularly saturated fat, and low in cholesterol. Use the following guidelines as you plan your new diet.

TO CUT BACK ON SATURATED FATS:

- ***Choose poultry, fish, and lean cuts of meat more often. Remove the skin from chicken and trim the fat from meat.***
- ***Drink skim milk, one-half percent, or one-percent milk. Eat cheeses with no more than 2–6 grams of fat per ounce (like low-fat cottage or low-fat farmer cheese) instead of processed, natural, and hard cheeses (like American, brie, and cheddar).***
- ***Use tub margarine or liquid vegetable oils that are high in unsaturated fat (like safflower, corn, and olive oil) instead of butter, lard, and hydrogenated vegetable shortening, which are high in saturated fat. Choose products that list more unsaturated fat than saturated fat on the label.***
- ***Cut down on commercially prepared and processed foods made with saturated fats or oils. Read labels to choose those low in saturated fats.***

TO CUT BACK ON DIETARY CHOLESTEROL:

- ***Eat less organ meat such as liver, brain, and kidney.***
- ***Eat fewer egg yolks; try substituting two egg whites for each whole egg in recipes.***

TO INCREASE COMPLEX CARBOHYDRATES (STARCH AND FIBER):

- ***Eat more whole grain breads and cereals, pasta, rice, and dried peas and beans.***
- ***Eat vegetables and fruits more often.***

TO LOSE WEIGHT:

- ***Eat fewer daily calories (cutting back on fat in your diet will really help).***
- ***Burn extra calories by exercising regularly.***

Remember, by closely following your diet and monitoring your progress with regular checkups, you can lower your blood cholesterol level and greatly reduce your risk of developing coronary heart disease.

Generally, both your total- and LDL-cholesterol levels will begin to drop 2–3 weeks after you begin your cholesterol-lowering diet. Over time you may reduce your cholesterol levels by 30–55 mg/dl or even more.

How much you reduce your blood cholesterol levels depends on how much fat, specifically saturated fat, and how much cholesterol you were eating before starting your cholesterol-lowering diet; how well you follow your new diet; and how responsive your body is to the diet. Also, the higher your blood cholesterol level is to begin with, the greater or more dramatic reduction you can expect with your new diet.

Your new cholesterol-lowering diet should be continued for life. While eating some foods high in saturated fat and cholesterol for one day or at one meal will not raise blood cholesterol levels, resuming old eating patterns will. Surprisingly, after a while your new way of eating won't seem like a diet at all, but simply like your regular routine—full of appealing and appetizing foods.

In most cases, a blood-cholesterol–lowering diet is the only step necessary to lower blood cholesterol levels. However, if your LDL-cholesterol level is still too high after you've been on your diet for six months, your doctor may decide to include medication as part of your treatment. In addition, if your cholesterol level is unusually high, or if you have other major risk factors for coronary heart disease, your doctor may prescribe medications to lower blood cholesterol even sooner.

If your doctor does prescribe medications, you must continue your cholesterol-lowering diet, since the combination may allow you to take less medication to lower your levels. And, because diet is still the safest treatment, you should always try to lower your levels with diet alone before adding medication.

❁ ❁ ❁

Need more help? Want to know more? There are many places you can go to get information about your new diet, your diagnosis, and the latest findings about treatment and medications for high blood cholesterol.

If you want some help following your recommended diet, talk to a registered dietitian or qualified nutritionist. They can explain the diet to you in greater detail and show you ways to follow it. They can give you advice on shopping and preparing foods, eating away from home and changing your eating habits to help you stay on your new diet. They will also help you set goals for dietary change so that you can successfully lower your high blood cholesterol levels without drastically changing your eating pattern and overall lifestyle all at one time. The Division of Practice of the American Dietetic Association (312-899-0040) can help you find a registered dietitian in your area. State and local branches of the American Dietetic Association, your local hospital, or your doctor can recommend a dietitian for you.

There are also other resources. The nurse in your doctor's office can answer questions you may have about your high blood cholesterol or your new diet. If your blood cholesterol level is not lowered within a reasonable amount of time, your doctor may refer you to a physician who is a lipid specialist. Lipid specialists are experts in the management of high blood cholesterol and other lipid disorders. If you have questions about drug therapy or the medication your doctor is prescribing, ask your doctor. Finally, pharmacists are also aware of the best ways to take medication, of ways to minimize side effects, and of the latest research about specific drugs.

If you would like more information to help you start your new approach to healthy eating, contact the National Cholesterol Education Program (NCEP) of the National Heart, Lung, and Blood Institute. Another NCEP pamphlet that can help you, "Eating to Lower Your High Blood Cholesterol," provides more specific information on how to lower your blood cholesterol levels through diet. NCEP also has developed a resource list of agencies and organizations that can answer your questions. These and other materials can be requested by writing to the National Cholesterol Education Program, National Heart, Lung and Blood Institute, C-200, Bethesda, MD 20892.

CHAPTER 6

SOYBEANS AND SOY PRODUCTS —A RICH SOURCE OF PROTEIN

Over 4,000 years ago, the Chinese discovered the value of the soybean as a readily available source of edible protein. Yet in the United States, the soybean's enormous potential as a nutritional resource remained virtually untapped until the 1920s, when U.S. farmers first began growing soybean crops in commercial quantities. Today more soybeans are grown in the United States than anywhere else in the world. In 1990, about 440,000 U.S. soybean farmers harvested 1.9 billion bushels of soybeans.

In a world faced with exponential population growth and rapidly dwindling resources, the soybean may provide a much-needed dietary miracle. It converts nutrients from the soil into quality edible protein with incredible efficiency, and it is the single largest nutritive source of both protein and oil in the world. Food technologists have extracted from the soybean an economical and highly nutritious food resource: soy protein.

The comparative cost of soy protein is significantly lower than other protein sources. For example, the cost of protein in ground beef is more than twenty times the cost of soy protein.

Furthermore, soy protein is acknowledged to be the highest quality form of vegetable protein and is one of the most abundant. The world produces more than 60 million metric tons of soybeans each year. The amount of soy protein produced per acre of land is a good indication of the soybean's value as a highly efficient source of edible protein.

For example, beef cattle grazing on one acre of land can produce 58 pounds of edible protein, enough to sustain a person for 77 days. The same acre planted in wheat can yield 180 pounds of protein, enough to sustain a person for 877 days. Yet one acre of soybeans can furnish 584 pounds of edible protein, enough to sustain an individual for 2,224 days.

Today thousands of soy protein products are on the supermarket shelves; they range from baby foods and formula to delicious entrees like cholesterol-free, all-vegetable Midland Harvest® Brand Burgers.

Midland Harvest Burgers® are becoming more and more available in supermarkets. If you can't find them in your supermarket, you can still order them by telephoning Harvest Direct, Inc., at 1-800-8-FLAVOR. This company also carries a full line of TVP® varieties.

TVP® is made by extruding or texturing defatted soy flour. TVP® is practically fat free and approaches the texture and chewy quality of meat. I have been involved in some serious debates over whether my Chile Con Carne and Spaghetti "meat" sauce were really fat free and truly meatless; they were, due entirely to the use of TVP®.

Here is a list of some available varieties:

(a) Ground Beef Style
(b) Strip Beef Style
(c) Chunk Beef Style
(d) Ground Poultry Style
(e) Chunk Poultry Style
(f) Flavored Ground Beef Style
(g) Flavored Chunk Beef Style
(h) Bacon Style Bits.

"Take thou also unto thee wheat, and barley,

and beans, and lentils, and millet

and fitches, and put them in one vessel

and make bread there of..."

—EZEK. 4:9

CHAPTER 7

EATING OUT

TRENDS IN EATING OUT

Americans are on the move. Busy lifestyles and tight work and travel schedules make eating out routine for many of us. According to recent surveys:

- ***Americans, excluding those who live in institutions, eat more than one of every five meals at away-from-home eating establishments.***
- ***Fast-food places serve four out of ten meals eaten at away-from-home eating establishments.***
- ***Four out of ten consumers say they have changed their eating habits to reflect nutritional concerns.***
- ***Adults eat roughly 30 percent of their calories away from home.***
- ***Americans spend more than 40 cents of every food dollar on food eaten away from home.***

What Guidelines Should You Follow When Eating Out or at Home?

The dietary guidelines for Americans are seven basic principles for developing and maintaining a healthier diet. The guidelines represent the best thinking in the field of nutrition information and education programs for healthy Americans. They were developed by the U.S. Department of Agriculture and the U.S. Department of Health and Human Services.

The dietary guidelines emphasize balance, variety, and moderation in the overall diet. The seven guidelines are:

- ***Eat a variety of foods***
- ***Maintain desirable weight (body fat content)***
- ***Avoid too much fat, saturated fat, and cholesterol***
- ***Eat foods with adequate starch and fiber***
- ***Avoid too much sugar***
- ***Avoid too much sodium***
- ***If you drink alcoholic beverages, do so in moderation***

Chapter 7

How does eating out affect your overall diet? That depends on where you eat, what and how much you order, and what extras you add to the foods you order—dressings, spreads, condiments, and so forth. Of course, how often you eat out is important, too. Where you eat out greatly affects the food choices available to you. It is a lot easier to follow guidelines-style eating at some restaurants than at others. For example, a greater selection of menu items gives you the opportunity to choose for variety. And if foods are prepared to order, you can have more control over the calories, fat, sugars, and sodium in your meal. Here's how eating places compare:

Full-service restaurants usually provide the greatest variety and flexibility in types of foods and preparation methods. Items are often prepared to order, so you can ask that foods be prepared differently than the menu specifies. One drawback of having foods prepared to order is the time it takes—what and how much do you eat while waiting for your order? For lunch in Kansas City, I choose The Soup Exchange because they offer good tasting, fat-free menu items. For dinner (supper to some) I might choose Bob Gaines Colony Steak House and Lobster Pot. I simply call ahead and tell them that I'm bringing my own butter and salad dressing. That is never a problem. When I arrive and order, I simply give my server a packet of Butter Buds® flavor granules so it can be served with my lobster. When my salad arrives, I whip out my small bottle of fat-free salad dressing and enjoy. Later, my boiled Maine lobster arrives with its bubbling hot "butter" for my baked potato and to dip my lobster in. I am apparently eating what everyone else is eating, however, my meal is essentially fat free! If I crave barbecue in Kansas City, I choose the Smokestack restaurant in Martin City. They grill everything over an open fire. I usually choose fire-grilled skinless boneless breast of chicken or fish, vegetable kebob also grilled, ranch beans (similar to recipe on page 207), and a tossed green salad with my own fat-free salad dressing. I simply ask that nothing is to be basted in butter or grease and I go real light on the wonderful beans. I am never deprived, nor do I stick out of the crowd. (I have my wife hide the dressing in her purse.) *Cafeterias, smorgasbords, and restaurant buffets also provide a wide variety of food selections.* Since foods are prepared in advance, there's no wait, but you are not able to order foods the way you want them. You do, however, have some control over portion size and the amounts of sauces, gravies, and dressings served with foods. Watch out for "all-you-can-eat" offers, though. You may be tempted to eat too much just to get your money's worth! Also, many cafeterias have fallen in love with butter-flavored oil which sometimes shows up in all of their vegetable dishes. Check it out! If it looks like green beans are swimming in grease, then they probably are. *Pizza parlors offer variety in toppings and crust types but an otherwise limited menu.* Toppings vary in calories, fat, and sodium content. Some parlors feature salad bars. In Kansas City, Gino Shiraldi's Pizza Company will always fix me a pizza with extra mushrooms, tomatoes, jalapenos, and some beef topping. I ask them to hold the cheese and oil and I end up with a super pizza. The beef topping at most pizza parlors contains TVP® and is much lower in fat than pepperoni or Italian sausage. *Convenience store "mini-meals" and vending machines are a growing source of food eaten away from home.* Offerings include chili, hot-dogs and Polish sausages, nachos with cheese sauce, prepackaged hamburgers and sandwiches, single-serving foods, candy, and snack foods. Fat, calories, sugars, and sodium are high in many of these items, especially in processed, prepackaged, and canned foods. Some refrigerated vending machines offer alternatives—yogurt, fruit, and fruit juices, for example. *Other people's homes can provide a real challenge to eating in the guidelines style.* How much control you have (or are willing to take) may depend on several factors, including the risk of offending your host or hostess! Buffet arrangements and informal parties permit you to be selective in what and how much you choose. However, there is often a tempting array of food and drinks that are high in fat, sugars, sodium, or alcohol. Family-style dinners may make it more difficult to avoid certain food selection, but you can still control serving sizes. Of course, formal sit-down dinners, where you're served a prepared plate of food, provide you with the least control. When people invite me to their homes to eat they understand that I have an ongoing battle with fat, so they always make provisions, usually in the form of breast of chicken, shrimp, or scallops. I suggest that when you are invited for dinner, be your own advocate and inform the person asking that you are, of necessity, on a very low-fat diet and inquire if this would cause embarrassment or undue problems. If not, then accept and enjoy the chicken. *Sub shops offer a varied selection of subs and sandwiches but usually little else.* Items are prepared to order so the amount of high-calorie, high-fat spreads can be limited. Sometimes smaller servings are available.

Many offer a variety of breads. Just make sure to stick to breast of turkey, breast of chicken, or lean beef. Skip the bologna, salami, and other fat meats. *Fast food restaurants offer an expanding but still rather limited menu.* Many items are deep-fat fried, including chicken and fish items, French fries, onion rings, and fruit pies. However, smaller servings are available for some sandwiches and side orders, and you can request that foods be prepared without sauces or other condiments. Salads, baked potatoes, and whole-grain rolls are now available at some fast-food restaurants, and low-fat milk and fruit juices are joining soft drinks and shakes as beverage options. Ask for a copy of the nutrition information sheet that most fast-food restaurants companies now offer. You'll be pleasantly surprised to find many with very low-fat items. Beware of Mexican food because they still insist on adding fat to refried beans, Spanish rice, and tortillas.

CHAPTER 8

THE IDEAL RESTAURANT

If, as a homemaker, you purchase and prepare food for others to eat, you are largely responsible for their long-term health, both physical and mental. When you make poor fat-filled food choices, oftentimes you inadvertently create a fat child that grows to become a fat adult with the attendant onslaught of various cancers and coronary heart disease. These food choices are made for the child at home, at school, and when eating out. You are responsible for what your children eat and their future health! If you have read this far, I assume that you have gained a lot of insight into no-fat cooking. I know you are well on your way to becoming a great no-fat cook, where everyone is happy with your food and no one feels short-changed or deprived. Eating out is a totally different matter, and to a certain extent you are at the mercy of the restaurateur. This chapter is designed as an aid to help you assist your local restaurateur in his effort to provide less disastrous food offerings. A guiding principal of my first book, *No Fat Please,* was that if you strive for a fat-free diet, you will actually end up with a low-fat diet from which approximately 10 percent of your calories will come from fat.

LOW-FAT DEFINITION

My understanding of the definition of a low-fat diet is as follows:

Various medical groups and associations have decided that 30 percent of your calories should come from fat, at least for the average person. If, from this, you categorize 30 percent as being "average" and you accept the current 45-50 percent as being "high" then it must surely follow that 10 percent is a good figure to be called a "low" fat diet.

Chapter 8

CURRENT MENU CHAOS

Current standards used in defining and designating certain foods as "low" fat are as variable as the wind. A good description would be wishy-washy. Consider the following terminology: ***Lo Fat, Low Fat, Low Calorie, Lean, Heart Healthy, Light, Lite.***

The first word, "Lo," is defined as Look! See! and the last word, "Lite," isn't even in my dictionary! Most items marked "Heart Healthy," or such, are in fact only "average" when it comes to fat content.

JUST NO FAT STANDARDS

Consider the dessert menu in *Figure 1* that I put together for a local upscale restaurant, and pay particular attention to the closing note. Also be aware of the fact that each menu item is clearly marked as to fat content. In this case each item is marked as containing less than one gram of fat per serving. Is this really possible? Not only is it possible, it is easy!

The displaying of the fat content per serving, and the guarantee that your host did not use any ingredients containing more than one gram of fat per serving, or with meat, fish, and poultry, one gram of fat per ounce is the standard that every restaurant should adopt when trying to serve low-fat menu entrees.

This standard is, in fact, only telling the customer what the restaurant owner is up to. If, in fact, a restaurant owner is just using low-fat descriptive words in an effort to increase his bottom line profit, while not providing pure low-fat menu items, then this becomes a disservice to his customers and is worthy of rejection.

The menu on page 41–45 is from a hypothetical restaurant that I put together as a topic of conversation for a popular Kansas City talk show. Please note that each low-fat entree carries the JNF symbol and that all entrees have the fat content clearly stated. When you eat at this restaurant there is no doubt about the fat content. It should also be pointed out that buffalo provides a truly low-fat red meat which makes most of the red meat entrees, especially the steaks, possible. Chapter 10 is devoted to buffalo and describes the taste as tasting like the best beef you've ever eaten. Everyone likes buffalo!

DESSERT OFFERINGS MOSTLY "JUST NO FAT"

JNF **STRAWBERRY SHORTCAKE**
AN OLD-FASHIONED SHORTCAKE SERVED WITH FRESH WHIPPED CHEESECAKE CREAM TOPPING AND PLENTY OF STRAWBERRIES PRESENTED ON A POOL OF STRAWBERRY SAUCE.
(CERTIFIED LESS THAN ONE GRAM OF FAT PER SERVING)

JNF **BLACKBERRY COBBLER**
A TRADITIONAL MIDWESTERN COBBLER SERVED WITH LOADS OF FRUIT AND HEAVY DESSERT CREAM SAUCE.
(CERTIFIED LESS THAN ONE GRAM OF FAT PER SERVING)

SUGAR-FREE ICE CREAM
SO RICH AND SMOOTH YOU WILL NEVER MISS THE SUGAR
(APPROVED BY THE AMERICAN DIABETES ASSOCIATION)

JNF **FAT-FREE ICE CREAM SUNDAE**
VANILLA ICE CREAM TOPPED WITH BERRIES-IN-SEASON AND OUR OWN CREAM FRAICHE. ASK YOUR SERVER ABOUT THE BERRIES.
(CERTIFIED LESS THAN ONE GRAM OF FAT PER SERVING)

JNF **FRUIT SORBETO**
SWEET, LIGHT AND REFRESHING. NO DAIRY PRODUCTS HERE. ASK YOUR SERVER ABOUT OUR FLAVOR OF THE DAY.
(CERTIFIED LESS THAN ONE GRAM OF FAT PER SERVING)

JNF **OUR SIGNATURE CHEESECAKE**
A TRADITIONAL RICH AND CREAMY TEXTURE WITH AN UNTRADITIONAL TWIST. WE HAVE TAKEN OUT THE FAT AND TOPPED IT WITH LUSCIOUS FRUIT. MADE EXCLUSIVELY FOR OUR RESTAURANT. ASK YOUR SERVER ABOUT OUR FLAVOR OF THE DAY.
(CERTIFIED LESS THAN ONE GRAM OF FAT PER SERVING)

JNF **CHOCOLATE DECADENCE**
FOR THOSE WHO CRAVE CHOCOLATE, WE OFFER CHOCOLATE POUND CAKE SITTING ON TOP OF A SCOOP OF CHOCOLATE ICE CREAM TOPPED WITH MORE ICE CREAM, CHOCOLATE SAUCE AND FRESH RASPBERRIES.
(CERTIFIED LESS THAN ONE GRAM OF FAT PER SERVING)

NOTE: JNF IS A REGISTERED TRADEMARK OF NORMAN ROSE COMPANY, INC., AND IS USED WITH PERMISSION.

BY THE USE OF THIS TRADEMARK YOUR HOST GUARANTEES THAT THE INGREDIENTS USED IN THE PREPARATION OF SUCH MARKED FOODS DO NOT EXCEED ONE GRAM OF FAT PER SERVING, AND WITH MEAT, FISH, AND POULTRY, 1 GRAM OF FAT PER OUNCE.

Figure 1

EDUCATING YOUR RESTAURANT OWNER/MANAGER

When you approach a restaurant owner or manager with your request for truly low-fat regular food, you will generally be met with a blank stare and his inability to understand what you are talking about. It is as though you are talking about baseball and he is talking about tennis. They are both sports, although vastly different. Until the restaurateur becomes educated, these vast differences will continue to exist.

OVERCOMING IGNORANCE

The quickest and best way for a restaurateur to become educated in the simple art of no-fat cooking is by enrolling in and graduating from the Kansas City No Fat Culinary Institute, which provides correspondence schooling and then two days of total immersion into the world of no-fat cooking in my kitchen. The correspondence portion is an education gleaned from this book and is the foundation for all Just No Fat cooking of regular food for regular people. Owners, managers, chefs, cooks, and just regular folks learn to prepare the broad spectrum of no-fat foods from creme fraîche to sausage gravy. Information and reservations can be obtained by writing directly to me:

Norman Rose
c/o Kansas City No Fat Culinary Institute
P.O. Box 8009
Prairie Village, Kansas 66208

THE KANSAS CITY BUFFALO COMPANY

APPETIZERS

JNF **SPICY BUFFALO SAUSAGE** **$5.95**
Combo served with cheese chunks, bread and spicy sauces (4 grams of fat per serving)

JNF **JERKY STRIPS AND CHEESE CHUNKS** **$4.95**
(2 grams of fat per serving)

JNF **NACHOS** **$4.95**
A great Southwestern treat (3 grams of fat per serving)

JNF **BUFFALO SAMPLER** **$8.95**
A unique taste of the Old West (3 grams of fat per serving)

ENTRÉES

All entrees are served with a pot of Hunter's Stew and choice of baked potato, mashed potatoes, smoked sweet potato, rice pilaf or ranch beans and warm homemade bread.
We serve only Promise® Ultra Non-Fat Margarine

STEAKS

(All meat is buffalo unless otherwise indicated)

JNF **BIG MIKE'S STEAK** **$19.95**
8-oz. sirloin grilled to perfection and topped with mushrooms and brown sauce (morels in season) (Entire dinner contains less than 14 grams of fat)

JNF **EDWARD ROSE STEAK** **$15.95**
8-oz. round steak, tenderized, sautéed and topped with cream gravy (Entire dinner contains less than 14 grams of fat)

JNF **JOHN COLTER STRIP STEAK** **$19.95**
8-oz. strip hickory grilled to your satisfaction (Entire dinner contains less than 14 grams of fat)

JNF **KIT CARSON FILET $22.95**
8-oz. mouth-watering tenderloin (Entire dinner contains less than 14 grams of fat)

MISS KITTY'S FILET (BEEF) $19.95
6-oz. lean Wisconsin beef tenderloin wrapped in turkey bacon and hickory grilled to your satisfaction (Entire dinner contains less than 16 grams of fat)

JNF **ROAST PRIME RIB $21.95**
8-oz. cut seasoned with our own secrets, then slowly roasted. Served with our own creamy horseradish sauce or raspberry sherbet (Entire dinner, lean only, contains less than 16 grams of fat)

OTHER MEAT ENTRÉES

JNF **POT ROAST AND GRAVY $14.95**
(6 grams of fat)

JNF **BEEF POT ROAST AND GRAVY $14.95**
(12 grams of fat)

JNF **TERIYAKI SIRLOIN EN BROCHETTE $14.95**
Tender cubes marinated with onions, new potatoes, peppers and pineapple served over brown rice (Less than 6 grams of fat)

JNF **STROGANOFF $14.95**
Lean pieces of round steak, simmered in a rich brown sauce with mushrooms and sour cream. Served over egg noodles (Less than 6 grams of fat)

JNF **TERIYAKI SHRIMP EN BROCHETTE $14.95**
Jumbo shrimp marinated, skewered with veggies and hickory grilled (Less than 5 grams of fat)

JNF **THE CHEF'S CATCH OF THE DAY $14.95**
(Ask server for fish variety) Served with mustard dill sauce (Fat content is always less than 10 grams)

JNF **SHRIMP ÉTOUFÉE** **$14.95**
For our Cajun friends we offer these jumbo shrimp smothered in seasoned sautéed onions and green peppers (Less than 5 grams of fat)

JNF **CHICKEN CHAMPAGNE** **$14.95**
Breast of Chicken in a creamy, savory champagne sauce (Less than 6 grams of fat)

JNF **CHICKEN EN BROCHETTE** **$14.95**
Chunks of white meat and veggies skewered and hickory grilled (Less than 6 grams of fat)

SOUTHWESTERN SPICY SPECIALTIES

Served with beans, rice, sour cream and warm corn tortillas.

JNF **GREEN CHILE CHICKEN** **$12.95**
Tender chunks of chicken breast in our zesty green sauce (Entire dinner contains less than 6 grams of fat)

JNF **CHILL VERDE** **$12.95**
Chunks of pork and beef simmered tender with green chilies and savory seasonings. Mixed with tidbits of Monterey Jack cheese just prior to serving. (Entire dinner contains less than 10 grams of fat)

JNF **CARNE ADOBADA** **$12.95**
Pork tenderloin marinated in our made-from-scratch red chile sauce, then simmered slowly. A favorite in northern New Mexico. (Entire dinner contains less than 8 grams of fat)

JNF **FILET TAMPIQUENA (4-OZ.)** **$15.95**
Hickory-grilled sirloin sliced thin on homemade bread, then topped with green chilies and cheese. (Entire dinner contains less than 6 grams of fat)

JNF **RED CHILE STEW** **$12.95**
Chunks of meat and potatoes swimming in a savory seasoned red sauce mixed with cubes of Monterey Jack cheese just prior to serving. (Entire dinner contains less than 5 grams of fat)

WORLD FAMOUS HUNTER'S STEW (JNF)

The trapper survived on the food he could catch, varying from buffalo meat in good times to skinny birds in lean times.
Try our stew—Buffalo makes it great!

HUNGRY HUNTER SPECIAL **$6.95**
(Bowl of stew, warm bread and salad) (Less than 6 grams)

DESSERTS

All our desserts are made with fat-free ingredients. Fat content, per serving in grams, is shown in parenthesis.

JNF HOMEMADE COBBLER OF THE DAY **$3.50**
with heavy dessert cream (Less than 1 gram)

JNF HOT CARAMEL DUMPLINGS **$3.50**
with heavy dessert cream (Less than I gram)

JNF BLUEBERRY, STRAWBERRY OR CHERRY CHEESECAKE **$3.50**
(Less than 1 gram)

JNF WHISKEY BREAD PUDDING **$3.50**
with bourbon sauce (Less than I gram)

JNF CHEF'S IN-SEASON SPECIAL **$3.50**
Ask about it (Always less than 1 gram)

WINES

We proudly feature only great American wines. Ask for a wine list.

BEER

We proudly feature the beers of KC's own local Boulevard Brewery.

*Buffalo is the meat of the 90s. Lean, tender, and very healthy. All our buffalo are raised in Beloit, Kansas, without the use of growth hormones or stimulants. Compare and decide, all statistics are based on a 100-gram sample (3.5 ounces).

TOP SIRLOIN

	BUFFALO	**ROASTED CHICKEN BREAST**	**BEEF**
Calories	*115*	*162*	*227*
Cholesterol	*55 mg.*	*85 mg.*	*88 mg.*
Fat	*2 grams*	*3.5 grams*	*19 grams*

FILET TENDERLOIN

Calories	*100*	*162*	*288*
Cholesterol	*55 mg.*	*85 mg.*	*98mg.*
Fat	*2.6 grams*	*3.5 grams*	*23.5 grams*

PRIME RIB (LEAN ONLY)

Calories	*100*	*162*	*382*
Cholesterol	*55 mg.*	*85 mg.*	*102 mg.*
Fat	*2 grams*	*3.5 grams*	*30.6 grams*

**Comparison based on USDA Research*

Note: JNF is a registered trademark of Norman Rose Company, Inc., and is used with permission. By the use of this trademark your host guarantees that the ingredients used in the preparation of such marked foods do not exceed one gram of fat per serving and in the case of meat, fish and poultry, 1 gram of fat per ounce.

CHAPTER 9

VENISON

In 1992, dramatic new evidence indicated that humans had crossed the Bering Straits and migrated at least as far south as Ft. Bliss (El Paso), Texas, by the year 28,000 B.C. and perhaps as early as 38,000 B.C. Those folks, as well as all other humans of that period, had adapted to a diet rich in vegetables, fruits, grains, grass seeds, and wild game. This was a diet very low in fat.

Most wild game is very lean due to the inability of the muscle meat to become marbled. As with turkey and chicken, wild game will become fat around the muscle, but not inside the muscle. Hence, when the exterior fat is removed, you've removed almost all of the fat.

For those who *must* have red meat in their diet, I strongly suggest New Zealand, farm-raised venison. Venison will allow you to return to one of the meat staples of your ancestors, a staple you were designed to operate on.

Once the fare of royalty, venison has recently gained new visibility and popularity among a growing number of chefs in America. These chefs are aiming to please discriminating diners on the lookout for healthy, flavorful alternatives to cholesterol-laden meats and high-calorie entrées.

Venison has been eaten for centuries, yet its nutritional benefits are a perfect match for an increasingly health-conscious modern society. This distinctive meat is higher in protein and lower in fat and cholesterol than lean beef, white or dark turkey meat, skinned chicken breasts, and even many seafoods.

Venison is often assumed to be a heavy, gamey-tasting meat obtained from deer captured in the wild. Actually, the majority of all venison served in restaurants around the world today comes from grass-fed deer raised on farms in New Zealand. The meat is delightfully mild but flavorful and extremely tender when prepared properly.

Venison can be obtained by calling Game Sales International, Inc., at (303) 667-4090.

Chapter 9

A NOBLE HISTORY

Today's farm-raised venison is a modern commodity that has evolved from an age-old tradition. Deer have been hunted by man since prehistoric times and were an important source, not only for food, but for tools and weapons fashioned from the antlers and bones of the deer.

European nobles depended on deer herds as a source of nourishment for their troops, but eventually cattle became more important for this purpose because they provided the high-fat content essential to soldiers who needed energy to stay warm during the winters.

For this same reason, beef became a food of peasants, while the leaner venison became a "royal food" for the gentry, who lived in warm, protected homes.

The influence of the early aristocratic connoisseurs of venison is still evident today in the type of venison dishes most commonly served by the world's finest restaurants. Royal palates preferred hearty, rich dishes. Lengthy marinating and heavy sauces were long considered necessary to increase the tenderness of the meat and cover up the wild game flavor and any inconsistencies created by the animal's age, composition, and diet. This is not necessary with farm-raised venison.

DEER INTRODUCED TO NEW ZEALAND

Deer were not found in New Zealand until the 19th century when the islands became a British colony. In the late 1800s and early 1900s, deer were brought to New Zealand from English parks and Scottish highlands to provide game for the English sportsmen who had settled there. No deer herds were native to New Zealand, but once introduced, the animals thrived under the ideal conditions—mild climate, plentiful food, and no natural predators.

Eventually, the rapidly multiplying herds became a problem. Hunters could not kill the deer quickly enough to stave off the problems they were creating in the forest and for farmers. These wild deer were causing a serious erosion problem and depleting the feed supplies on the lower hills, creating a food shortage for local livestock.

From the 1930s until the beginning of World War II, the government enlisted professional hunters to shoot the deer to stabilize the population and control the massive growth. The problem abated until the hunting was stopped during the war. Once again, the surplus deer became a problem.

In the 1960s, a few entrepreneurs recognized an opportunity to ship the deer to Europe where venison was traditionally a favored dish. Deer hunting eventually became so lucrative and sophisticated that helicopters were used as a foolproof method of capturing the animals.

Export tonnage surged to a peak of nearly 10,000,000 pounds in 1972. Ironically, once the European market for New Zealand venison was highly developed, supply began to be a problem. So many deer had been killed that the wild herds had been diminished to a point where helicopter hunting could no longer support the rapidly increasing number of operators.

Reluctant to turn their backs on a lucrative business opportunity, exporters turned to deer farming as a way to ensure future supplies of venison to newly developed markets. Helicopter operators switched from shooting deer to capturing them as foundation breeding stock for deer farms.

MODERN-DAY DEER FARMING IN NEW ZEALAND

The first license for a deer farm was issued in March 1970. Today, there are more than a million and a half deer on more than 5,000 deer farms throughout New Zealand.

Initially, New Zealand exported its product mainly to West Germany and European countries. But in the past 10 years, there has been a demand for venison in the United States. From 1976 to 1984, imports of New Zealand venison increased from 175,000 pounds to 600,000 pounds, with an estimated 1.5 million pounds of exports of New Zealand venison importing 1.2 million pounds, up 43 percent from 1989.

The deer are slaughtered in New Zealand, butchered, and conveniently packaged in an array of meat cuts to ship worldwide. More than 60 percent of the product today is shipped chill-packed for freshness. In the United States, venison is sold primarily to restaurants, but also increasingly to a growing number of specialty gourmet shops and meat stores in major cities.

U.S. chefs are beginning to recognize that venison offers substantial health benefits to Americans who love red meat, but who are becoming more concerned about trimming high fat and cholesterol diets. Surprisingly, venison is lower in fat, cholesterol, and calories than beef, skinned chicken breast, light or dark turkey meat, and baked salmon. In fact, venison offers 50 percent more protein than lean beef, with only half the calories.

Chefs at trendy, upscale American restaurants are experimenting with new ways of preparing venison, sans the heavy, rich, caloric sauces of the past. Some of the new dishes now available are: venison salads, grilled venison, venison kebabs, Cajun-style venison, etc.

Evolving from a food of kings to a food of the upscale and nutrition-conscious, venison promises to become a popular item in the American diet.

CUTS AVAILABLE:

1. ***Hind leg cuts can be purchased bone-in or boneless. Boneless leg cuts include topside, thick flank, rump, and silverside. Shoulder cuts are available mainly in boneless form and can be purchased from many suppliers as shepherd steaks or diced.***
2. ***Both shoulders and legs are good for steaks, schnitzels, kebabs, roasts.***
3. ***The saddle is traditionally considered the premier quality venison cut, offering the highest quality and requiring little trimming. Saddle is good for roasts, steaks, or fillets.***

PREPARATION:

- ***Keep raw meat refrigerated on a covered plate. Don't use plastic—the meat should not sweat.***
- ***Carefully remove any sinew or skin before pan "frying" or grilling. (Many cuts can be purchased fully de-sinewed.) Boneless cuts need to be separated into individual pieces by following the seam of each muscle and removing the silverskin. It is crucial to remove the muscle-coating skin for tender, quality steaks.***
- ***Always slice meat across the grain, not with it.***
- ***Allow up to 6–8 ounces of meat per main course serving and about***

3–4 ounces for smaller entrée portions and small plates.

- *Cook venison quickly, at high heat.*
- *Always serve venison rare or medium rare, because it is a lean meat. Medium or well-done venison can be tough and dry, unless cooked tender as in a stew.*
- *Cook steaks, medallions, and sautés at the last minute when everything else is ready.*
- *Never attempt to reheat venison except as an addition to the stew pot.*
- *A marinade involves three elements—acid, seasonings, and oil. The acid assists in tenderizing the meat; herbs, spices, and seasonings act to impart complementary flavors; and oil will allow the transfer of flavors through the meat. When marinating venison skip the oil and:*
  - *Marinate small cuts only briefly to complement flavor.*
  - *Marinate large cuts no longer than four hours.*
  - *Try wine, vinegar, lemon juice, beer, or buttermilk as a marinade for juicy venison steaks.*
  - *Tart fruits, such as kiwi fruit, pineapple, and raspberry make excellent marinades for venison.*

SERVING IDEAS:

- *Venison is excellent as steaks, roasts, charcoaled, or in kebabs, gyros, ragouts, salads, and sandwiches.*
- *Serve New Zealand venison kebabs, patties, or stir-fries with black rice, wild rice, or baked vegetables such as kumeras or potatoes.*
- *Make mountain man sandwiches with large loaves of French bread: Fill with grilled or roasted venison, steaks or patties, plum sauce or chutney, sour cream, sprouts, and sliced tomato.*
- *Serve barbecued venison with beer, champagne, or a chilled Gerwerztraminer.*
- *Use tart fruits as accompaniments in sauces for venison, or as light marinades to accent flavor.*
- *When venison dishes are richly sauced, serve noodles or bland potatoes as accompaniment.*
- *Accompany New Zealand venison dishes with a range of sweet to dry wines to suit your cooking style. Often, white wines enhance venison dishes.*

- ***Venison can be grilled over mesquite, stir-fried, wind-dried, roasted, and sautéed.***
- ***Venison is also tasty when served blackened Cajun-style.***
- ***Use venison to give Southwestern dishes an authentic and flavorful twist.***
- ***Venison can be a unique pasta filling for tortellini or ravioli.***

CHARCOALED MESQUITE VENISON STEAKS

Make sure everything else for your meal is ready and on the table before starting to cook your steaks.

Individual steaks are fine, but I like to cook one big thick steak and then slice it in 1/4" slices at the table.

Season your steaks with salt, pepper, or your favorite seasoned salt or a salt-free herb seasoning mix. Then place them over a hot mesquite charcoal fire and cook to a rare or medium-rare doneness.

NOTE: ***for a real New Mexico treat, dust each steak with a generous amount of chili powder or dry enchilada mix before charcoaling. Serve with Spanish rice and warm tortillas.***

SOUTH-WESTERN MESQUITE SMOKED VENISON

Generously coat a venison roast with chili powder, some salt, and insert a meat thermometer. Place meat on charcoal grill *away* from the direct heat of the charcoal and cover, allowing the smoke to circulate around the roast. Add *wet* mesquite wood chips periodically to create smoke. When thermometer indicates rare or medium-rare, remove and serve immediately. This smoking may take several hours. If impatience sets in, move meat closer to hot coals to expedite cooking.

HICKORY CAJUN VENISON STEAKS

Generously powder steaks with your favorite blackening spices and place them over a hot bed of hickory charcoal. Grill until rare or medium-rare and serve immediately.
NOTE: Can be cooked inside on a cast iron griddle or heavy skillet. Just be sure to cook steaks quickly. Serve with a baked potato, sour cream and chives, and a hearty warm bread.

VENISON SWISS STEAK

1 1/2 pounds venison round steaks
1/2 cup tomatoes, canned, chopped
1/4 cup onions chopped
1/4 cup beef stock or water
~ vegetable spray
~ season to taste

Pound steaks to tenderize and cut into serving-size pieces. In Dutch oven or heavy skillet that has been veggie-sprayed, brown steaks. Add remaining ingredients. Cover and simmer for 1 1/2 hours until tender. Stir often.

PINEAPPLE TERIYAKI VENISON

1 pound venison cut into 1-inch cubes
1/2 cup teriyaki sauce
1 cup pineapple chunks
1/2 cup pineapple juice
1/2 tablespoon cornstarch
~ vegetable spray

In Dutch oven or heavy skillet that has been veggie-sprayed, brown venison, add teriyaki sauce and pineapple chunks, and simmer until meat is done. (Medium-rare 5-10 minutes) Meanwhile, mix pineapple juice and cornstarch together and pour over meat. When thickened, serve over steamed rice.

VENISON-ONION ROAST

1 two or three pound venison roast
1 packet onion soup mix
~ vegetable spray

Preheat oven to 350° F. Brown roast in veggie-sprayed Dutch oven. Sprinkle with soup mix and cover with water. Bake until tender.

(Courtesy of Judy Hall, Lenexa, Kansas)

HUNTER'S STEW (VENISON)

4 OR 5 SERVINGS

1 *pound venison, cut into 1-inch cubes*
3-4 *medium potatoes*
1 *small to medium onion, chopped*
1 *can beef broth*
3 *cups water*
2 *tablespoons flour*
~ *vegetable spray*

Veggie spray a Dutch oven or heavy skillet, add meat, and brown. Sprinkle 1 tablespoon flour over meat and bottom of pan. Stir and continue browning until flour turns dark brown, but not burnt. Add 1/2 can of beef broth a spoonful at a time as the browning continues. When well browned, add water and onions. Cover and simmer until meat is tender. Add potatoes and continue simmering until potatoes are tender, about 30 minutes. Meanwhile mix 1 tablespoon flour and 1/2 can beef broth and pour into meat and potatoes. When thickened serve with fresh warm bread.

VENISON SMOTHERED IN ONIONS

1 *pound venison steak*
2 *medium onions, sliced*
~ *flour*
1 *can beef broth*
1 *teaspoon vinegar*
1/4 *teaspoon thyme*
1 *small bay leaf*
1 *teaspoon parsley*
1/2 *teaspoon garlic*
~ *water*
~ *vegetable spray*
~ *salt and pepper to taste*

Over medium/high temperature in a veggie-sprayed Dutch oven or heavy skillet, place onions on one side and 1 teaspoon flour over the other side and brown. When flour is brown add floured and seasoned steak. Brown meat and turn over. Add beef broth, vinegar, thyme, bay leaf, parsley, garlic, and enough water to just cover the meat. Reduce temperature to where the meat is just simmering and cook for about 2 hours until meat is tender. Serve, topped with onions, with mashed potatoes, (page 137), your veggie choice, and warm fresh bread.

CHAPTER 10

BUFFALO

It tastes like the best beef you've ever eaten! Forget gamey, sweet, or other peculiar tastes. It simply tastes like a well-aged prime piece of beef, and if you spring a cookout featuring T-bones, rare to medium-rare, your guests will wolf them down with thanksgiving gusto. Now if you don't tell them what they are eating, they will undoubtedly enjoy it more and be the better for it. Even when you've gone so far as to let your guests select their steak, they will marvel at the attractiveness of the meat and relish the flavor. If you crave red meat and the doctor says no, no, then you should definitely consider buffalo. Here is why: 70 percent less fat and 50 percent less cholesterol.

HOW IS THIS POSSIBLE?

The benefits of buffalo meat lie in the basic nature and biological or genetic attributes of buffalo.

BUFFALO MEAT DOES NOT MARBLE!

"Marble," meaning fat in the muscle. When you see a lean cut of buffalo, you can believe that it is lean. About 97.2 percent lean, or just under 1 gram of fat per ounce of roasted lean meat (according to the Human Nutrition Information Service of the USDA). The fat content of lean buffalo meat puts it in the same category with chicken or turkey breast meat. However, buffalo clearly wins the cholesterol battle. Three ounces of roasted buffalo has just 39 mg of cholesterol, compared to chicken breast at 73 mg, turkey breast at 72 mg, and beef at 79 mg. For you "clogged-arteries" folks, buffalo makes a lot of sense, and it should make sense for those who don't have (or want) clogged arteries.

WHERE TO BUY

The Denver Buffalo Company, Denver, Colorado, 1-800-BUY-BUFF
Butterfield Buffalo Meat Company, 1-800-321-5528
(In Kansas City, I buy my buffalo from McGonigles Market, 1307 W. 79th Street)

COOKING TIPS

Buffalo is cooked in much the same way you would cook beef, with only a couple of important differences. You shouldn't cook a buffalo steak well done because it gets tough; if cooking stews or soups, it takes longer for the buffalo to reach the tender stage. Steaks or roasts should be rare or medium-rare.

The lack of fat guarantees that your buffalo will cook faster than beef. Since fat is an insulation, and not present in buffalo, the meat cooks quicker. Well-marbled beef cooks slower, pound for pound, than lean commercial-grade beef. Since buffalo lacks marbling, the meat has a tendency to be done well before what you are used to. In this regard, it takes some trial and error to effectively master this quick-cooking phenomenon.

When broiling buffalo, move your rack about a notch farther away from the heat; that way it will be done in about the same amount of time.

If you would normally roast your beef at 325° F., turn the heat down to 275° F. for buffalo, and plan on the roast being done in about the same amount of time.

When roasting, always use a meat thermometer and remove when rare to medium-rare for best results.

Ground buffalo is also leaner than what you are used to. You should figure about 10 percent fat; in a 1/4 pounder that means about 11 grams of fat per serving. The thicker the patty, the juicier the meat.

A very interesting taste develops with the combining of chicken broth and buffalo. I demonstrate it in the green chili burrito and the smothered minute steaks. I don't think any finer-flavored foods are available anywhere, and for them to be healthy and good for you is an amazing extra.

Steaks recommended for grilling include minute steaks, rib eyes, T-bones, and New York strips:

Sear both sides of your steak on a hot grill to keep the juices in the steak, then you can lower the heat on the stove or move the meat to a cooler spot on the outdoor grill.

Don't use a fork when turning meat; use tongs instead. That way the juices stay inside your steak.

When cooking a roast, low temperatures and moist heat is recommended. Remember, your roast is best cooked either rare or medium-rare. The next step after medium-rare requires a lot of cooking time to reach the fork-tender stage.

Don't be apprehensive about preparing buffalo. Use as a direct substitute for fatty beef and have a healthier heart for your effort. Enjoy.

GREEN CHILE BUFFALO BURRITO

- 1 *pound buffalo meat cut into small bite-size pieces*
- 1 *can chicken broth*
- 2 *Anaheim green chili peppers, chopped*
- 1 *medium onion, chopped*
- ~ *salt and pepper to taste*
- ~ *water to process*

In saucepan, brown meat. Add chicken broth, 1/2 of the green pepper and 1/2 of the onion. Simmer for hours, adding water as needed, until fork-tender. Cook down the juice until the bottom of pan is just covered and add remaining peppers and onions. Continue to simmer until peppers are tender. Season and serve with warm flour tortillas.

MESQUITE SMOKED BUFFALO ROAST

- ~ *Buffalo roast with all visible fat removed*
- ~ *salt and pepper to taste*

On outdoor grill, place roast that has been peppered (but not salted yet) away from mesquite fire. Cover grill and allow to smoke meat for at least an hour. Place roast over fire and allow to brown on all sides and add salt. When you think that the meat is about done, insert meat thermometer. When center of meat is rare to medium-rare, remove and serve.

ONION-SMOTHERED BUFFALO MINUTE STEAKS

FOR TWO

2 *minute steaks, tenderized, seasoned, and floured*
1 *large onion, sliced*
1 *can chicken broth, defatted*
~ *flour*
~ *salt and pepper to taste*
~ *vegetable spray*

In large veggie-sprayed skillet on medium-high heat, place onion slices and grill for 2 or 3 minutes, push over to one side, and splash on top of onions 3 or 4 tablespoons chicken broth. Place steaks in skillet and brown. After turning once, splash on several tablespoons of broth under steaks, allow to cook off and brown but not burn. Mix 1 tablespoon of flour to remaining broth. Stir until smooth and pour into skillet. Stir as gravy thickens. Remove steaks when just barely done to your satisfaction. Top with onions and gravy and serve.

RED CHILE CON CARNE BUFFALO

FOR TWO

1 *pound buffalo roast, cut into bite-size pieces*
1 *dry red chili, seeds removed*
~ *water to process*
~ *salt to taste*

In heavy saucepan or Dutch oven, brown meat thoroughly. Add water to cover meat by at least 1 inch and add chili broken in pieces. Simmer for 4 or 5 hours adding water as needed. When meat is very tender, allow water to boil down until meat is not quite covered. Salt to taste and serve with warm tortillas. Note: For a more fiery chili, leave the chili seeds in.

Chapter 11

EQUIPMENT

I assume that most folks reading this book have access to a pretty well-supplied kitchen. Therefore, I will point out a few items that I find indispensable in the preparation of a full fat-free menu that you may not have.

CAST-IRON COOKWARE

Non-stick cookware doesn't hold up under the strain of no-fat cooking. Cast-iron cookware, when seasoned and used in conjunction with a nice, strong, stainless steel pancake turner, is practically indestructible. Cast iron can be purchased at your local discount department stores and is priced quite reasonably.

When preparing meats that need to be floured and then browned, it is crucial not to burn the drippings and flour. For example, a fricassee, a ragout (ra-goo), soups, stews, and many Cajun dishes require a well-browned flour for color and seared meat for flavor. This can be accomplished easily in cast-iron cookware. Depending on the number of people for whom you are cooking, I would recommend a selection from the following:

- ***Small Dutch oven with top, 10-inch diameter x 4 inches deep***
- ***Large Dutch oven with top, 13-inch diameter x 5 inches deep***
- ***Large skillet, 12-inch diameter x 2½ inches deep***
- ***Medium skillet, 10-inch diameter x 2 inches deep***
- ***Small skillet, 7-inch diameter x 2 inches deep***
- ***Griddle, 10-inch diameter***

A Dutch oven is just a cast-iron pot with a lid. It can be placed close to an open fire for baking bread or simmering a hearty stew. I use the large Dutch oven in preparing whole turkeys with stuffing and for big family get-togethers.

To season your cast-iron cookware: Just coat lightly with vegetable oil and bake the pans empty at 300° F. for an hour. Don't put oil on the outside of the pans when seasoning. This procedure results in a non-stick coating closely resembling commercial non-stick cookware.

The big difference is that if you scratch the coating on your seasoned pan, you can always re-season it by coating lightly with oil and baking it again.

Tips on cast-iron cookware maintenance: First, don't wash it in an automatic dishwasher. Second, don't allow really acidic foods like tomatoes to stand very long in a cast-iron pot. Third, never put your cast-iron cookware away while it is wet as it will rust. Cast-iron pots always add minute amounts of dietary iron to your food. This is considered an advantage for those folks who need extra iron.

STAINLESS STEEL WHISK

A 12-inch whisk is regularly used to blend flour (which is used as a thickening ingredient) and liquid. Since we no longer make a roux in the traditional sense of adding flour to grease, we now must mix our flour in another liquid. These liquids can be water, milk, broth, etc. After the flour and liquid are mixed in a bowl with a whisk, they generally are then added to whatever we wish to thicken.

Egg whites can be quickly broken down into a liquid with a quick whisking.

STAINLESS STEEL PANCAKE TURNER

Invaluable in preparing hash browns, burgers, pancakes, etc.

STAINLESS STEEL SKEWERS

You should get to know "kebobs," if you are not already acquainted with them.

PORTABLE ELECTRIC HAND MIXER

You need a mixer of some sort. An inexpensive hand mixer works well with a minimum of clean-up and storage time.

SPRING-FORM PAN

If you don't make cakes, you won't need this, but if you want an occasional cheesecake, you will. (See our recipe.)

Chapter 11

STAINLESS STEEL MIXING PANS

If you are going to make bread, you need mixing pans. I recommend a set of three, measuring in diameters of 10 inches, 13 inches, and 16 inches. When making bread for two, I generally use the 13-inch pan and do the kneading right in the pan. I don't like to clean up a floured board or countertop if I don't have to.

CHAPTER 12

NO-FAT QUICK COOKING

One-half the time spent being a cook is used in cleaning pots, pans, and the kitchen in general. This chapter will help you eliminate a lot of clean-up and some preparation time.

The basic idea is to prepare a complete meal in the skillet or Dutch oven, which not only cooks all the ingredients, but doubles as a serving dish also. Electric crock-type cooking has been well-expounded on in other books and is an excellent cooking method for soups, stews, and beans.

I'll give you a few examples, and then you can let your imagination create those meals that appeal to you.

FISH FILETS, BROCCOLI, & GOLDEN SAUTE™

FOR TWO

In large skillet bring water required for one package of Lipton® Golden Saute™ to a boil. Add dry ingredients, place fish filets on top and broccoli florets around edges. Cover and simmer until fish flakes. Sprinkle fish with paprika, place skillet in center of dining table and enjoy.

MEAT STEW & DUMPLINGS

FOR TWO

In veggie-sprayed Dutch oven, brown enough meat or poultry cut into bite-size pieces for two people, add one cup water, and a handful each of your favorite frozen veggies. Simmer until tender and add one can chicken broth to which has been added one tablespoon of flour. Place one can of low-fat biscuits on top of stew, cover and simmer for 20 minutes. Garnish and serve.

BAKED BREAST OF CHICKEN, STUFFING, VEGGIES, & GRAVY

In Dutch oven prepare one box stuffing mix. Push to one side and place three or four cups of large cut chunky veggies such as carrots, broccoli, cauliflower, etc. Spoon stuffing on top of veggies and place seasoned chicken on top of stuffing. Add one tablespoon flour to one can of defatted chicken broth and pour into bottom of pan. Cover and bake in 350° F oven for one hour. Remove to dining table and serve. ※

BLACKENED FILETS, CAJUN RICE, & KALE

FOR TWO

In medium veggie-sprayed skillet, place two filets covered with blackening spices. (Filets could be turkey breast, chicken breast, venison, buffalo, or beef eye of round) Sear meat, cook until done, and remove. In same skillet, place water required to cook one packet of Lipton® Cajun Rice, add a couple of handfuls of fresh leafy kale or spinach, and boil for five minutes before adding rice. Push greens off to one side and add rice and follow directions. When rice is done, place filets on top with a couple of thick slices of homemade bread, cover and allow to warm. Serve. ※

SAUTÉED MEAT, RICE, BEANS, & YAMS

In medium veggie-sprayed skillet, brown your choice of tender meat or poultry. Add ½ can chicken broth and simmer until meat is done. Remove meat. In same skillet with meat juices prepare one packet Lipton® Rice & Beans with sauce. Add a drained can of yams to one area of the skillet and cook until rice is done. Put two thick slices of bread on top of rice along with cooked meat, garnish, and serve. ※

MEAT, POTATOES, & WHOLE KERNEL CORN

In medium veggie-sprayed skillet, brown meat (your choice of very lean items), add a chopped small onion and 1/2 can chicken or beef broth. Push meat and onion off to one section of skillet and place three medium potatoes cut to bite-sizes. In skillet add one cup water, cover and simmer until potatoes are done. Combine one tablespoon flour to 1/2 can broth and pour over potatoes. Continue simmering uncovered until gravy is thickened. Push potatoes together in order to make room for one small can of well-drained canned corn. Remove from heat, cover and allow corn to warm. Garnish with fresh parsley and serve.

OPEN-FACE BARBECUE SANDWICH

FOR TWO

In small veggie-sprayed skillet, brown filets of choice, adding a small amount of chicken broth to facilitate browning. Allow broth to cook off, leaving a brown residue as meat cooks. Add 1/2 can chicken broth and two thick slices of a big onion (break down into onion rings). Simmer until onion rings are tender and meat is done. Top the filets with 1/4 cup of your favorite barbecue sauce allowing to mix with onions and broth. Uncover and simmer slowly until sauce is thick, remove from heat.

At the table, spoon filets onto 3/4 inch thick slices of fresh bread and top with onion and barbecue sauce.

I'm sure by now you realize that you have only one pan to clean up. That's nice and it saves time.

Chapter 13

THE 10 MASTER TIPS TO GUARANTEED NO-FAT COOKING SUCCESS

TASTE/FLAVOR

No-Fat food must be real food!

These 10 master tips will assist you in presenting real food at the dinner table. The no-fat food you prepare should be bursting with flavor, and it should taste exactly like its fat-filled relatives. Contrary to public opinion, fat has almost no flavor. If you don't believe me then just eat a big spoonful of shortening. No taste, no flavor there. FAT ADDS NO FLAVOR TO YOUR FOOD. The flavor of meat comes from the blood and juices contained in the meat. If you roast a chunk of meat, cover it with boiling water, cool, and then skim off the fat, what you'll discover is that the remaining liquid contains all the flavor you expect to find in gravy made from roasted meat drippings, sans fat!

TEXTURE

Your no-fat food must "feel" like the real thing when you eat it. A buttermilk biscuit must tear apart and have the "bite" of its fatty cousin. Scrambled eggs must be scrambled. A hot dog must "snap" when you bite it and ice cream must feel creamy. Give some artificial crab meat to a crab cake eater from the Chesapeake Bay area. He will tell you it has somewhat the taste of crab meat, but it doesn't "feel" like crab meat and it doesn't look like crab meat. To some it is an acceptable substitute, but to many it is not even close.

CHAPTER 13

APPEARANCE/PERCEPTION

Your no-fat food must "look" like the regular food you are used to. Your sausage gravy on the top of biscuits should be perceived as just that—biscuits and gravy. A no-fat chili dog topped with melted cheese should be unmistakably a chili dog topped with melted cheese. A thick, dark brown Cajun gumbo should appear the same regardless of the fat content. Taste, texture, and appearance are easy to learn, as you will see. Some say it is simple after attending my standard two sessions of No-fat Cooking 101. Those two sessions consist of the following menus and fat analysis:

FIRST SESSION
NO-FAT COOKING - 101
MENU

BREAKFAST

Buttermilk Biscuits

Sausage Gravy

Omelet

Smoked Sausage

LUNCH

Beef Burritos

Beans & Cheese

SUPPER

Pizza

DESSERT

Cake with Berries & Cream

FIRST SESSION FAT ANALYSIS

MEAL (FOR TWO)	TOTAL GRAMS OF FAT	GRAMS PER SERVING (½ Total = 1 serving)
BREAKFAST		
Biscuits	2.5	1.25
Gravy	Trace	~
Scrambled Eggs	0	~
Smoked Sausage	7	3.5
Cheese	Trace	~
LUNCH		
Beef Burrito	10	5
Beans & Cheese	2	1
SUPPER		
Pizza Crust	3	1.5
Pizza Sauce	Trace	~
Veggies	Trace	~
Cheese	Trace	~
Meat Toppings	11	5.5
DESSERT		
Cake	Trace	~
Ice Cream	Trace	~
Chocolate Sauce	Trace	~
Berries	Trace	~
TOTALS	36 Grams	18 Grams

SECOND SESSION
NO-FAT COOKING-101 MENU

BREAKFAST

Butter Pecan Cinnamon Rolls

LUNCH

Nachos

Chili Dogs

SUPPER

"Fried" Buffalo Steak

Mashed Potatoes and Cream Gravy

DESSERT

Cherry or Strawberry Pie

SECOND SESSION FAT ANALYSIS

MEAL (FOR TWO)	TOTAL GRAMS OF FAT	GRAMS PER SERVING (1/2 Total = 1 serving)
BREAKFAST		
Butter Pecan Cinnamon Rolls	3	1.5
LUNCH		
Nachos	2	1
Chili Dogs	10	5
SUPPER		
"Fried" Buffalo Steak	8	4
Mashed Potatoes	Trace	~
Cream Gravy	Trace	~
DESSERT		
Cherry or Strawberry Pie	0.5	0.25
TOTALS	24	12

The recipes and techniques for each of these entrées are provided in this book with two exceptions: First, the scrambled eggs are egg whites that have been colored with a few drops of yellow food coloring, or fat-free egg substitutes. Second, the smoked sausage is fried smoked sausage from Healthy Choice®. We use 7 ounces of this sausage, and with 1 gram of fat per ounce, this comes to just 7 grams of fat. We use some for breakfast and some as a topping for our pizza. We also cook plenty of sausage for our sausage gravy (see page 73). The meat toppings for our pizza are listed as containing 11 grams of fat. These toppings consist of 4 ounces of extra lean beef (4 grams of fat) and 7 ounces of smoked sausage (7 grams of fat). From the appendix you will find that 2½ cups of white flour contains

$2\frac{1}{2}$ grams of fat, and egg whites are fat free. Other no-fat items are listed as containing a "trace" of fat. If you eat enough "traces" you'll end up with a gram of fat or more, and that is the reason this total is different than the sum of the parts.

TIP NUMBER ONE

Purchase only items containing one gram of fat or less per serving, and with meat, fish, and poultry, 1 gram of fat or less per ounce.

Almost everything contains some fat or oil. For practical reasons let's lump these two items together and call them fat. Even your drinking water can contain fat. As an example, I relate how a brand new swimming pool when filled with water for the first time displayed small beads of rainbow colored fat floating on the surface. It wasn't much, but it was there, and it is found in almost everything you eat. So when you see the words Non-Fat, Fat Free, etc., it is really a misnomer. There is some fat in "them thar" cookies or sour cream or whatever. However, when you reduce this fat to less than $\frac{1}{2}$ gram per serving, by government regulation, you may call them Fat Free or Non-Fat. If you adhere to this rule, you will lose fat (if you are too fat) without ever dieting. Dieters, Dieting, Diet! These words rarely bring joy to those involved, and oftentimes create more problems than they solve!

Instead of dieting, just take the fat out and keep it out!

This tip will increase your food bill by *3%–5%* but will automatically reduce your percent of calories from fat to approximately 10%.

TIP NUMBER TWO

Purchase a set of cast iron cookware.

Thin bottomed cookware just won't get the job done. Heating is uneven and foods tend to stick and burn. Thick-bottomed stainless steel with wooden handles doesn't work well in the oven when you want to make a deep dish pizza or giant crepe for a pastry crust. Also the wooden handles turn to charcoal in the oven. For what to purchase see chapter 11, then wander on in to your friendly store and buy some cast iron cookware.

TIP NUMBER THREE

Purchase and use Wondra® Quick-Mixing Flour from Gold Medal® for perfect gravy every time.

The very first thing I teach my students to cook is sausage gravy! In fact, some folks have attended class just to learn how to make this gravy. This gravy is loaded with flavor, has the right texture, and looks like real sausage gravy. I like to brown the ground beef, which results in a light brown gravy. If you want a whiter gravy don't brown the meat. Wondra® Quick-Mixing Flour is a joy to use. If you looked at regular flour under a magnifying glass it would appear to have jagged edges; however, Wondra® flour appears to have rounded edges. These rounded edges allow you to sprinkle Wondra® in a boiling liquid without it clumping and becoming unsightly. Just sprinkle, stir, and thicken. It's that simple.

SAUSAGE GRAVY

FOR TWO

- 1/4 *lb. Healthy Choice® Extra Lean low-fat ground beef*
- 1 *teaspoon ground sage*
- 1 *teaspoon chicken bouillon*
- 1 *teaspoon beef bouillon*
- 1 *tablespoon Thick & Chunky salsa*
- ~ *black pepper to taste*
- ~ *ground red pepper to taste*
- 1/8 *cup water*
- 1 *cup skim milk*
- ~ *Wondra® Quick-Mixing Flour added to desired thickness.*

In a small (8 inch) cast iron skillet cook first seven ingredients over high heat. If you desire a rich brown gravy then be sure to brown meat mixture thoroughly. After browning add water to loosen brown glaze on the bottom of the skillet. (It's called "de-glazing" your pan). Add skim milk and begin adding Wondra® Quick-Mixing Flour. Stir, and cook until desired thickness is obtained, then cook an additional 3 minutes. For double the amount, just double the ingredients.

(I put this following recipe below because biscuits certainly go with sausage gravy.)

BUTTERMILK BISCUITS

- 2 1/4 *cups self-rising flour*
- 1 *cup Buttermilk*
- ~ *veggie spray*

Preheat oven to 400° F.
In a large 13-inch stainless steel

mixing bowl combine ingredients, mix and form into a ball, Press, flatten and shape ball into a 9 inch diameter disc, which lies in the bottom of the mixing bowl. Cut into biscuits and place in a 9-inch veggie-sprayed cake pan. Bake for 20 minutes. (The whole pan of Biscuits contains less than 4 grams of fat!)

TIP NUMBER FOUR

Store your Chicken Broth in the refrigerator.

Since canned chicken broth is such a wonderful source of flavor, purchase plenty of it and store it in the refrigerator. Chicken broth contains fat, and by cooling it, the fat congeals on top and can be easily removed. Spooning the congealed fat into the garbage results in the most efficient fat-loss program in the world!

CHICKEN GRAVY

- 1 *$10^1/_2$ ounce can chicken broth*
- 1 *fat-free saltine cracker, crumbled*
- 1 *teaspoon flour*
- ~ *pepper to taste*
- ~ *Wondra® Quick-Mixing Flour to desired thickness*

In a small cast iron skillet over medium high heat, brown crumbled cracker and flour. Stir frequently to keep from burning. When well browned add chicken broth. Thicken with Wondra® Quick-Mixing Flour. For cream gravy, add some evaporated skim milk.

TIP NUMBER FIVE

When cooking with no-fat cheese always use high-moisture heat.

Pizza should be topped with thick, stringy cheese. The secret here is when to put the cheese on the pizza. When pre-heating your oven, place a cookie sheet in the bottom of your oven. Prepare your pizza but don't add the cheese yet. Bake pizza for 15 minutes and remove from oven. Top with shredded no-fat mozzarella cheese and place back in oven. Splash 1/4 cup hot water into cookie sheet on bottom of oven. Close oven door and allow resultant steam to heat and melt cheese. Remove when done and serve. Your cheese will appear to be and act like regular cheese.

When Healthy Choice® came to market with a two-pound, non-fat pasteurized process cheese product, it became possible to make really great non-fat nachos. Let's define our nachos as corn chips with chile con queso, otherwise known as chiles with cheese. Of course, in the free-wheeling realm of Tex-Mex cooking, you can put anything on a pile of corn chips and call them nachos. Recently, at a popular Mexican restaurant, I saw a six-inch high pile of corn chips covered with: ***(a) chili con carne, (b) jalapeno peppers, (c) chopped onion,(d) black olives, (e) diced tomatoes, (f) melted cheese with green chiles (chile con queso), (g) sour cream.***

On the menu, this item was listed as an appetizer priced at $6.95. If you desire this type nacho, use the chili recipe on page 159, purchase fat-free sour cream such as Land O'Lakes® no-fat sour cream, and skip the black olives. The recipe for corn chips is on page 171 and the chile con queso recipe follows:

CHILES CON QUESO (CHILES WITH CHEESE)

- 1/4 *cup Thick & Chunky salsa*
- 1/2 *lb. Healthy Choice®; non-fat pasteurized process cheese product*
- 1 *Anaheim fresh green chile, chopped (Use jalapenos if you like hotter)*

In a small cast iron skillet, over medium heat, cover bottom with salsa and green chile pepper. Dice cheese over salsa and peppers, allow salsa to come to a gentle simmering boil. Cover and turn heat off. Allow cheese to melt, turning heat back on, if necessary. Remember, you want moist heat to melt the cheese. Slow and gentle is better than fast and furious.

TIP NUMBER SIX

When craving medium-rare or rare red meat, buy some Buffalo.

It tastes like the best beef you've ever eaten. It is much higher in protein and the lean red meat is much, much lower in fat than beef. The fat that does show up in the lean portion is much higher in polyunsaturated fats and much lower in saturated fats. Lower in fat than breast of chicken or turkey, buffalo would appear to be a near perfect food for humans. Besides, a buffalo never gets cancer, I'm told. When traveling through Denver, Colorado, I always try to arrange my schedule to include a meal at either the Mountain Man Steakhouse in Commerce City or the Denver Buffalo Company in downtown Denver. Both are excellent and both specialize in buffalo steaks. If you can't find a close-by source for buffalo meat you can call:

Butterfield Buffalo Meat Co., 1-800-321-5528, or
The Denver Buffalo Company, 1-800-BUY-BUFF

Ask for a free catalog and explore a whole host of buffalo and buffalo meat products. Very interesting!

TIP NUMBER SEVEN

For Cajun greatness learn to make a roux without grease.

The problem with Cajun food is the cook that prepares it!

Most cooks believe that the only way to prepare a roux (pronounced "rew" as in crew) is to combine flour and grease and heat until mixture is brown and has a nutty flavor. This brown color and flavor is essential to many Cajun dishes.

To obtain the brown color and toasty flavor without using grease is actually quite easy. When I say "brown the flour" in a recipe, I suggest you simply place flour in a cast iron cooking utensil, turn the heat on and stir until degree of browness is obtained. I guarantee you that it will toast and brown, and if you heat it long enough it will turn black. Somewhere between brown and black, remove your pan from the heat and add something to stop the browning process. If you burn the flour, start over. No one likes burnt flour.

TIP NUMBER EIGHT

Learn where to purchase and how to use textured vegetable protein, otherwise known as TVP®.

TVP®, made from soybeans, can provide the texture factor in many no-fat recipes, while adding almost no flavor or fat. It can be the ground beef in a chili recipe or it can become pecan nut meats in our Butter Pecan Cinnamon Rolls on page 212. TVP® is the great mimic of the food world as it can take on the appearance and absorb the flavors of many diverse foods. The advantage, of course, is the fact that TVP® contains only a trace of fat! Read chapter 6 for more information.

Most health food stores sell TVP®. If you can't find it locally you may want to telephone Harvest Direct at 1-800 8-FLAVOR. Ask for a free catalog. This company carries a full line of TVP® varieties.

TIP NUMBER NINE

Learn how to dilute fatty foods.

Of all the food groups, desserts are among the easiest to make no-fat! When a new no-fat product becomes available, you should give some thought as to how you can use it to create "new" regular no-fat dishes. As an example on page 242, I use a one-gram-of-fat-per- serving, "light" brownie mix in order to create a chocolate cherry cheesecake that ends up containing about 1½ grams of fat per serving. This same brownie mix is also used to make chocolate-covered cherry cookies and chocolate raisin cookies. The sugar cookie recipe on page 246 demonstrates how you can take a reduced fat or "lite" or "light" cake mix and further reduce the per-serving fat content by adding self-rising flour, sugar, and egg whites. If, for instance, your cake mix contains 2 grams of fat per serving and you add an equal amount of fat-free ingredients, the per-serving fat content is lowered to one gram per serving. Another example would be to purchase a "lite" or "light" blueberry muffin mix, prepare as directed, and then add an additional cup of big, plump, juicy fresh blueberries. Folks eating these muffins will delight in the extra berries and you have automatically reduced the per serving fat content.

TIP NUMBER TEN

Learn to serve the flavor.

I know this tip sounds a bit strange, but please bear with me. Many times a cook will throw away a flavorful portion of the item being prepared. In my first example, it is the browned juices and small particles of meat from an all-beef patty. This browned material is a source of intense flavor and should be served on the cheeseburgers. Generally, cooks throw this away. The following cheeseburger, when prepared as directed, will be more flavorful than what you are used to eating.

CHEESE BURGER

FOR ONE (6 GRAMS OF FAT)

- 1/4 *lb. Healthy Choice® Extra Lean Low-Fat ground beef*
- 1 *slice fat free cheese*
- 1 *teaspoon granulated chicken bouillon*
- ~ *black pepper to taste*
- 4 *tablespoons water*
- ~ *Wondra® Quick-Mixing Flour*
- ~ *fat free bun*
- ~ *slice tomato, pickle, onion, and lettuce as desired, along with catsup, mustard, and fat-free mayonnaise.*

In a small cast iron skillet over medium-high heat, place 1/4 lb. beef pattie and sprinkle with chicken bouillon and black pepper. Cook to desired doneness, top with cheese, and remove from skillet. To skillet add water to loosen browned meat and juices from the bottom of pan, sprinkle with Wondra® flour to thicken to consistency of gravy. If needed, add more water and cook for two minutes; then remove from heat. You should now have a small amount of dark brown gravy in your skillet. Use this gravy to moisten each bun half by swishing bun half in the gravy. Place cheese-topped meat pattie on bun half, garnish and flavor as desired. Serve hot.

A second example of throwing the flavor away would be the discarding of leftover charcoal-cooked pieces and parts. If you cook a bone-in buffalo sirloin or T-bone, save the bone by freezing it and use the excellent flavor for your next gumbo, jambalaya, or ranch beans. To get that smoked flavor into your Cajun dishes, you should always add several extra links of Healthy Choice® smoked or Polish sausage to the grill when cooking outside. Add some hickory chips to the fire and allow sausage to become well infused with this hickory flavor. Somehow a goodly portion of this sausage always ends up on someone's plate instead of in my freezer. The water used to boil potatoes or other veggies can be used as the flavorful start of a soup or stew. Leftover veggies always go well in soup, and, unfortunately, they are often allowed to turn to garbage in the refrigerator and thrown out.

CHAPTER 14

RECIPES & PREPARATIONS

RECIPE ANALYSIS

The individual analysis of each of over 400 recipes was deemed to be a very redundant exercise. From a logical perspective, if you strictly adhere to the purchasing principles expounded in earlier chapters *(i.e., buy only products which contain no more than 1 gram of fat per serving or with meat, fish and poultry products, no more than 1 gram of fat per ounce)*, then the following recipes should provide you with a diet that derives less than 10% of its calories from fat.

APPETIZERS

Fat-free appetizers can make a positive statement at any function, whether a cozy fireside meal with your mate, the local bridge club, or a corporate Christmas party. ❧ *Cold appetizers can be presented on fat-free crackers, breads, or as dips. Vegetables such as mushrooms, celery, or cherry tomatoes may be stuffed early in the day, covered with plastic wrap, and refrigerated.* ❧ *Hot appetizers should be prepared later, towards mealtime, and in sufficient volume.*

DIPS & SPREADS

A plate of icy-cold raw vegetables is always appropriate, appreciated, and they won't spoil your appetite. Serve with these tasty no-fat dips and spreads.

ONION DIP

- ~ *Lipton® dehydrated onion soup mix*
- ~ *no-fat sour cream*

Mix and blend quantity to taste. For more color add chopped green onion tops.

MEXICAN SOUR CREAM DIP

- 1 *cup no-fat sour cream*
- 2/3 *cup fat-free mayonnaise*
- 1/3 *cup your favorite chunky salsa or taco sauce*
- 1/2 *teaspoon minced garlic*
- 2 *tablespoons minced sweet onions*
- 1 *tablespoon chopped parsley* **or** *cilantro*
- ~ *salt and pepper*

Mix and season to taste.

EASY BEAN DIP (REFRIED BEANS)

- ~ *pinto* **or** *black beans*
- ~ *taco seasoning*

Mash beans and add taco seasoning to taste.

PINTO BEAN AND GREEN CHILE DIP

- 2 *cups mashed pinto beans*
- 1/2 *cup chopped green chilies (well drained)*
- 1/4 *cup thick and chunky salsa or taco sauce (your favorite)*

Mix all ingredients thoroughly. Can be served hot by topping with fat-free cheese singles and warming in oven.

TUNA SPREAD

7 *oz. canned tuna in water*
1 *tablespoon sweet onion*
2 *tablespoons fat-free mayonnaise*

Puree tuna and onion in blender; add the rest and chill.

MEXICAN SALSA

2 *cups your favorite salsa* **or** *taco sauce*
1 *Anaheim (green) chili, finely diced*
1/4 *cup finely diced sweet onion*

Mix and chill.

DEVILED EGGS

1/2 *cup Egg Beaters® egg substitute scrambled*
4 *hard boiled eggs*
2 *tablespoons fat-free mayonnaise*
1 *tablespoon Dijon mustard*
1 *tablespoon minced parsley*
~ *paprika*
4 *tablespoons pickle relish*

Scramble Egg Beaters® and allow to cool. Peel hard-boiled eggs and cut in long halves. Discard yolks. Mix in blender scrambled Egg Beaters®, mayonnaise, relish, mustard, and parsley. Fill hard-boiled egg halves with mixture and sprinkle lightly with paprika.

SMOKED TURKEY SPREAD

1 *cup finely chopped smoked turkey breast*
2 *tablespoons fat-free mayonnaise*
2 *tablespoons chopped dill pickle*

Mix and chill.

CLAM DIP

2 *cups no-fat sour cream*
6 1/2 *oz. can minced clams*
1/4 *cup fat-free mayonnaise*
1 *tablespoon Worcestershire sauce*
1 *tablespoon grated onion*
~ *dash cayenne pepper*

Mix all ingredients and chill.

RANCH DIP

2 *cups fat-free ranch dressing*
1/4 *cup finely diced red* **or** *orange bell pepper*

Mix together.

ROQUEFORT & HAM DIP

2 *cups fat-free Roquefort dressing*
1/4 *cup finely minced turkey ham*
~ *dash of cayenne pepper*

Mix and chill. ▩

CHICKEN SPREAD

7 *oz. canned white chicken meat packed in water*
1 *tablespoon grated sweet onion*
1 *tablespoon sweet pickle relish*
4 *tablespoons fat-free mayonnaise*

Puree chicken in blender; add rest of ingredients and chill. ▩

CREAM CHEESE & MARASCHINO CHERRY SPREAD

1/2 *cup Healthy Choice® fat-free cream cheese*
1/4 *cup maraschino cherries, minced*
1 *packet artificial sweetener or sugar*

Mix well and serve on warm fresh bread or slice of cake. ▩

CREAM CHEESE & CELERY SPREAD

4 *tablespoons celery, finely chopped*
1 *tablespoon onion, finely chopped*
1/4 *cup Healthy Choice® no-fat cream cheese*
~ *paprika*

Mix well and sprinkle with paprika. ▩

CREAM CHEESE & PIMENTO SPREAD

1/4 *cup Healthy Choice® no-fat cream cheese*
2 *tablespoons pimento, finely chopped*
~ *salt and pepper to taste*

Mix and serve. ▩

CREAM CHEESE & GREEN CHILE SPREAD

1/4 *cup Healthy Choice® no-fat cream cheese*
3 *tablespoons Anaheim green chili, finely chopped*

Mix and serve on baked corn tortilla chips.

CREAM CHEESE & PICKLE SPREAD

1/4 *cup Healthy Choice® no-fat cream cheese*
2 *tablespoons pickle, your choice*

Mix and serve.

CREAM CHEESE & WATERMELON RIND SPREAD

1/4 *cup Healthy Choice® no-fat cream cheese*
3 *tablespoons pickled watermelon rind, finely chopped*
1 *packet artificial sweetener* **or** *sugar*

ITALIAN TOMATO SAUCE & BREAD STICKS

1 *27 1/4-oz. can of Hunt's® Chunky Style Spaghetti Sauce with tomato chunks*
1 *cup diced green pepper*
1 *cup diced sweet onion*
1 *cup diced fresh mushrooms*
~ *loaf bread (homemade preferred, but fat-free Italian or French will do)*

Mix sauce and veggies and simmer until veggies are done. Slice loaf bread one-inch thick and then cut each slice into one-inch sections forming bread sticks. Sprinkle with Butter Buds® Sprinkles and garlic powder and toast under broiler. Serve beside sauce.

MEATLESS ITALIAN MEATBALLS

~ *Italian tomato sauce*
1 *package ADM Midland Harvest Burger® mix*

Reconstitute Burger mix with water; form into meatballs and simmer in sauce for 20 minutes. Serve hot.

ITALIAN MUSHROOMS

- ~ *Italian tomato sauce*
- 2 *cups medium to large mushrooms*

Simmer mushrooms in sauce for 20 minutes. Serve hot.

CORNBREAD STUFFED MUSHROOMS

- 1 *pound large stuffing size mushrooms*
- 1 *6-oz. package Stove Top® cornbread stuffing mix*

Remove stems carefully from mushrooms. Set caps aside. Dice finely the stems and add to 1½ cups water and vegetable seasoning packet in a saucepan. Bring to a boil. Reduce heat and let stand for 5 minutes. Stir in stuffing crumbs. Fluff with fork, then stuff mushroom caps. Place stuffed mushroom caps on cookie sheet and broil for 5 to 8 minutes until tops are lightly browned. Garnish with parsley and serve hot.

MEATLESS BURRITOS

- 4 *ten-inch fat-free flour tortillas page 211*
- 1 *pound ADM Midland Harvest Burger® mix*
- 1 *packet taco seasoning*
- ¼ *cup chopped tomatoes*
- ¼ *cup chopped green chilies*
- ¼ *cup chopped sweet onions*
- 6 *oz. package Healthy Choice® fat-free mozzarella (grated)*

Reconstitute burger mix. Add taco seasoning, green chilies, onions, and tomatoes. Simmer in skillet for 10 minutes. Spoon mixture onto tortillas, sprinkle with cheese, roll up and wrap with aluminum foil. Place in warm oven to hold till serving time. Platter and allow guest to cut to desired lengths with sharp knife.

BARBECUE WIENERS

- 1 *package Hormel Light & Lean® frankfurters*
- 1 *cup barbecue sauce*

Cut frankfurters into bite-size pieces, add barbecue sauce, heat and serve.

SOUPS & SALADS

In Exeter, New Hampshire, you can sit down at a crooked table placed on a slanting, uneven floor at the famous Loaf and Ladle restaurant and enjoy hearty homemade soups and thick slabs of homemade bread. When you leave, your tummy smiles and your mind is at peace with the world. You have just satisfied all the basic instincts of the ancestral hunter-gatherer. ❀ *In this case all you gathered was enough money to pay for the soup, but for those cooks behind the counter, it has been the combining of the things "gathered" and the things successfully "hunted" into a triumphant, simple meal.*

SOUPS

Try this one for pure satisfaction; prepare a soup in a Dutch oven, cover and set pot next to an open fire (fireplace, campfire, etc.). At mealtime, preferably after dark, ladle up bowls of soup and serve with hot fresh sourdough rolls (page 207). I guarantee satisfaction!

BEAN & VEGETABLE SOUP

- *1 1/2 cups dried pinto beans*
- *2 quarts water*
- *2 cans beef broth, defatted*
- *1/2 cup tomato sauce* **or** *1 cup chopped fresh tomato*
- *1/2 cup chopped carrots*
- *1 cup shredded cabbage*
- *1/2 cup chopped onion*
- *1 chopped medium potato*
- *2 tablespoons chopped parsley (optional)*
- *1 cup chopped kale, spinach, or other green*
- *~ salt and pepper to taste*

Wash and soak beans overnight in water. Simmer beans until tender, adding more water if necessary. Put in vegetables and cook until done. Season to taste.

BLACK BEAN SOUP

- *1 lb. black beans*
- *1 onion*
- *2 cloves*
- *1 bay leaf*
- *1 teaspoon dry* **or** *fresh parsley*
- *1 chopped medium onion*
- *1 chopped green pepper*
- *1 tablespoon minced garlic*
- *1 can defatted chicken broth (page 104)*
- *1 teaspoon oregano*
- *1 teaspoon sugar*
- *1 teaspoon vinegar*
- *1 8-oz. can tomato sauce*
- *1/2 cup red wine*
- *~ chopped green onion tops*

Clean and soak beans overnight. Add onion with two cloves stuck into it, bay leaf, parsley, and boil until tender. In skillet, cook chopped onion, green pepper, and garlic in chicken broth. Add to beans and cook until thickened. Pour in red wine and simmer for 5 minutes. Garnish with chopped green onion tops.

CREAM OF MUSHROOM SOUP

1 *lb. sliced fresh mushrooms*
1 *can defatted chicken broth*
2 *cups evaporated skim milk*
1/2 *medium chopped onion*
1 *tablespoon parsley flakes*
1 *tablespoon flour*
1 *tablespoon red wine*
~ *salt and pepper to taste*

In saucepan, sauté mushrooms and onions in chicken broth. Add parsley and red wine. Combine milk and flour thoroughly and add to mushrooms. Simmer to thicken and season to taste. For thinner soup, add more skim milk.

MEXICAN CHICKEN SOUP

2 *boneless, skinless chicken breasts*
1 *can defatted chicken broth (page 104)*
1 *cup water*
1 *cup Mexican-style stewed tomatoes* **or** *tomatoes and green chilies*
2 *fresh chopped Anaheim green chilies*
1 *medium chopped onion*
2 *cups* **or** *1 can drained pinto beans*
~ *salt and pepper to taste*

Dice chicken into bite-size pieces and simmer in large saucepan with chicken broth until tender. Add other ingredients and simmer until onions and peppers are tender. Season to taste. Serve with tortillas.

CHICKEN NOODLE SOUP

4 *cans defatted chicken broth (page 104)*
1 *stalk celery*
1/4 *cup diced onions*
2 *oz. dry pasta (your choice, but no egg noodles)*
3 1/2 *ozs. canned white chicken in water*
2 *tablespoons chopped parsley*
~ *salt and pepper*

Simmer broth, celery, and onions 5 to 7 minutes. Add pasta and cook until tender. Add chicken and salt and pepper to taste.

CHICKEN DUMPLING SOUP

Prepare chicken noodle soup but replace pasta with spoonfuls of vegetable cobbler dough (page 228). Simmer until dumplings are done.

VEGETABLE BEEF SOUP

6 *oz. defatted roast beef, leftovers,* **or** *6-oz. package deli oven-roasted, cured beef – 98% fat-free*
4 *cans defatted beef broth (page 104)*
2 *scraped and sliced carrots*
~ *leftover vegetables such as string beans, corn, peas, etc.*
1 *small bunch of fresh greens (kale, spinach, etc.)*
1 *small zucchini* **or** *yellow squash*
1 *cup chopped onions*
~ *salt and pepper to taste*

Add all ingredients and simmer until carrots are done. Season with salt and pepper after cooking.
NOTE: ***for beef barley soup add 3 tablespoons barley and cook until tender (about 45 minutes).***

NAVY BEAN SOUP

2 *cups dried navy beans*
~ *water to process*
1 *large diced onion*
1 *slice stalk celery*
4 *slices cubed turkey ham – 96% fat-free*
~ *salt and pepper to taste*

Soak beans overnight; add water to make 2 quarts in soup pot. Add all ingredients except salt and pepper and simmer for 3 to 4 hours until beans are soft. Add more water to replace any that evaporates. Remove 3 cups of beans from pot and place in blender; reduce to liquid and put back into soup. Salt and pepper to taste.

SEAFOOD CHOWDER

3 *medium sliced potatoes*
1 *large diced onion*
1 *$3^1/_2$-oz. can minced clams*
1 *$3^1/_2$-oz. can crab meat*
2 *lbs. frozen* **or** *fresh cod fish*
1 *can evaporated non-fat milk*
1 *teaspoon Butter Buds® butter-flavor sprinkles*
2 *slices diced turkey ham*
1 *can defatted chicken broth (page 74)*
1 *cup water*
~ *salt and pepper to taste*

In soup pot, combine potatoes, onion, clams, crab meat, turkey ham, chicken broth, and water. Simmer until potatoes are almost done; then add fish and cook until fish and potatoes are done. Add milk but do not boil. Salt and pepper to taste.

NEW ENGLAND CLAM CHOWDER

4 *cups strained chowder clams (reserve juice and add water to make 2 cups)*
3 *slices turkey ham - 96% fat free*
1 *medium chopped onion*
3 *peeled and diced potatoes*
3 *cups non fat milk*
1 *tablespoon Butter Buds® butter-flavor sprinkles*
3 *tablespoons flour*
~ *salt and pepper to taste*
~ *dash of paprika*

Combine clams and juice, ham, onion, and potatoes in soup pot and simmer until potatoes are done. In a bowl, combine milk, butter-flavor sprinkles, and flour. Use a whisk or mixer to thoroughly blend flour into mixture. Add to soup pot and simmer to thicken. Sprinkle paprika on each bowl of chowder.

SALADS

The traditional tossed green salad we leave to your imagination and personal tastes. It is important that you always use fat-free dressings with any salad. Oil is a bad no-no, as are avocados. We include some of the hearty salads that are sometimes served as a side dish with a meal instead of being served as a lonely first course. Also included are main course salads.

CHEF'S SALAD

FOR TWO

- ~ *lettuce* **or** *greens of choice*
- ~ *radishes*
- ~ *celery*
- ~ *tomato wedges*
- 3 *slices Healthy Choice® fat-free cheese, cut into strips*
- 1 *slice turkey ham, cut into strips*
- 2 *slices breast of chicken* **or** *turkey lunch meat, 98% fat free, cut into strips*
- 2 *deviled egg halves (page 85) (optional)*
- ~ *your favorite fat-free dressing*
- ~ *salt and pepper to taste*

SUNDAY SUPPER SALAD

SERVES 6 TO 8

- 4 *slices turkey bacon, fried crisp and fat pressed out*
- 1 *teaspoon minced garlic*
- 1 *bunch watercress*
- 1/2 *lb. spinach*
- 1/2 *head lettuce*
- 1 *head endive*
- 2 *stalks chopped celery (not 2 bunches)*
- 5 *sliced radishes*
- 3 *quartered tomatoes*
- 12 *finely diced green onions*
- 2 *finely sliced carrots*
- ~ *salt and pepper to taste*
- ~ *fat-free dressing of choice* **or** *your own homemade fat-free dressing*

Crumble bacon and add to garlic-rubbed salad bowl. Break cleaned, dry greens with fingers and mix all other ingredients in bowl. Chill before serving.

COLE SLAW WITH CELERY SEEDS

- 3 *cups shredded cabbage*
- 1/2 *cup cole slaw dressing (page 166)*
- 1 *tablespoon minced onions (optional)*
- 1 *tablespoon chopped pimento*
- 1/2 *teaspoon dry mustard*
- 1/2 *teaspoon celery seeds*
- ~ *salt to taste (optional)*

Combine and chill until serving time.

NOTE: *For cole slaw with green peppers, replace celery seeds with 1/2 teaspoon chopped green pepper.*

MIXED VEGETABLE SALAD (CANNED)

- 1 *can mixed, drained vegetables*
- ~ *fat-free mayonnaise to taste*

Mix and chill until serving.

MIXED VEGETABLES SALAD (FRESH FROZEN)

- 1 *16 oz. package frozen mixed vegetables*
- 3 *tablespoons fat-free mayonnaise*
- 1 *teaspoon dried sweet basil leaves*
- ~ *salt and pepper to taste*

Cook veggies per directions and drain. Combine with mayonnaise, basil, salt, and pepper. Mix well and chill before serving.

NOTE: *Instead of mayonnaise try your favorite fat-free salad dressing, also try marjoram or rosemary instead of basil.*

WALDORF SALAD

- 2 *cups unpeeled, sliced apples*
- 1 *cup diced celery*
- 1/2 *cup raisins*
- 1/2 *cup seedless grapes*
- 1 *teaspoon lemon juice*
- 1 *packet artificial sweetener (or sugar)*
- 1/2 *cup Healthy Choice® fat-free cream cheese* **or** *1/4 cup no-fat yogurt*

Mix and serve.

DILLED SHRIMP SALAD

1 *lb. shrimp, cooked, cleaned, and deveined*
1 *tablespoon minced onion*
1/2 *cup sliced water chestnuts*
2 *tablespoons creamy Italian salad dressing, fat free*
~ *tomato wedges*
~ *sliced mushroom*
~ *lettuce leaves*

Toss shrimp with onion, water chestnuts, and salad dressing. Serve with tomato wedges and mushroom slices on lettuce leaves.

BEET & ONION SALAD

1 *can sliced beets*
1 *medium sliced onion*
1/2 *cup vinegar*
1 *packet artificial sweetener (or sugar) to taste*

Combine and chill in refrigerator at least an hour before serving. A real hot weather dish.

TUNA SALAD

Crab may be used instead of tuna, but never salmon.

1 *7-oz. can tuna in water, well drained*
1/4 *cup chopped celery*
1 *tablespoon your favorite chopped pickle*
1 *tablespoon fresh lemon juice*
1 *tablespoon fat-free mayonnaise*
~ *minced parsley*

Combine well; may be served on crisp lettuce leaves, shredded lettuce, or stuffing in tomato or green pepper or as a sandwich. Garnish with minced parsley.

CHICKEN SALAD

2 *cups white meat chicken cooked, defatted, and sized to choice*
1/4 *cup diced celery*
1/4 *cup diced tomato*
3 *tablespoons fat-free mayonnaise*
~ *salt and pepper to taste*

Combine ingredients, adding more mayonnaise if desired. Season to taste. Serve on crackers, toast points, as a sandwich, or stuffing for tomatoes, peppers, or mushrooms. Chopped onions are optional.

CARROT SALAD

2 *cups shredded carrots*
~ *coleslaw dressing (page 166)*
1/4 *cup raisins*

In mixing bowl, add carrots, raisins, and coleslaw dressing to taste. Cover and chill.

WILTED GREENS & BACON SALAD

1 *large skillet of your favorite greens (spinach, kale, collards, etc.)*
4 *strips turkey bacon*
~ *water sufficient to wilt greens in skillet (approx. 1/4 cup)*

Cook bacon until crispy; remove and press with paper towels. Remove all grease from skillet. Wilt greens and drain off all water, add crisp bacon broken into bite-sizes and toss. Serve with red wine or Balsamic vinegar.

PASTA & VEGGIE SALAD

2 *cups cooked and drained pasta of your choice*
1 *cup mixed steamed veggies*
~ *fat-free ranch dressing*

Mix pasta and veggies. Add dressing to taste.

RICE & WHATEVER SALAD

3 *cups cooked rice*
3 *oz. turkey ham cut into small strips*
1/2 *cup uncooked frozen green peas*
3 *tablespoons chopped green onion tops*
1 *tablespoon chopped parsley*
1 *teaspoon mustard*
1 *tablespoon red wine vinegar*
~ *salt and pepper*
1 *cup your imagination*

Mix ingredients. 1 cup your imagination might be shrimp, lobster, clams, crab, zucchini, tomatoes, or peppers.

POTATO SALAD

- 4 *cups diced baked potatoes (boiled is okay)*
- 4 *tablespoons fat-free mayonnaise*
- 2 *tablespoons yellow prepared mustard*
- 2 *tablespoons sweet pickle relish*
- 1/4 *cup diced celery*
- ~ *salt and pepper*

Mix and add more ingredients to taste if desired.

SEAFOOD SALAD

- 2 *cups cooked seafood of your choice (no-fat fish)*
- 2 *tablespoons fat-free mayonnaise*
- 1 *teaspoon capers*
- 2 *tablespoons lemon juice*
- 2 *tablespoons diced dill pickle*
- 1/4 *cup finely diced celery*
- 1/4 *cup diced red bell pepper*
- ~ *salt and pepper*
- ~ *dash of cayenne pepper*

Mix ingredients and balance to your taste.

COMBINATION FRESH FRUIT SALAD

- 2 *cups mixed fresh fruit of your choice in bite-sizes*
- 1 *tablespoon fat-free mayonnaise*
- 2 *tablespoons vanilla fat-free frozen yogurt*

Mix, cover, and chill. Toss just before serving. Garnish with Grape Nuts® and a sprig of fresh mint.

FRUIT & JELL-O® PARFAIT SALAD

- 2 *packages peach Jell-O® gelatin*
- 2 *cups fresh, chopped peach slices (canned will do)*

Prepare two mixing bowls of peach Jell-O® and chill until almost set. Remove from refrigerator and beat one bowl with electric mixer for four or five minutes until very foamy. Mix in one cup of peaches. In the other bowl, combine unbeaten bowl of Jell-O® and one cup peaches. In parfait or ice cream soda glasses, spoon in alternate layers of beaten Jell-O® and the unbeaten Jell-O.® Chill until set.

TOMATO & BREAD SALAD

3 *cups, 1-inch pieces, no-fat French* **or** *Italian bread*
2 *tomatoes, cut in bite-size pieces*
1 *teaspoon finely minced garlic*
1 *tablespoon basil*
1 *medium sliced onion*
1 *green pepper, cut into bite-size pieces*
1 *sprig fresh* **or** *dried parsley*
4 *tablespoons Balsamic vinegar*
~ *salt and pepper to taste*
2 *tablespoons mock blue cheese crumbles (see recipe below)*

Mix tomatoes, bread, garlic, onion, green pepper, basil, and parsley. Sprinkle with vinegar and toss. Cover and refrigerate for two hours. Garnish top with mock blue cheese crumbles, or cheese flavor sprinkles.

MOCK BLUE CHEESE CRUMBLES

2 *wafers melba toast*
2 *tablespoons fat-free blue cheese dressing*
1 *teaspoon dried parsley*

Crumble melba toast and mix in parsley and blue cheese dressing.

MEAT & POULTRY

PURCHASING

When the decision to eat meat has been made, purchases should be carefully considered. ❧ First consideration should be given to meats or poultry products that fit the "1 gram of fat per ounce" rule. ❧ Breast of turkey, breast of chicken, buffalo, Healthy Choice® extra lean ground beef, and venison are at the top of our list. ❧ Buffalo and venison, genetically, biologically, can not marble. This means that when you eat a piece of this lean meat it is not loaded with a lot of hidden fat. These two are so important to the red-meat eaters that they are covered separately in chapters 9 and 10. Please refer to those chapters for cooking instructions.

BEEF OR LAMB

Buy only whole roasts that appear very lean. Some grocers market them as "Lite" or "Lean" or similar language. Eye of the round is a good cut. If ground beef is desired, your first choice should be frozen one-pound tubes of Healthy Choice® extra lean ground beef.

PORK

Again, buy only roasts, preferably the fresh ham or loin, and have your butcher trim it. It should appear as 100% lean pork.

POULTRY

On a day-to-day basis restrict purchases to only breast meat. For special occasions buy the whole bird.

LUNCH MEAT

Labels that read "98% or 99% Lean" produced by a reputable company are acceptable. They include turkey and chicken breast products, some hams, and some beef items. Check the grams of fat per serving and purchase those containing 1 gram of fat or less per serving.

BACON

Buy only turkey bacon. Most brands are labeled 2 grams of fat per slice. When cooked crisp and toweled dry, only about 1/2 gram of fat remains.

MEAT SUBSTITUTES

Purchase ADM Midland Harvest Burgers® from a company called Harvest Direct. The telephone number is 1-800-835-2867. This excellent product is available in some stores. Also purchase a small bag of textured vegetable protein, also called TVP®, from your local health food or specialty store, or order it from Harvest Direct also. More about this product in Chapter 6.

PRIMARY DEFATTING PROCESS

This process applies to all meats and poultry products. It can be done in the oven or on top of the stove. As an example, let's prepare a pork or beef roast. ❧ Place roast and ½ inch of water in oven-proof cookware. A cast iron pot with a lid is preferred. Roast meat in 400° oven for approximately 20 minutes per pound. Cover roast with boiling water and continue in oven for an additional 30 minutes. Remove and allow to cool on top of stove. Make sure roast is completely covered with water. Place in refrigerator and chill overnight. ❧ Next day skim off congealed fat on top of liquid and remove roast. Boil stock to reduce to good flavor, add bouillon if necessary. Thicken gravy. Season to taste. Warm roast in gravy. Serve with mashed potatoes. ❧ When we purchase our beef roast, there is no visible fat. Meat packers say that even when no fat shows, the product is at least 5% fat. This means that in a quarter-pound serving there was originally about 6 grams of fat. We have baked the roast and rendered (removed) a portion of the fat, but not all. If cooked well done we have removed about half the fat which means a ¼-pound serving now has about 3 grams of fat. ❧ For ground beef patties, purchase Healthy Choice® extra lean ground beef and fry in a greaseless skillet. Refer to cheeseburger recipe on page 78.

SECONDARY DEFATTING PROCESS

This process simply repeats the first process on top of the stove and does not require a cooling and congealing step. It primarily applies to leftover meat, but could be used for all meat if desired. As an example, let's make shredded beef for Mexican Tacos (page 171). ❦ Slice leftover roast beef into thin 1/2-inch strips. Place in saucepan, cover with water, and boil rapidly for 1 hour. Don't run out of water! Pour water off and discard. With two forks, shred beef. ❦ Add your favorite salsa and bouillon (either chicken, beef, or vegetable). Add chopped onions and peppers and heat until onions are done, being careful to add water to keep mixture from burning. ❦ We have, with this second process, removed most of the fat and some flavor. With the addition of the bouillon we put the flavor back in. When this mixture is placed on a crisp baked corn tortilla and then topped with a thin slice of fresh tomato, mozzarella cheese, and sliced jalapeno peppers, it fairly bursts with rich and exotic flavors, but essentially no fat! ❦ Although these two examples use beef, the same processes apply to pork, lamb, chicken, and turkey dark meat. Skinless breast of chicken and turkey may be used fresh if desired; however these two defatting processes will remove fat.

BEEF & CHICKEN BROTH DEFATTING PROCESS

Store canned broth in a refrigerator at least overnight before using. After opening with can opener remove congealed fat on top of broth. Some beef broth is already fat free and therefore requires no refrigeration or defatting.

MEAT RECIPES

SMOTHERED BEEFSTEAK

- 2 *lbs. cooked defatted beef cut one inch thick*
- 2 *tablespoons garlic*
- 2 *large onions*
- 1 *can beef broth*

In heavy skillet (cast iron preferred) place ¼ inch of water and two large sliced onions. Sprinkle with ¼ cup beef broth and pepper to taste. Place one-inch thick defatted cooked beef cuts on top of onions. Spread 1 tablespoon garlic (per pound) on top of beef. Cover and simmer gently for 1½ hours. Remove beef cuts to serving dish. To remaining defatted beef broth add two tablespoons flour and mix thoroughly. Add to onions, stir and thicken. Spoon onions and gravy on top of beef cuts. Serve. If desired, pack whole mushrooms around meat in skillet.

RED WINE-FLAVORED STEW

- 2 *lbs. beef* **or** *buffalo (very lean roast) cut into large pieces*
- 1 *cup red wine*
- 1 *medium onion quartered*
- 1 *carrot, cut in half*
- 1 *teaspoon garlic, chopped*
- 1 *small piece orange peel*
- 1 *clove*
- ½ *small bay leaf*
- ¼ *teaspoon thyme*
- 1 *small tomato, chopped*
- 1 *teaspoon bacon flavoring*
- 1 *tablespoon flour*
- ~ *salt and pepper to taste, when done*

Combine all ingredients (except salt and pepper) in a slow crock cooker and allow to marinate overnight. Next morning set cooker to "low" and allow to cook all day. Remove meat chunks, skim off any fat and strain the juice if desired. Just remove the orange peel and bay leaf, season to taste, and serve over elbow macaroni.

CAJUN GREAT FILET

FOR TWO

- 2 *venison filets, regular size* **or** *4 small ones*
- 3 *green onions* **or** *1 small regular onion, sliced*
- 1 *teaspoon garlic, minced*
- ~ *Cajun blackening spices, (your favorite)*
- ~ *flour*
- ¼ *cup chicken stock, defatted*
- ~ *vegetable spray*

In veggie-sprayed skillet on medium-high heat, brown onions and garlic. Season filets with blackening spice and dust each filet with flour. Push onions off to the side and brown filets. Pour some of this chicken stock on onions and around filets. Turn filets as browned and continue adding chicken broth in order to brown and cook meat. Serve with salad, parsley buttered rice (page 139), and warm bread.

GOURMET BARBECUE TENDERLOIN OF VENISON OR BUFFALO

FOR TWO

- 1/2 *lb. meat sliced 1/4 inch thick*
- 1/2 *cup chicken broth*
- 1/4 *large onion, sliced thick*
- 1 *cup sweet barbecue sauce*
- ~ *Sourdough bread sliced 1 inch thick. (Sourdough oatmeal raisin, page 208, works wonderfully)*

Brown meat in skillet, add onions and broth, and cover. Simmer until onions are tender. Add barbecue sauce, cover, and lower temperature to very low. Let meat sit for 5 or more minutes. Spoon meat onto slices of bread, top with onions and sauce.

HUNGARIAN MEAT & POTATOES

- 4 *oz. (1/4-lb.) diced lean pork, chicken,* **or** *turkey breast (skinless)*
- 2 *cans chicken broth (defatted)*
- 1 *medium onion, chopped*
- 2 *lb. potatoes, peeled and sliced*
- 1/8 *teaspoon black or white pepper*
- 1 *teaspoon sweet Hungarian paprika*
- 2 *tablespoons flour*

In cast iron Dutch oven or skillet, brown meat and flour, adding enough chicken broth to keep from burning. When meat and flour are well browned add rest of the ingredients and simmer uncovered until potatoes are tender.

This is an excellent "left-over," as the flavors mingle and the dish takes on its own identity.

POT ROAST BEEF SOUP & SANDWICH

- 1 *lb. eye of round roast beef and broth defatted (page 104)*
- ~ *water to process*
- 2 *bay leaves*
- 1 *large tomato, peeled and diced*
- 1/2 *cup whole kernel corn*
- 1/2 *cup okra, frozen*
- 1/2 *cup green peas, frozen*
- 2 *medium potatoes, peeled and quartered*
- 1 *cup greens, chopped*
- 1/4 *cup leftover beans*
- 3 *medium carrots, cut in 2-inch chunks*
- 1 *can beef broth, defatted*
- 1 *medium onion, diced*
- 1/2 *stalk celery, chopped*
- ~ *salt and pepper to taste*

In heavy kettle or Dutch oven, combine beef, beef broth, bay leaves, onion, carrot, celery, and tomato. Boil on medium heat for 1 hour, add corn, okra, peas, potatoes, greens, and beans and simmer for 30 minutes more or until potatoes are tender. Remove roast beef to cutting board. Correct liquid in soup by adding water or broth. Slice beef and serve on slices of Potato-Oatmeal Bread (page 196).

MEATLESS SALISBURY STEAK

- 1 *packet Midland Harvest Burger® Mix*
- 1 *cup chopped sweet onions*
- 2 *tablespoons dry onion soup mix*
- 1 *can defatted beef broth*
- 1/2 *bell pepper*
- 1 1/2 *tablespoons flour*
- ~ *veggie spray*

Reconstitute Burger Mix as per instructions (let sit 15 minutes). Add sweet onions and onion soup and mix thoroughly and form into four patties.
Spray cast iron skillet lightly with veggie spray and brown patties on both sides. Blend broth and flour thoroughly and pour over patties. Lift patties to allow broth to underside. Top with green pepper rings and let simmer for 15 minutes.
Serve over a bed of rice or with mashed potatoes.

CAJUN BEEF

2 *cups shredded beef (page 104)*
1 *can defatted beef broth*
1/4 *cup chopped green onions*
1 *cup whole fresh mushrooms*
1 *tablespoon minced garlic*
1 *tablespoon Louisiana Hot Sauce*
1/2 *teaspoon paprika*
1/2 *cup diced fresh tomatoes*
~ *cayenne, salt and pepper to taste*

In large cast iron skillet combine everything except the mushrooms and beef. Simmer slowly for 1 hour. Add mushrooms and beef and simmer for 30 minutes. Goes great on top of instant white rice.

CREOLE BEEF HASH

1/2 *cup defatted beef broth*
2 *cups leftover beef*
1 *medium to small onion*
1 *cup chopped, uncooked potatoes*
~ *dash ground clove*
~ *cayenne, salt and pepper to taste*

Mince beef very fine but do not puree. Combine all ingredients in heavy skillet and simmer gently for about 30 minutes until potatoes are done. Add hot water if necessary to maintain simmer.

BEEF POT ROAST

3–4 lb. beef roast
1 *carrot, sliced*
1 *turnip, diced*
1 *stalk celery, sliced*
6 *medium potatoes, peeled and halved*
1 *can defatted beef broth*
2 *tablespoons flour*
1 *tablespoon chopped parsley*
1 *bay leaf*
3 *cups water*

In a heavy cast iron pot or Dutch oven place roast on top of carrots, turnips and celery. Add parsley, water and bay leaf. Cover and heat on medium-high burner for three hours. During last 1/2 hour cover mixture completely with hot water and add potatoes. Remove from heat and allow to cool. Refrigerate overnight. Next day remove congealed fat and discard. Remove roast and potatoes from pot. Reduce liquid to a tasty broth by boiling. Mix flour and defatted canned beef broth thoroughly and add to boiling stock. Thicken, add roast and potatoes to reheat. Simmer until roast is hot. Serve.

BEEF STROGANOFF

- 2 *cups defatted roast beef (page 103), sliced thin, 1-inch wide*
- 1 *tablespoon minced onion*
- 1 *tablespoon Butter Buds® butter flavor sprinkles*
- 1 *cup sliced fresh mushrooms*
- 1/2 *cup no-fat sour cream*
- 1/2 *cup defatted beef broth*
- ~ *dash of nutmeg*
- ~ *salt and pepper to taste*

In heavy skillet add onions and beef broth; boil for 3 or 4 minutes and add beef, Butter Buds®, and mushrooms, and simmer for 5 minutes. Add nutmeg and salt and pepper to taste. Add sour cream, but do not allow to boil. Serve immediately.

GRILLADES (FRIED BEEF STEAK OR FRICASSEE)

- ~ *eye of the round roast, thinly sliced*
- 1 *can defatted beef broth*
- ~ *flour*
- ~ *cayenne, salt and pepper to taste*

Slice beef as thin as possible, pepper to taste. Flour each steak on both sides. In cast iron skillet spray lightly with butter-flavored veggie spray. Heat skillet to medium-high temperature. Have the beef broth and a tablespoon on top of stove next to skillet. Place steaks in hot skillet. After 1 minute lift each steak with pancake turner and put one tablespoon of the beef broth under each steak. Put several tablespoons of beef broth around perimeter of the skillet. Turn steaks over and repeat process. When done remove steaks.

NOTE: *Pork, venison, buffalo, or poultry can also be prepared like this.*

GRILLADES WITH GRAVY (FRIED BEEF STEAK WITH GRAVY)

Prepare steaks as in preceding recipe, leaving sauce in skillet.

GRAVY

- 1 *tomato, diced*
- 1 *medium onion, chopped*
- 1 *teaspoon minced garlic*
- ~ *remaining beef broth* ***or*** *1 cup water*
- 1 *tablespoon flour*
- 1 *teaspoon Louisiana Hot Sauce*

To sauce already in skillet add the onions, tomatoes, garlic, and hot sauce and simmer until onions are done. To leftover beef broth add the flour and mix thoroughly; then add to skillet and thicken the gravy, simmering for 2 or 3 minutes. Remove and serve.

PORK STEAK & ROASTS

Prepare pork as you would beef (page 102–104), substituting chicken broth for the beef broth.

PORK STEAK & SWEET POTATOES

- 2 *Sweet potatoes, peeled and sliced*
- 8 *oz. thinly sliced pork tenderloin*
- 2 *tablespoons flour*
- ~ *salt and pepper to taste*
- ½ *cup water*

Boil sweet potatoes for 20 minutes until tender, drain and set aside. Prepare pork as for Fried Beef Steak (page 109), using defatted chicken broth. When steaks are done remove. Combine ½ cup water and flour, mix thoroughly; add to skillet and stir well to make gravy. Add sweet potatoes and place steaks on top. Simmer briefly to reheat steaks and serve from skillet.

POLISH PORK & KRAUT

Same recipe as for Pork Steak and Sweet Potatoes substituting:

- 1 *cup shredded cabbage and*
- 1 *cup sauerkraut for the sweet potatoes. Omit gravy.*

SWEET & SOUR PORK

- 1 *lb. defatted roast pork (page 103)*
- ½ *cup soy sauce*
- 2 *bell peppers sliced*
- 1 *medium onion quartered*
- 1 *cup pineapple chunks*
- 1 *cup sweet & sour sauce*
- ¼ *cup defatted chicken broth*

Marinate pork slices in soy sauce for an hour or so, turning meat several times. In hot skillet add chicken broth, peppers, and onions and boil vigorously for one minute stirring constantly. Remove from skillet. Drain pork and add to skillet along with pineapple, bring to boil and simmer 3 minutes. Add peppers, onions, and sweet and sour sauce. Simmer for 1 minute. Serve with steamed rice.

HUNGARIAN PORK & EGG NOODLES

4-6 oz. lean pork tenderloin, all fat trimmed, and cut into bite-size pieces
1 cup onions, chopped
2 cans defatted chicken broth
1/8 teaspoon black pepper
2 tablespoons flour
1 teaspoon paprika (sweet Hungarian)
6 oz. no-yolk egg noodles

In Dutch oven brown pork with flour, add broth from time to time as needed to keep from burning. Add the rest of broth and other ingredients and cook until onions are done.

Cook noodles according to directions and add to pork mixture. Remove from heat and allow to sit for an hour or so if possible.

BOUDINS

Boudins were originally a Cajun or Creole blood sausage. Government controls have virtually eliminated this use of blood in sausage-making. Modern recipes have added rice and green onions. Instead of stuffing the meat in animal casings, this recipe calls for the making of sausage patties. Original recipes called for the mixture to be "seasoned highly" with cayenne and black pepper. Use your own judgment when it comes to the use of very hot cayenne pepper, as it can always be added later. ❧ This sausage, when used as a base flavoring agent in gumbos, jambalayas, and other Cajun or Creole dishes, adds a very distinctive flavor and texture.

HOT BOUDIN PATTIES

- 1 *lb. ground buffalo (lean)*
- 1 *lb. turkey sausage*
- 1 *lb. packet ADM Midland Harvest Burger® mix*
- 1 *cup green onion tops, chopped*
- 1 *teaspoon parsley, chopped*
- 1 *teaspoon garlic*
- 1/2 *teaspoon each of finely ground:*
    - *allspice*
    - *sage*
    - *thyme*
    - *nutmeg*
- 1 *bay leaf*
- 2 *cups water*
- ~ *salt, pepper, cayenne pepper to taste*
- 1/2 *cup cooked rice*
- 1/2 *cup beef broth, defatted*
- ~ *vegetable spray*

In 2 cups water simmer turkey sausage, buffalo, and bay leaf for 30 minutes. Remove from heat and chill. Remove congealed fat. In mixing bowl add onions, garlic, parsley, rice, and spices. Mix spices thoroughly. Add turkey sausage along with its broth, the rice, and the beef broth. Add Burger Mix and mix thoroughly. Allow to sit for 15 minutes. Form into patties and fry in veggie-sprayed skillet. Freeze and store excess patties to be used in Cajun or Creole recipes calling for sausage. ❧

SAUSAGE

Sausage consists of parts of an animal and seasoning. Our sausage consists of extra lean beef from Healthy Choice® and seasoning from:

Planters Seed & Spice Co.
513 Walnut
Kansas City, Missouri 64106
Telephone: 1-816-842-3651

The extra lean beef from Healthy Choice® is clearly marked on the label as containing 4 grams of fat per 4-oz. serving. That meets our fat requirement for meat. (i.e. 1 gram of fat per ounce or less). This is an extremely versatile product, and if you are a meat eater it should always be available to you in your refrigerator. ❦ *Planters Seed & Spice Co. is a unique establishment. When you walk in the front door you'll think you are in a turn-of-the-century store. There are lots of old-fashioned counters, barrels of good stuff, and wonderful service. This business dates back to 1926 and they will be happy to mail you a retail spice list which details the ingredients in their spice mixes. We'll be using two of their sausage-seasoning spice mixes.* ❦ *The following sausage mixtures can be stuffed into casings if desired; however, I just use them in patty form. You will get a better blending of flavors if you allow your sausage to set overnight in the refrigerator, although it is not necessary. Also you can use ground turkey breast for about 50% of your meat. It will create a lighter-colored sausage.*

BREAKFAST SAUSAGE PATTIES

FOR TWO

½ *lb. Healthy Choice® extra lean ground beef*
2 *teaspoons Planters Special Sausage Seasoning (For ordering see address on previous page)*
~ *ground red chilies optional for hot sausage*

Combine ingredients and form into patties and fry.

ITALIAN SAUSAGE

FOR TWO

½ *lb.Healthy Choice® extra lean ground beef*
2 *teaspoons Planters Sweet Italian Sausage Sesoning (To order, see previous page)*

POULTRY

HOLIDAY ROAST CHICKEN OR TURKEY & STUFFING

Prepared the day before:

~ *bird or birds, not self-basting or basted*
~ *chicken broth*
~ *salt and pepper to taste*
~ *stuffing (page 119–121)*
~ *hot boiling water*

Remove skin from bird, rub with salt and pepper, and place in cast iron Dutch oven. Make sure there is enough room on top to facilitate covering with hot water. A large turkey will need to be quartered. Roasting chickens may need to be split. In 325° F oven, cover and cook about 25 minutes per pound or until meat thermometer shows 185° F in thigh meat, then cover entire bird with hot boiling water and bake for an additional 15 minutes. Remove to top of stove and allow to cool. Chill overnight, removing congealed fat from top of water next morning.

Remove bird from water. Boil water until reduced to flavorful stock. Remove from heat. Pour stock into a saucepan. Prepare stuffing. Place bird and stuffing back into Dutch oven with top on. Place in oven at 325° F. Thicken stock with flour. When stuffing is done and turkey is heated, remove from oven to top of stove. Serve. In post pilgrim times, the large Dutch oven would have been placed in the middle of the dining table. ※

CRISPY CHICKEN FILETS

1 *lb. chicken breast filets*
~ *Shake 'n Bake® seasoning and coating mixture, original recipe for pork*

Follow directions on box. ※

CHICKEN OR TURKEY ENCHILADAS

1 *lb. shredded defatted breast meat (page 104)*
1 *cup chunky salsa (your favorite)*
1/4 *cup onion, chopped*
1 *tablespoon minced garlic*
1 *small can green chilies, chopped*
1/2 *can defatted chicken broth*
6-8 *slices fat-free cheese*
12 *corn tortillas*

In medium skillet on medium-high heat, add onion, garlic, and 1/2 can chicken broth. Simmer for 3 minutes. Add salsa, green chilies and meat. Simmer for 15 minutes. Remove from heat. Spoon mixture onto corn tortillas and roll up. Place in 8" x 14" baking pan. Pour leftover juices on top of rolled tortillas. Top with cheese slices. Bake in 350° F oven for 25 minutes, or until cheese is bubbly hot and starting to brown. ※

HUNGARIAN CHICKEN OR TURKEY

1 *lb. breast meat, cubed*
1/2 *cup onion, chopped*
1 *tablespoon Butter Buds® butter-flavor sprinkles*
1/4 *cup tomato, chopped*
1/4 *cup water*
1 *can chicken broth*
3 *tablespoons flour*
1/2 *cup no-fat sour cream*
2 *tablespoons sweet Hungarian paprika*
~ *salt to taste*

In medium skillet add onion and a little broth. Brown onions carefully and add breast meat. Continue adding a small amount of broth so as to allow meat to brown. When meat is browned, add tomato, paprika, and water and simmer on low heat for 30 minutes, uncovered. Mix flour with remaining broth and Butter Buds® and add to skillet. On medium heat simmer for 3 minutes. Turn off heat and add sour cream but do not boil. Serve on your favorite pasta. ※

MEXICAN CHICKEN OR TURKEY

- 1 *lb. breast meat, cubed*
- 1 *cup salsa* **or** *taco sauce (your favorite)*
- 1/2 *cup chopped onion*
- 1 *tablespoon minced garlic*
- 2 *long green chilies (Anaheim), sliced thin*
- 1 *can defatted chicken broth*
- 1/4 *cup red bell pepper*
- 2 *slices fat-free cheese*
- ~ *salt and pepper to taste*

In large skillet brown breast meat using a little broth. Watch carefully and don't burn. Use medium to high heat. Add salsa, onion, garlic, bell pepper, and the rest of the broth. Simmer for 25 minutes. Add green chilies and cheese and stir until cheese is melted. Remove from heat and serve with rice and beans. (pages 138 and 158)

CHICKEN OR TURKEY CACCIATORE

- 1 *lb. breast meat, cubed*
- 1 *tablespoon flour*
- 1 *cup whole, medium-small mushrooms*
- 1 *medium onion, chopped*
- 1/4 *cup dry white wine (optional)*
- 1 *cup defatted chicken broth*
- 1 *teaspoon garlic, minced*
- 1 *small can tomato sauce*
- 1 *large fresh tomato, chopped*
- 1/4 *teaspoon allspice*
- 1 *bay leaf*
- 1/4 *teaspoon thyme*
- ~ *salt and pepper to taste*

In large skillet add breast meat and 2 tablespoons broth. Allow to brown but *not* burn. Add more broth as needed. When meat is somewhat brown on all sides add flour and allow flour to brown but not burn. When brown, add the rest of the broth, onion, wine garlic, tomato sauce, tomato, allspice, bay leaf, and thyme. Simmer for 15 minutes. Add mushrooms and simmer 15 minutes more. Salt and pepper to taste and remove from heat. If possible, allow to sit for 30 minutes to one hour before serving.

CHICKEN OR TURKEY JAMBALAYA

3 *tablespoons flour*
1 *lb. boneless, skinless breast meat, cubed*
1 *can chicken broth, defatted*
2 *slices ham, cut into thin strips*
1/2 *bell pepper, chopped*
1 *large onion, chopped*
2 *tablespoons celery, chopped*
2 *tablespoons garlic, minced*
1/4 *cup parsley, chopped*
1 *bay leaf, finely chopped*
1/4 *lb. hickory grilled Healthy Choice® smoked sausage*
1/2 *teaspoon thyme*
1 *14-oz. can diced tomatoes*
1 *tablespoon Louisiana Hot Sauce*
1 *tablespoon jalapeno peppers, chopped*
~ *salt, cayenne and black pepper to taste*
1 *cup instant rice (uncooked)*

In 10-inch Dutch oven or large cast iron skillet brown flour until a dark brown. Add breast meat and ham and continue to brown. Add chicken broth to accelerate browning; then add the rest of the ingredients except for the rice. Simmer for 30 minutes and season to taste. Add rice and remove from heat. Allow to set for 10 minutes or longer. This dish is actually better the second day after allowing the various flavors to mingle.

CHICKEN OR TURKEY FAJITAS

8 *oz. breast, shredded*
1/4 *cup salsa, your choice*
1 *medium onion, sliced*
1/2 *bell pepper, sliced*
~ *salt and pepper to taste*
6 *flour tortillas, fat free* **or** *see page 211*

In medium skillet add onions, peppers, salsa, and breast meat. Simmer on medium heat until peppers are tender. Remove from heat, spoon onto tortilla, and serve.

CHICKEN STEW & DUMPLINGS

1 *lb. chicken breast, cubed*
2 *medium potatoes, diced*
1 *cup kale (or other greens of choice)*
1 *medium onion, chopped*
2 *carrots, sliced*
1/4 *large turnip (optional), chopped*
3 *cans chicken broth, defatted*
2 *cups water*
~ *salt, pepper and chicken bouillon granules to taste*
2 *tablespoons flour mixed with*
1 *cup water*
1 *package biscuits, (the cheap ones)*
~ *paprika*

In Dutch oven combine the chicken, potatoes, kale, onion, carrots, turnips, chicken broth, 2 cups of water, and simmer briskly for 20 minutes. Season to taste and add flour mixture. Stir and place biscuits on top of stew, cover and simmer for another 20 minutes. Correct liquid if necessary. When done, sprinkle biscuits with paprika.
Since this is a stew, add whatever vegetables you desire. ❖

QUICK TURKEY OR CHICKEN STEW

- 1 *lb. cooked white meat defatted and cubed*
- 2 *cans chicken broth, defatted*
- 1 *teaspoon garlic, minced*
- 1/4 *teaspoon thyme, dried*
- 2 *tablespoons parsley, fresh*
- 1/8 *teaspoon black pepper*
- 1 *bay leaf*
- 1/2 *cup onions, diced*
- 1 *cup baby carrots, cooked*
- 1 *cup potatoes, cubed and cooked*
- 3 *tablespoons flour*
- 1 *teaspoon lemon juice*
- 1/4 *cup dry white wine (optional)*

In large skillet simmer onions, garlic, bay leaf, and 1 can of broth until onions are about tender. Add flour to remaining can of broth and mix thoroughly. Add to skillet along with the rest of the ingredients. Simmer gently for 10 minutes. If gravy is too thick, add water. If to thin, mix 1 tablespoon flour to 1/2 cup water and add. Serve with hot crusty French bread. ❖

GLAZED TURKEY HAM WITH RED-EYE GRAVY

- 1 *turkey ham*
- 1 *cup orange marmalade (as needed)*
- ~ *whole cloves*
- 1 *teaspoon instant coffee*
- ~ *water*

In a pan that fits the ham add water to cover and bring to boil. Simmer for 45 minutes, making sure ham is totally covered with water. Remove and chill, Spoon off congealed fat from the water and remove ham. Dot ham with whole cloves and spoon on marmalade. Place in 350° F oven for 30 minutes. Remove. Boil water to reduce to a good strong broth and add coffee. Red-eye gravy isn't usually thickened; however, if desired, thicken with flour or cornstarch. ❖

POPOVER CHICKEN

2 *chicken breasts, skinless*
~ *popover batter (page 210)*
1 *teaspoon dry parsley*
1 *teaspoon chicken bouillon granules*
~ *salt and pepper to taste*

Brown chicken and place in veggie-sprayed casserole dish. To popover batter, stir in parsley and chicken bouillon granules. Pour over chicken and place in a 350° F preheated oven for 50 or 60 minutes until done. Serve with mushroom sauce. (page 165)

LIVER, ONIONS & BACON

Chicken liver and beef liver contain about 1.1 grams of fat per ounce; however they are high in cholesterol.

~ *chicken livers*
~ *flour*
~ *salt and pepper, to taste*
~ *chicken broth, defatted (page 104)*
~ *turkey bacon, cooked crisp and pressed with paper towel, then crumbled.*
~ *sliced onions*
~ *vegetable spray*

Flour livers, salt and pepper, and brown in veggie-sprayed skillet. Turn, continue to brown and add some chicken broth. As broth boils off, add some more. When browned, add bacon pieces and onion slices, continue cooking until done. Add more broth to maintain sufficient cooking liquid.

MOM'S OYSTER STUFFING

MAKES ABOUT 2 QUARTS

1 *cup turkey* **or** *chicken broth (defatted)*
1 *cup water*
2 *cups chopped onion*
1/2 *cup chopped celery*
12 *cups non-fat bread, cubed*
1 *8-oz. can oysters*
2 *teaspoons poultry seasoning*
1/2 *teaspoon salt*
1/4 *teaspoon black pepper*
1/2 *teaspoon ground sage*

Boil water, onions, and celery until tender. Remove oysters from can and strain juice through a cloth to remove gritty particles. In large mixing bowl combine all ingredients. Toss and mix well. If you prefer a more moist stuffing add more broth.

CORNBREAD STUFFING

- 1/2 *cup turkey* **or** *chicken breast, chopped (optional)*
- 1/2 *cup onion, chopped*
- 2 *cups cornbread, crumbled*
- 1 *can chicken broth, defatted*
- 2 *tablespoons celery, chopped*
- 1 1/4 *teaspoon poultry seasoning*
- 1/2 *cup Egg Beaters® egg substitute*
- ~ *salt and pepper to taste*
- 1/2 *cup water*

In skillet simmer turkey, onions, celery, and a half-can chicken broth until onions are tender. Add cornbread, water, the rest of the chicken broth, sprinkle with poultry seasoning, and toss to mix. Add Egg Beaters® and spoon into a veggie-sprayed casserole dish. Bake at 350° F for 45 minutes.

NOTE: *For Cajun cornbread stuffing use Cajun cornbread from page 214 or add 2 tablespoons of sugar to this recipe.*

BACON & SWEET POTATO STUFFING

FOR POULTRY

- 4 *cups mashed, cooked sweet potatoes*
- 8 *Slices turkey bacon, fried crisp, grease removed with paper towel, then crumbled*
- 1 *cup water*
- 1 *medium onion, chopped*
- 1 *cup celery, chopped*
- 2 *cups dry bread, crumbled*
- 1 *teaspoon salt*
- 1/4 *teaspoon paprika*

Sauté onions, celery, salt, and crumbled bacon in water until tender. Pour over bread crumbs, add sweet potatoes, sprinkle with paprika and mix well.

BACON-VEGGIE STUFFING

- 8 *slices turkey bacon, fried crisp and grease pressed out with paper towels and crumbled*
- 10 *cups stale bread, broken in small bite-size pieces.*
- 1 *medium onion*
- 1 *cup greens, chopped (spinach, kale, collards, etc.)*
- 1 *cup asparagus* **or** *other veggie, chopped*
- 2 *teaspoon vegetable bouillon granules*
- 1 *can chicken broth, defatted*
- 1 *8-oz. can oyster pieces and broth*
- 2 *teaspoons poultry seasoning*
- 1 *cup water*
- ~ *salt and pepper to taste*

In skillet, sauté onions, veggies, and greens in some of the broth until tender. In large mixing bowl or pan combine all ingredients and mix well. Season to taste. Use as stuffing with meat, fish, or fowl, cooking until meat is done. If stove-top stuffing is desired, just boil all ingredients before pouring on top of bread pieces, then mix and serve. ▩

APPLE & BREAD STUFFING

- 1/4 *cup chicken broth, defatted*
- 1 *tablespoon onions, finely chopped*
- 1/2 *cup celery, chopped*
- 1 *cup soft bread cubes*
- 2 *cups tart apples, finely chopped*
- 1/2 *teaspoon salt*
- 1/4 *teaspoon paprika*

Sauté onions and celery in chicken broth until tender, pour over bread cubes and mix with apples, add salt and paprika and mix thoroughly.
NOTE: *add more chicken broth if needed.* ▩

CRABMEAT STUFFING

- 1 *6 1/2 -oz. can crabmeat*
- 1/2 *cup Egg Beaters® egg substitute, slightly beaten*
- 1/4 *cup chicken broth, defatted*
- 1/2 *cup onion, chopped*
- 3/4 *cup celery, chopped*
- 4 *slices turkey bacon, fried, grease removed with paper towel, then crumbled*
- 1 *cup soft bread cubes*
- ~ *salt and pepper to taste*

Sauté onion, celery, cooked bacon in chicken broth, cook until tender reducing liquid to about 2 tablespoons. Pour over bread cubes then add crabmeat and egg substitutes. Mix well. Bake this stuffing with meat, fish, or fowl until eggs are thoroughly done. ▩

CHESTNUT STUFFING

- 3 *cups chestnuts, boiled until soft*
- 1/4 *cup raisins*
- 1 *tablespoon Butter Buds® flavored granules*
- 1 *teaspoon salt*
- 1/8 *teaspoon pepper*
- 1/4 *cup evaporated skim milk*
- 1 *cup dry bread crumbs*
- 2 *tablespoons parsley, chopped fresh*
- 1/2 *cup celery, chopped*
- 1 *tablespoon onion, finely chopped*

Peel shells and chop chestnuts in food processor until the size of rice; combine with rest of ingredients and mix well. Bake with poultry. Recipe may be doubled or tripled for a big turkey. ▩

FISH & SHELLFISH

The selections of fish should be limited to varieties having a small amount of fish oil or fat. Some acceptable varieties are: **Flounder, Haddock, Halibut, Snapper, Sole, Cod, Tuna, Orange Roughy, Sea Bass, Scrod.** *Some high-fat varieties include:* **Jack Mackerel, Salmon, Herring, Catfish, Sardines, canned Tuna in oil, Trout, White Fish.** ❀ *Shrimp and crab are low in fat, but shrimp are high in cholesterol. Scallops, on the other hand, are low in fat with less than half the cholesterol of shrimp. Fresh oysters contain about 1/2 gram of fat and 14 milligrams cholesterol per ounce. If you are watching your dietary cholesterol, keep a close watch on shrimp consumption, and make substitutions in your recipes calling for shrimp. If you are not watching cholesterol intake, then shrimp are a nice low-fat food item.* ❀ *All breaded and prepared seafood, unless it passes the 1 gram of fat per ounce test, should be avoided. Some frozen entrées or dinners that contain only 2 or 3 grams (or more) per 8-oz. dinner should be considered.*

CRISPY FISH FILLETS

1 *lb. raw fish*
~ *Shake 'n Bake® seasoning and coating mixture original recipe for fish*

Follow instructions on box.

SHRIMP ÉTOUFFÉE

1 *lb. uncooked shrimp, peeled and deveined*
1/4 *cup chicken broth*
1/2 *cup finely chopped onion*
1/4 *cup finely chopped celery*
1/4 *cup finely chopped green pepper*
1 *tablespoon minced garlic*
1/2 *tablespoon cornstarch*
3/4 *cup water*
1 *teaspoon Butter Buds® butter-flavor sprinkles*
~ *salt, pepper, and cayenne pepper to taste*

Split shrimp, season with salt, pepper, and cayenne pepper, and set aside. Simmer onions, celery, green pepper, garlic, and chicken broth until onions are tender. Dissolve cornstarch in water, add butter flavor and add to onions along with shrimp. Simmer for 10 minutes until shrimp are just done. Correct seasoning and serve over cooked rice.

BAKED CRAB MEAT & SHRIMP

FOR SIX

1 *medium chopped green pepper*
1 *medium chopped onion*
1/2 *cup chopped celery*
1 *small can (6–7 oz.) white crab meat*
1 *lb. cooked, deveined shrimp*
1/2 *teaspoon salt*
1/8 *teaspoon black pepper*
~ *dash cayenne pepper*
1 *teaspoon Worcestershire*
1 *cup fat-free mayonnaise*
1/4 *cup cornflake crumbs*

Preheat oven to 350° F. Except for cornflake crumbs, combine all ingredients and spoon into individual oven-proof cookware. Sprinkle with cornflake crumbs and bake for 30 minutes.

CRISPY SHRIMP

~ *Raw shrimp, deveined and well dried*
~ *Shake 'n Bake® seasoning and coating mixture, original recipe for fish*

Follow instructions on box for fish.

SHRIMP CREOLE

1 *lb. deveined shrimp*
1 *medium chopped onion*
1 *cup beef broth*
1 *teaspoon minced garlic*
1 *cup diced tomatoes*
1 *cup chopped okra*
2 *tablespoons finely diced celery*
1 *tablespoon flour*
1 *teaspoon Louisiana Hot Sauce*
1/4 *teaspoon thyme*
1 *finely chopped bay leaf*
~ *salt, pepper, and cayenne to taste*

In medium skillet on medium heat add onion, garlic, and flour. Brown but do not burn. Add rest of ingredients except shrimp. Simmer for 20 minutes. Add shrimp. Simmer for 10 minutes and season to taste. Serve with boiled rice.

SHRIMP & SAUSAGE GUMBO

3 *tablespoons flour*
1 *lb. medium deveined shrimp*
1/2 *lb. Healthy Choice® smoked sausage, sliced*
1 *teaspoon paprika*
1/2 *cup chopped onion*
1/4 *cup chopped green pepper*
1 *cup okra*
1 *sliced jalapeno pepper*
2 *tablespoons finely chopped celery*
1 *tablespoon minced garlic*
1 *finely chopped bay leaf*
1 *teaspoon Creole seasoning*
1/4 *teaspoon thyme*
1 *teaspoon Louisiana Hot Sauce*
1 *teaspoon Worcestershire sauce*
1 *bunch chopped green onion tops*
1 *can chicken broth*
1 *8-oz. can oysters and juice, strained*
4 *cups hot water*

In Dutch oven, first brown flour then add sausage, garlic, and onions (well browned but not burnt). Add green peppers, jalapeno pepper, celery, okra, and paprika. Simmer for 10 minutes. Except for the shrimp, add the rest of ingredients and simmer for 40 minutes. Remove and cool. Then store overnight in refrigerator. Remove congealed fat from top of liquid. Heat to simmer and add shrimp. Simmer for 10 minutes and remove from heat. Serve with hot homemade rolls and hot cooked rice. If a thicker gumbo is desired, use flour or cornstarch to thicken after chilling and removing fat.

BLACKENED SHRIMP

- ~ *shrimp, deveined*
- ~ *blackening spices*

Skewer shrimp on wooden or stainless steel skewers. Cover abundantly with blackening spices. In heavy cast iron skillet on high heat, spray lightly with veggie spray and place shrimp. Turn over in 3 minutes and blacken other side for 3 minutes. Do not burn.

BROILED CRAB CAKES

- 1 *lb. crab meat, lump back fin*
- 4 *tablespoons fat-free mayonnaise*
- 1/8 *teaspoon white pepper*

Fold ingredients gently together and spoon into individual oven-proof serving dishes. Broil for 10 minutes. Sprinkle with paprika and garnish with chopped parsley if desired.

BAKED FISH FROM MEXICO

- ~ *cod fillets*
- ~ *picante sauce (your favorite)*
- ~ *slices fat-free cheese*

In individual oven-proof serving dishes, place pieces of fish. Spoon on liberally picante sauce and top with cheese. Bake until fish flakes apart.

CREOLE FISH (OR SHRIMP) & MUSHROOMS IN A WHITE CREAM SAUCE

- 1 *lb. raw fish (or shrimp)*
- 3/4 *cup chopped green onion (about 1 small bunch)*
- 1 *tablespoon Butter Buds® butter-flavor sprinkles*
- 1/2 *lb. mushrooms sliced to bite-size*
- 1 *cup white wine*
- 1 *cup evaporated skim milk*
- 1 1/2 *tablespoons flour*
- ~ *salt, pepper, and cayenne pepper to taste*

Sauté onions and mushrooms in wine for five minutes. Add fish, and simmer for another five minutes. Meanwhile, combine milk and flour and mix thoroughly. Pour into fish and simmer for 2 or 3 minutes. Season to taste and serve over rice or pasta.

BAKED FISH IN CREOLE GRAVY

FOR TWO

2 *fish filets*
2 *tablespoons flour*
1 *stalk celery*
1 *green bell pepper*
1 *medium onion*
1 *8-oz. can tomato sauce*
1 *cup water*
~ *salt, pepper, and cayenne to taste*

Preheat oven to 350° F. In medium cast iron skillet brown flour to dark brown but not burnt. Add onion, celery, water, bell pepper, and tomato sauce and simmer until onions are tender. Season to taste. Place fish filets in skillet on top of gravy and bake in oven until fish flakes apart (about 15 minutes). Serve on steamed rice.

Since my favorite fish is the ugly orange roughy, I present more "roughy" recipes than you've ever seen before. Although I specify orange roughy, any similar fish can be substituted.

TERIYAKI ROUGHY

FOR TWO

1/4 *cup teriyaki sauce*
1 *tablespoon sugar*
2 *orange roughy filets*

In small skillet, mix teriyaki sauce and sugar and bring to a boil. Place fish in sauce and simmer for 5 minutes, turn fish and simmer until fish flakes apart. Serve with rice.

CRAB-STUFFED ROUGHY

FOR TWO

1 *6-oz. can crab meat*
1/4 *cup green bell pepper diced*
1 *tablespoon fat-free mayonnaise*
1 *orange roughy filet cut in half*
~ *paprika*

Preheat oven to 400° F. Combine crab meat, pepper, and mayonnaise and spoon into two individual oven-proof dishes. Place fish on top, sprinkle with paprika and bake until fish flakes apart (12-15 minutes).

STUFFED ROUGHY

FOR TWO

- 1 *orange roughy filet (enough for 2)*
- 1 *box stuffing mix*
- 2 *portions vegetable of choice*
- 1 *can defatted chicken broth*
- ~ *paprika*

Preheat oven to 400° F. In a large skillet, add broth, stuffing seasoning, and vegetable and simmer on top burner until tender. Correct the amount of liquid in skillet according to stuffing mix directions. (If stuffing mix calls for 1⅔ cups of water, just make sure you have 1⅔ cups of liquid in your skillet by adding water.) Push vegetables off to one side of skillet and add stuffing bread.
Place fish on top of stuffing, sprinkle with paprika, and pop into the oven to bake until fish flakes apart (10-12 minutes). Remove and serve in skillet. ▩

GENTLE ROUGHY

FOR TWO

- 1 *orange roughy filet (enough for two)*
- ~ *white sauce from page 162*
- 1 *tablespoon chopped fresh parsley*

In a small skillet, place fish in a little water, and over medium heat, simmer for 5 minutes. Turn fish and pour white sauce over fish. Continue simmering for another 5 minutes or until fish flakes apart. Remove from heat, top with parsley, and serve from the skillet. ▩

DRUNKEN ROUGHY

FOR TWO

- 1 *orange roughy filet (enough for two)*
- ½ *cup white wine*
- ~ *white clam sauce from page 163*
- ~ *chopped green onion tops or chives*

Preheat oven to 400° F. Place fish in an oven-proof serving dish pour on the wine. Bake until fish flakes apart (12-15 minutes). Remove, spoon on sauce, and sprinkle with green onion tops. Serve hot. ▩

TEQUILA ROUGHY

FOR TWO

- 1 *large orange roughy filet (enough for two)*
- 1 *chopped Anaheim green pepper*
- ½ *medium chopped onion (green onions are fine)*

1 *medium chopped tomato*
1 *very optional chopped jalapeno pepper (if you don't like it hot, don't add the jalapeno pepper)*
1 *oz. tequila*
~ *salt to taste*

In skillet, sauté onions with a little water until tender. Add pepper and tomato and simmer for 5 minutes. Add tequila and simmer for another minute or so. Salt to taste and remove from heat. Broil fish in oven-proof dish until it flakes apart. Remove and top with pepper/tomato mixture. Serve hot.

BROILED ROUGHY WITH HERBED WHITE BUTTER SAUCE

FOR TWO

1 *large orange roughy filet (enough for two)*
~ *White clam sauce from page 163*
1/2 *teaspoon chopped chives **or** green onion tops*
1/2 *teaspoon parsley*
1/2 *teaspoon tarragon*
1 *teaspoon butter flavoring*

Combine sauce, chives, parsley, tarragon, and butter flavoring. Broil fish until it flakes apart in oven-proof serving dish. Remove from oven and top with sauce mixture. Serve hot.

BROILED GARLIC BUTTER ROUGHY

FOR TWO

1 *orange roughy filet (enough for two)*
1 *packet Butter Buds® butter-flavor sprinkles prepared as per directions*
1 *teaspoon minced garlic*
~ *salt and pepper to taste*
~ *cracker crumbs*
~ *fresh parsley*

In oven-proof dish or individual dishes, place fish. Mix garlic and butter flavoring and pour over top of fish. Add salt and pepper to taste, top with cracker crumbs, and place under broiler until fish flakes apart. Garnish with fresh parsley and serve.

MUSHROOM ROUGHY

FOR TWO

1 *orange roughy filet (enough for two)*
~ *mushroom sauce from page 165*
~ *fresh mushroom caps*
1 *tablespoon chopped parsley*

Simmer fish, mushroom caps, and mushroom sauce in a covered skillet for 5 minutes. Turn fish and sprinkle with parsley and continue simmering until fish flakes apart. Serve in skillet.

CAJUN ROUGHY, VEGGIES, BEANS, & RICE

FOR TWO

1 *packet Lipton® Rice and Beans with Sauce*
1 *cup cut okra*
1 *medium chopped tomato*
1 *cup chopped broccoli*
½ *medium thinly sliced onion*
1 *orange roughy filet (enough for two)*
~ *Cajun seasoning to taste*

Prepare Lipton® Rice and Beans per directions (minus any butter or margarine) in a large cast iron skillet. Add tomato, onion, okra, and broccoli and simmer for 5 minutes. Season orange roughy with Cajun spices and place on top of rice and vegetables. Cover and continue cooking until orange roughy flakes apart. Add favorite bread on top of rice, cover and place skillet in center of dining table and enjoy. Goes well with cheddar cornbread. (page 214)

ORIENTAL ROUGHY

FOR TWO

¼ *cup water*
½ *medium thinly sliced onion*
½ *thinly sliced green bell pepper*
½ *thinly sliced red bell pepper*
½ *teaspoon minced garlic*
1 *teaspoon parsley*
~ *salt and pepper to taste*
1 *box Lipton® Golden Sauté™ Oriental Style*
~ *orange roughy filets for two*
~ *snow pea pods for two*

In large cast iron skillet, sauté onion in water until tender. Add peppers, garlic, parsley, salt, and pepper. Cook for 3 or 4 minutes stirring several times. Remove mixture from skillet and set aside. Prepare Golden Sauté™ in skillet and simmer for 5 minutes. Place orange roughy on top and spoon pepper mixture on top of fish. Add pea pods, cover, and continue simmering until fish flakes apart.

SCALLOPS

If you have ever seen the Shell Oil symbol, you've seen a scallop shell. In days gone by, the scallop shell was used as a plate to eat out of or a cup from which to drink. ❦ There are two types of scallops available in most large supermarket fish sections. The sea scallop is from the deeper sea and is larger than the bay scallop. Bay scallops are smaller and more tender. Both are prepared in the same manner. ❦ Scallops are very low in fat, about 1/4 gram per ounce and, as such, are a welcome variation to our diet.

BROILED SCALLOPS

FOR TWO

- ~ *scallops for two*
- 2 *tablespoons white wine*
- 2 *teaspoons minced garlic*
- ~ *salt and pepper to taste*

In each of two individual oven-proof serving dishes, place one half of the scallops, one tablespoon of white wine, and one teaspoon of garlic, as well as salt and pepper to taste. Broil close to heating element or flame. ❦

BAKED SCALLOPS

FOR TWO

- ~ *scallops for two*
- 1 *teaspoon Butter Buds® butter-flavor sprinkles*
- 1 *teaspoon minced garlic*
- 1 *teaspoon minced green onion tops*
- 1 *tablespoon chopped parsley*
- 1 *teaspoon lemon juice*
- ~ *fat-free cracker crumbs*
- ~ *salt and pepper to taste*
- ~ *paprika*

Preheat oven to 400° F. In each of two individual oven-proof serving dishes, place one half of the scallops and one half of the Butter Buds®, minced garlic, green onion tops, and lemon juice. Sprinkle tops with cracker crumbs and salt and pepper to taste. Bake 10-12 minutes. Remove, sprinkle with paprika, and serve. ❦

SAUTÉED SCALLOPS WITH DILL

FOR TWO

- 1/2 *lb. scallops*
- 1/2 *cup defatted chicken broth*
- 1 *teaspoon Butter Buds® butter-flavor sprinkles*
- 1 *teaspoon chopped onion*
- 1 *teaspoon dill*
- ~ *dash of Tabasco*
- 1 *tablespoon white wine*
- ~ *pepper to taste*

In a medium skillet on medium heat, add chicken broth, Butter Buds®, onions, dill, and Tabasco. Reduce liquid to about 4 tablespoons. Add white wine, scallops and toss. Simmer only until scallops are heated through. Do not overcook!

BLACKENED SCALLOPS

FOR TWO

- 1/2 *lb. scallops*
- ~ *your favorite Cajun blackening spices for fish*
- ~ *vegetable spray*

Place scallops on individual skewers. Dust with Cajun blackening spices and place on hot veggie-sprayed griddle or skillet. Turn over after 3 or 4 minutes and continue cooking until scallops are heated through. Serve on top of a bed of Cajun rice.

CREOLE SCALLOPS

FOR TWO

- 1/2 *lb. scallops*
- 1 *tablespoon flour*
- 1 *can defatted chicken broth*
- 2 *tablespoons chopped onion*
- 1 *tablespoon minced garlic*
- 1/2 *cup chopped tomatoes*
- 1 *teaspoon Tabasco sauce*
- ~ *salt, pepper, and cayenne pepper to taste*

In a medium skillet over medium-high heat. Put in the flour and brown while stirring. Add a little chicken broth and allow to cook off and brown. Continue to stir, splashing on a little more broth until liquid is quite brown but not burnt. Add rest of broth, onion, garlic, tomatoes, and Tabasco sauce. Simmer until onions are tender and season to taste. Add scallops and bring to a simmer for 5 or 6 minutes until scallops are heated through. Serve over rice.

SEAFOOD MEDLEY IN DILL/ TARRAGON SAUCE

FOR TWO

- 1/2 *lb. cod (or your choice of fish)*
- 1/2 *lb. large shrimp, peeled and deveined*
- 1/2 *lb. scallops*
- 2 *tablespoons flour*
- 1/2 *cup evaporated skim milk*
- 2 *teaspoons Butter Buds® butter-flavor sprinkles*
- 1 *tablespoon oyster sauce*
- 2 *tablespoons clam sauce*
- 1/8 *teaspoon pepper*
- 1/2 *teaspoon dry tarragon*
- 1/2 *teaspoon dry dill weed*
- 2 *tablespoons white wine*

Clean fish, cut into bite-size pieces, and along with shrimp, place in a skillet with water, oyster sauce, clam sauce, pepper, tarragon, dill weed, and white wine and bring to a slow simmer until shrimp are heated through. Remove fish and shrimp with slotted spoon and set aside. Reduce broth to about one cup. In a separate bowl, combine and mix thoroughly the milk, Butter Buds®, and flour. Add the flour/ milk mixture to the simmering broth and stir as sauce thickens. Simmer sauce until it is slightly thicker than desired. Add scallops, shrimp, and fish. Barely simmer (don't boil) until scallops are heated through. Remove from heat and serve over pasta or toast. ❖

POTATOES, RICE, PASTA & DRIED BEANS

This section is dedicated to four of your staunchest allies. If you replace these carbohydrates in part with protein (as in meat) or fat, (as in any kind) then fat loss is slowed, or in extremes, is reversed (as in gaining). So load up on these four horsemen and let them carry the day.

POTATOES

BAKED POTATOES

Never wrap a potato in aluminum foil. It will steam your potato and you'll miss the truly "baked" flavor and texture. Heat oven to 450° F. Clean potatoes by using a vigorous scrub brush. Apply salt and coarse ground black pepper to potato. Place on oven rack apart from each other. Bake for 1 hour. If thicker crust is desired continue baking for another hour.

FRENCH FRIED POTATOES

- ~ *potatoes, peeled and cut to even size*
- ~ *Shake 'n Bake® seasoning and coating mixture, original recipe for pork*

Preheat oven to 400° F. Coat potatoes liberally with coating mixture and place separated on baking sheet. Bake for approximately 30 minutes until potatoes are brown and crisp.

POTATOES AU GRATIN

- 2 *cups potatoes, sliced*
- 1/2 *medium onion, sliced*
- 1 *can chicken broth, defatted*
- 1 *tablespoon powdered milk*
- 4 *slices fat-free cheese*
- 3 *tablespoons flour*

Preheat oven to 400° F. In casserole dish combine potatoes, onion, 2 slices of broken up cheese. Mix flour, milk and broth thoroughly, pour on casserole, and top with 2 slices of cheese. Bake 40 minutes or until potatoes are tender and top is browned.

TWICE-BAKED POTATO

- 1 *large potato, baked*
- 2 *slices fat-free cheese*
- 1/8 *teaspoon onion powder*
- 2 *tablespoons evaporated nonfat milk*
- 1 *teaspoon chives* **or** *green onion tops, minced*
- 2 *teaspoons Butter Buds® butter-flavor sprinkles*
- ~ *salt and pepper to taste*

Preheat oven to 400° F. Split potatoes in long halves. Carefully scoop out potato, being cautious not to tear up potato shell. Set shell aside. Combine other ingredients and mash, DON'T BEAT. Spoon into potato shell and bake for 20 minutes or until brown on top and hot inside. ⁂

POTATO SKINS

1 *baked potato (left over)*
1 *slice fat-free cheese*
½ *jalapeno pepper, fresh and sliced*
1 *tablespoon green onion, chopped*
~ *slice tomato, chopped*
1 *tablespoon no-fat sour cream*

Preheat oven to 400° F. Slice potato in half lengthwise. Scoop out part of the potato and discard. Lay cheese on top of potato; then add peppers and onion. Heat in oven for 10 minutes. Remove, top with tomatoes and sour cream. Serve hot. ⁂

MASHED POTATOES

2 *cups potatoes, fresh cooked or instant cooked*
~ *evaporated skim milk as needed for creamy potatoes*
1 *tablespoon Butter Buds® butter-flavor sprinkles*
~ *salt and pepper to taste*

Combine ingredients and whip if necessary. ⁂

RICE

It is said that brown rice is better than white rice and white rice is better than instant rice. But if you are in a hurry, instant rice is great. Wild rice is not rice at all, but is grass seed. As one of the four horsemen carrying your carbohydrate load, rice is deserving of your close attention and HIGH usage.

BOILED RICE

Whether white, brown or instant prepare as per directions.

BAKED CHEESE & RICE WITH YOUR CHOICE OF VEGETABLE

- 2 *cups rice, cooked*
- 1 *can chicken broth, defatted*
- 3 *tablespoons flour*
- 6 *slices fat-free cheese*
- 1 *cup vegetables, cooked (your choice)*

Preheat oven to 400° F. Combine ingredients and spoon into a casserole dish. Bake for 20 minutes.

RICE & LEMON RAISINS

- 1 *cup instant rice, uncooked*
- 1 *cup water*
- 1/4 *cup maple syrup (maple-flavored)*
- ~ *juice of 1/2 lemon*
- 1/2 *cup raisins*

In saucepan bring water, raisins, syrup, and lemon juice to a boil for 3 minutes. Add rice, cover, and remove from heat. Let sit for 5 minutes. Fluff with fork and serve. Goes well with baked poultry.

SPANISH RICE

- 2 *cups instant rice, uncooked*
- 1 *cup chicken broth, defatted*
- 1 *cup canned tomatoes, diced*
- 1 *teaspoon garlic, minced*
- 2 *tablespoons onions, diced*
- 1 *fresh jalapeno pepper, diced*
- 1/2 *teaspoon paprika*
- ~ *salt to taste*

In saucepan bring to boil all ingredients *except* rice. Boil for 3 minutes. Add rice, cover and remove from heat. Let sit for 5 minutes. Fluff and serve.

PARSLEY BUTTERED RICE

For each cup of cooked rice, add one teaspoon Butter Buds®, one teaspoon chopped parsley, and salt and pepper to taste. Add during the cooking process.

DIRTY RICE

2 *chicken livers*
1 *can chicken broth, defatted (page 104)*
3 *green onions, finely chopped (tops and all)*
1 *teaspoon garlic, minced*
1 *cup instant rice*
salt and pepper to taste

In saucepan, simmer ingredients (except for rice) until livers are done. Remove livers, chop, and return to pan along with rice. Simmer to allow rice to absorb liquid, remove from heat.

SHRIMP FRIED RICE

1 *6.7-oz. Package Lipton® Golden Sauté™, oriental or beef style*
1/2 *cup bean sprouts*
1/2 *cup Egg Beaters®, scrambled*
1/2 *cup green onion tops, sliced*
1/4–1/2 *lb. shrimp, peeled and de-veined*

Prepare Lipton® Saute™ as directed in pan *without* butter or margarine. After three minutes boiling time add shrimp to pan and continue simmering for 7 minutes or until rice is tender. Remove from heat and let sit for 5 minutes. Add green onions, Egg Beaters®, (already scrambled) and bean sprouts. Toss gently and serve.

WILD RICE

Wild rice or Mahnomen, as the Indians call it, has been harvested in the lakes and streams of the Great Lakes area since long before the dawn of written history. It is found in great abundance in the shallow, cool lakes of northern Minnesota and the adjacent area of Canada. Recently, successful wild-rice farming has been developed in the same geographic areas. Now an increasing farm harvest is becoming available to supplement the ancient Indian harvest. ❧ *The wild rice produced on the wild rice paddies is identical and indistinguishable in both appearance and taste from the lake harvest from which the paddy seed is derived—if both types are identically processed. Differences in color and flavor are a result of processing techniques.* ❧ *In harvesting the lake crop, a boat or canoe is poled through the wild rice by one person. A second person bends the heads of the wild rice plant over the boat with a flailing stick and strikes them with another such stick to dislodge the plump, ripe kernels. The unripe kernels adhere to the stem until ripe, requiring several trips, some days apart, to complete the harvest.* ❧ *The wild rice grown in paddies is harvested in the most careful, modern method in order to secure the highest possible yield. The water is released in the late summer allowing sufficient time for the ground to firm and yet not impede the growth of the wild rice plant. Large, efficient grain combines are used to harvest the kernels eliminating as much waste as possible.* ❧ *Wild rice used to be scarce and expensive, but now it's more available and affordable. You'll enjoy the nutty, toasted flavor, the firm, crunchy bite of this elegant grain. A nutritious, high-fiber carbohydrate with only 70 calories per half-cup serving, it goes with today's smarter, "in-style" menus.*

A LITTLE MAKES A LOT

1 cup wild rice = 3–4 cups cooked = 6–8 servings!

EASY TO PREPARE

Wash wild rice thoroughly. In a medium saucepan, cover 1 cup wild rice with 3 to 4 cups water. Add 1 teaspoon salt, if desired. Bring to a boil and simmer. Check it after 45 minutes. If most of the grains have split and the inner, lighter part is visible, it's just right. At this stage, it's got good texture and bite. ❧ *It you prefer a softer rice, simply cook it a few moments longer, until most of the grains are puffed and some are curly. (But don't let it get mushy.) Most of the water will be absorbed, and the rest can be drained off.*

KEEPS WELL

Dry wild rice keeps for months in a dry, tight container. Plain, cooked wild rice should be drained well and stored air-tight. Refrigerated, it will keep well for a week. Frozen, it will keep for months.

VERSATILE

Wild rice adds a special touch to many recipes. ❧ *To make a creamy Wild Rice Soup: Add 2 tablespoons cooked wild rice, for each serving to cream of mushroom soup, page 91. To make a Wild Rice Waldorf Salad: Add cooked wild rice to Waldorf Salad recipe, page 95.* ❀ *To make a Wild Rice Chicken Salad: Add cooked wild rice to Chicken Salad recipe, page 96.* ❀ *To make Wild Rice Tabbouleh Salad: Substitute cooked wild rice for the bulgur in your favorite Tabbouleh recipe.* ❀ *The preceding information, along with the following recipes, have been provided by the Minnesota Paddy Wild Rice Council, St. Paul, Minnesota. I have modified the recipes by removing fatty ingredients.*

WILD RICE SAUTÉ

4-6 *cups cooked wild rice*
1 *large onion, chopped*
1/4 *lb. fresh mushrooms, sliced*
1 *large bell pepper, cut into strips (use half red and half green pepper)*
1/2 *cup chicken broth*
~ *salt* **or** *seasoning salt*
1/4 *teaspoon garlic salt*
~ *pepper, as desired*

Sauté the onion, mushrooms, and bell pepper in the chicken broth, adding salt, garlic salt, and pepper as desired. Cook only until vegetables are tender, but still crisp. Add the wild rice, stir, and when wild rice is heated through, serve. Serves 6 to 8, depending upon the amount of wild rice used. ❀

WILD RICE AU GRATIN

4 *cups cooked wild rice*
2 *cups sliced fresh mushrooms, about 1/4 lb.*
1/4 *cup chicken broth*
2 *cups grated non fat cheese*
~ *vegetable spray*

Sauté the mushrooms in the broth until the mushrooms soften slightly. Toss wild rice with sautéed mushrooms and cheese: spoon into a veggie-sprayed 2-qt. casserole. Cover and bake at 325° F about 20 minutes. Uncover and bake 10 minutes longer. Serves 4 as a main dish, up to 8 if used as a side dish with meat. ❀

WILD RICE STUFFING

Use with poultry, game, roast or chops

3 *cups cooked wild rice*
4 *slices turkey bacon*
1/2 *cup chicken broth, defatted*
1 *medium onion, chopped*
1/2 *lb. mushrooms, sliced*
3 *ribs celery, chopped*
1 *teaspoon crushed leaf oregano*
1/2 *teaspoon crushed leaf sage*
2 *cups bread crumbs*
~ *salt and pepper, if needed*

Fry bacon crisp, remove, and press grease from bacon using paper towels. Cut bacon into one-inch pieces and sauté with onions, mushrooms, celery, and chicken broth until tender. Add this to the wild rice, along with the oregano, sage, and bread crumbs. Adjust seasonings with salt and pepper if needed. Makes enough stuffing for a 10 to 14 lb. turkey. (If cooking separately, bake, covered, in a casserole at 350° F for 30 to 40 minutes. Add more chicken stock, if needed, for moisture.)

WILD RICE ORIENTAL SOUP

1 1/2 *cups cooked wild rice*
8 *cups chicken stock, seasoned to taste*
1 *whole chicken breast, skinless, de-boned*
24 *fresh, small pea pods*
18 *carrot curls** **or** *1/4-inch diagonal carrot slices*
2 *teaspoons ginger juice, (press fresh ginger pieces through a garlic press)*

Poach the chicken breast in stock; remove chicken breast and cool. Cut into julienne strips. Poach pea pods in chicken stock until just tender, about 6 minutes; remove from stock.

Poach carrot curls in stock about 1 minute (do not overcook). Remove from stock and let cool; remove picks, being careful to maintain "curls."

Strain chicken stock through cheese cloth until it is clear. Add ginger juice to stock and adjust seasonings to taste. Reheat stock to serving temperature.

Meanwhile, arrange wild rice and chicken strips in the bottoms of 6 soup bowls. Place 6 poached pea pods in each bowl and divide the stock between bowls, pouring slowly into the sides of bowls. Arrange 3 carrot curls in the center of each serving and serve immediately. Serves 6, as a first course soup or a light entrée.

*** TO MAKE CARROT CURLS:** *Large, thick carrots are best for these. Scrape carrots. With a vegetable parer, cut wide, thin slice down the length of carrot. Roll slice around index finger, fasten with a toothpick.*

LEMON-TARRAGON WILD RICE

- 4 *cups cooked wild rice*
- 1/4 *cup chicken broth*
- 1 *tablespoon instant chicken bouillon granules*
- 1 *tablespoon fresh lemon juice*
- 1-2 *tablespoons chopped fresh tarragon*
- ~ *salt and pepper to taste*
- ~ *strips of lemon peel and sprigs of fresh tarragon, for garnish*

Mix chicken broth, bouillon granules, lemon juice, and tarragon. Cook over low heat until bouillon granules are dissolved, adding a tablespoon of water, only if necessary. Add the wild rice, adjust seasonings if desired, and continue cooking until wild rice is thoroughly heated. Garnish with strips of lemon peel and sprigs of fresh tarragon. Serves 6.

WILD RICE QUICHE FLORENTINE

- 1 1/2 *cups cooked wild rice*
- 1/2 *cup finely chopped leek*
- 1/4 *cup chicken broth (defatted)*
- 1/4 *cup finely chopped parsley*
- 1 *cup finely chopped fresh spinach,* ***or*** *1/2 (9 or 10-oz.) pkg. frozen chopped spinach, thawed and drained well*
- 3/4 *teaspoon salt*
- 1/4 *teaspoon pepper*
- 1/4 *cup finely chopped raisins*
- 1 *cup Egg Beaters® egg substitute (lightly beaten)*
- 1 *cup evaporated skim milk*
- 1 *(9-inch) pie crust, (uncooked) (page 222)*
- ~ *non-fat plain yogurt* ***or*** *sour cream*

Sauté the leek in the chicken broth about 2 minutes. Combine this with the wild rice, parsley, spinach, salt and pepper, and raisins. Add the egg substitute and milk and mix well. Pour the mixture into the pie crust. Bake at 425° F for 10 minutes, then reduce heat to 325° and continue baking 30 minutes, or until a knife inserted near center comes out clean. Let set about 15 minutes before slicing. Serve as a main dish with a dollop of yogurt or non-fat dairy sour cream. Serves 6 to 8.

LOBSTER WILD RICE BISQUE

- 1 *cup chopped onions*
- 1 *4 1/2-oz. jar sliced mushrooms, drained*
- 2 *tablespoons flour*
- 1/2 *teaspoon salt*
- 1/2 *teaspoon pepper*
- 2 *teaspoons crushed rosemary*
- 4 *cups chicken broth*
- 1/4 *cup cooking sherry*

1 *cup evaporated skim milk*
1 *cup chopped tomatoes, fresh or canned*
2 *cups cooked wild rice*
8 *oz. imitation lobster, cut in 1" chunks*
6 *oz. yolk-free egg noodles, cooked*
2 *cups shredded fat-free cheese*

Sauté onion and mushrooms in 1/4 cup broth. Stir in flour, salt, pepper and rosemary. Cook until bubbly. Gradually add rest of chicken broth, heat until boiling, stirring often. Stir in sherry and milk. Add tomatoes, wild rice, lobster, and noodles. Heat thoroughly. Fold in cheese. 8 servings.

TURKEY WILD RICE CHILI

1 *medium onion*
1 *garlic clove, minced*
1 *lb. turkey breast slices, cut in 1/2" pieces*
2 *cups cooked wild rice*
1 *15-oz. can great northern white beans, drained*
1 *11-oz. can white corn, whole kernel*
2 *4-oz. cans diced green chilies*
1 *14 1/2-oz. can chicken broth, defatted*
1 *teaspoon ground cumin*
~ *hot pepper sauce*
6 *oz. fat-free cheese, shredded*
~ *parsley (optional)*

Heat 2 tablespoons of chicken broth in large pan over medium heat; add onion and garlic. Cook until tender. Add turkey, wild rice, beans, corn, chilies, rest of broth and cumin. Cover and simmer over low heat 30 minutes or until turkey is tender. To serve, stir hot pepper sauce into chili to taste. Serve with shredded cheese. Garnish with parsley. 6 to 8 servings.

WILD RICE GOURMET BURGERS

4 *lb. lean ground buffalo*
3 *cups cooked wild rice*

Mix well. Form into 22 to 24 patties. Freeze in quantities to suit your family. Defrost before pan frying or broiling.
SEASONED BURGERS – *add seasoned salt, minced onion, parsley, or other seasonings before freezing.*
CHEESEBURGERS – *add a slice of fat-free cheese.*

WILD RICE LEMON SEAFOOD SALAD

1 *cup cooked wild rice*
6 *imitation crabmeat sticks, cut in one-inch pieces*
1 *cup cooked yolk-free egg noodles*
1 *cup cubed jicama*
1 *medium avocado, cubed*

DRESSING:
3/4 *cup lemon yogurt*
1/2 *cup sour cream (fat free)*
1/2 *teaspoon curry powder*

Lightly toss together salad ingredients. In small bowl, blend dressing ingredients. Top salad with dressing. 4 servings.

ARTICHOKE WILD RICE SALAD

2 *cups cooked wild rice*
1 *cup frozen peas, thawed*
1 *8-oz. can sliced water chestnuts, drained*
1 *6-oz. jar marinated artichoke hearts, drained*
4 *oz. fat-free cheese, cubed*
1 *2-oz. jar diced pimento, drained*
6 *tablespoons fat-free Italian salad dressing*

In large bowl, combine salad ingredients and mix with dressing. Chill 4 hours or overnight, to blend flavors.
6 to 8 servings.

DILLY WILD-RICE CRABWICH

12 *oz. imitation crab meat, shredded*
1 *cup fat-free cheese, shredded*
1/2 *teaspoon dill seed*
1 *cup cooked wild rice*
3 *oz. cream cheese, non-fat*
1/2 *teaspoon garlic powder*
6 *drops hot sauce*
10 *slices French bread, cut in 1/2" slices*

Mix first 7 ingredients. Set aside. Spread crab mixture on 5 bread slices. Make a sandwich by topping each with second piece of French bread. Grill until warmed through and browned, about 6 minutes each side. Makes 5 sandwiches.
VARIATION: ***Use cocktail rye bread for a grilled mini-sandwich appetizer.***

TURKEY WILD RICE MEATBALLS

- 1 *lb. ground turkey breast*
- 1 *cup cooked wild rice*
- 1/4 *cup beef broth (from 15-oz. can)*
- 2 *egg whites, slightly beaten*
- 1/4 *cup chopped leeks* **or** *green onions*
- 1 *garlic clove, minced*
- 1/4 *teaspoon salt*
- 1/8 *teaspoon pepper*
- ~ *vegetable spray*
- 6 *oz. spaghetti, cooked*

SAUCE:

- 1 3/4 *cups (or remaining) beef broth*
- 1 *6-oz. can tomato paste*
- 1 *4 1/2-oz. jar sliced mushrooms, undrained*
- 1/2 *cup chopped green pepper*
- 1/4 *cup chopped onion*
- 2 *tablespoons chopped parsley (or 1 tablespoon dried)*
- 2 *tablespoons oregano leaves (or teaspoon dried)*

Mix meatball ingredients except for spaghetti. Shape in one-inch balls. In veggie-sprayed skillet using medium-high heat, brown meatballs; move to side of pan. Add sauce ingredients and carefully stir to blend. Stir sauce and meatballs together. Simmer, covered, about 30 minutes, until sauce is thickened and vegetables are tender. Prepare spaghetti as directed on package. Serve meatballs over spaghetti. 6 servings.

VARIATION: ***make smaller meatballs and serve as an appetizer.***

WILD RICE TETRAZZINI

- 1 *cup chopped green pepper*
- 1 *cup chopped onion*
- 1 *8-oz. jar sliced mushrooms, drained*
- 1 *lb. ground turkey breast*
- 1 *teaspoon salt*
- 1 *teaspoon pepper*
- 2 *teaspoons garlic powder*
- 3 *tablespoons flour*
- 2 *cups chicken broth, defatted*
- 2 *cups milk, evaporated, skimmed*
- 1/2 *cup cooking sherry*
- 2 *cups spaghetti, cooked and drained*
- 3 *cups cooked wild rice*
- 2 *cups shredded fat-free mozzarella cheese*
- ~ *parsley flakes*

Preheat oven to 350° F. Sauté green pepper, onion, and mushrooms in 1/4 cup chicken broth. Add turkey, brown. Add seasonings. Mix flour with remaining broth and milk, stir and cook 5 minutes. Add sherry. Heat thoroughly. Place spaghetti and wild rice in a 5-quart, veggie-sprayed casserole. Mix in 1 cup cheese. Pour turkey mixture in casserole; lightly mix. Top with remaining cheese and parsley. Cover with foil. Bake 30 minutes. Remove foil, continue to bake approximately 10 minutes to brown.

WILD STUFFED PEPPERS

1 *lb. lean ground buffalo*
2 *cups cooked wild rice*
1 *medium onion, chopped*
1/2 *cup dried fruit bits **or** raisins*
1 *cup fat-free Swiss cheese, shredded*
1 *teaspoon salt*
1 *teaspoon pepper*
1 *teaspoon cinnamon*
6 *green peppers*

Preheat oven to 350° F. Cut green peppers in half and remove stems and seeds. Combine the rest of the ingredients. Lightly stuff the green pepper halves with the wild rice mixture. Place in baking dish and loosely cover with foil. Bake 30 minutes. Uncover, bake 10 minutes or until pepper is tender. 6 servings.

WILD RICE TURKEY OSCAR

1 *lb. turkey breast tenderloins*
6 *oz. imitation crab meat*
4 *oz. fat-free cheese, shredded*
1 *tablespoon lemon juice*
1 *teaspoon Dijon mustard*
4 *cups water*
1 1/2 *cups uncooked wild rice*
1 *tablespoon instant chicken bouillon*
1 *tablespoon chopped fresh tarragon **or** 1 tsp. dried*
1/2 *cup raisins*
1 *15-oz. can asparagus spears*
~ *Vegetable spray*
~ *White wine sauce from page ?*

Preheat oven to 325° F. Spray 9" x 13" pan with vegetable spray. With a sharp knife make a pocket in the long side of tenderloin pieces; cut to within one-half inch of each end. In a medium bowl combine crab, cheese, lemon juice, and mustard. Stuff about one-third of the crab filling in each pocket. Pin together with toothpicks. Place in prepared pan. Spoon remaining filling over top of stuffed tenderloins. Cover with foil and bake about 45 minutes. Uncover; bake 15-20 min. until turkey is done.

Meanwhile, in large saucepan bring water to a boil. Add wild rice, bouillon, and tarragon. Cover and simmer 45 minutes, or until rice is tender and grains are starting to puff open. Drain. Stir in raisins. Heat asparagus spears. Spoon wild rice onto large serving platter. Slice each turkey tenderloin into 6 slices. Arrange slices over wild rice. Top with wine sauce and asparagus spears; garnish with fresh tarragon, if desired. 6 servings.

WILD RICE BREAKFAST BREAD

- 1/4 *cup brown sugar*
- 4 *egg whites*
- 1 *teaspoon vanilla*
- 1 1/2 *cups well-cooked wild rice*
- 1/2 *cup chopped raisins*
- 3/4 *cup whole wheat flour*
- 3/4 *cup white flour*
- 1 *teaspoon baking powder*
- 1 *teaspoon salt*
- 2 *teaspoons cinnamon*
- 3/4 *cup skimmed milk*
- ~ *vegetable spray*

Preheat oven to 325° F. Add eggs and sugar and beat until fluffy. Add vanilla. Stir in wild rice and raisins. Mix dry ingredients together; combine everything and stir just until dry ingredients are moistened. Pour mixture into an 8" x 4" veggie-sprayed loaf pan. Bake 55-60 minutes. Serve with raspberry jam.

*** NOTE: *When combining sugar and wild rice, it is essential to cook wild rice very well. Wild rice has a unique property; combining with sugar causes the wild rice to revert to a hard kernel. "Over" cooking the wild rice prior to combining with sugar solves this problem.***

NORTHWOODS BUTTERMILK CAKE

- 2 *cups well-cooked wild rice*
- 1 *cup whole wheat flour*
- 2 *cups all-purpose flour*
- 2 *teaspoons baking soda*
- 1/2 *teaspoon salt*
- 1/2 *teaspoon nutmeg*
- 1 *cup prunes* **or** *dates, pureed in*
- 1/2 *cup water*
- 1 *cup packed brown sugar*
- 1 *teaspoon vanilla*
- 8 *egg whites*
- 1/2 *cup raisins*
- 1/3 *cup applesauce*
- 1 *cup buttermilk*
- ~ *vegetable spray*

Preheat oven to 350° F. Veggie spray and lightly flour 9" x 13" pan. In medium bowl stir together flours, baking soda, salt, and nutmeg.

In another bowl add brown sugar and vanilla; add eggs, one at a time, beating one minute after each (batter will look curdled). Add raisins, prunes or dates, and applesauce, blending well after each. Add dry ingredients and buttermilk alternately to mixture, blending well. Stir in wild rice. Turn into prepared pan. Bake 45-50 minutes or till done. Do not overbake. Cool. Frost with a favorite frosting or top each serving with whipped cream. (page 252)

NORTH COUNTRY WILD RICE PANCAKES

1 cup Egg Beaters® egg substitute
1¹/₄ cups buttermilk
¹/₂ teaspoon baking soda
1¹/₄ cups all-purpose flour
1 teaspoon baking powder
¹/₂ teaspoon salt
1 teaspoon sugar
1 cup cooked wild rice
~ vegetable spray

In a large bowl, whisk together the eggs, buttermilk, and baking soda. In another bowl mix flour, baking powder, salt, and sugar and add to the egg mixture. Whisk in the wild rice. Cook pancakes on hot veggie-sprayed griddle until golden on both sides. Serve with maple syrup.
NOTE: *For thicker pancakes, use only ¹/₂ cup egg substitute.*

WILD RICE FANCY

1¹/₂ cups cooked wild rice
¹/₂ cup packed brown sugar
¹/₂ cup dates, chopped
¹/₂ cup maraschino cherries, halved
~ whipped cream from page 252

Combine wild rice, brown sugar, dates, and cherries. Chill. Serve with whipped cream from page ?.
NOTE: *Prepare in advance to let flavors blend. 4 to 6 servings. Variation: also good served with milk as a cold cereal.*

MEXICALI WILD RICE CASSEROLE

This quick-to-make casserole features the popular ingredients of Mexican foods with wild rice in a meatless, main dish entree. Vegetarians, as well as those who are trying to eat foods which are low in cholesterol, will like this recipe!

2 cups cooked wild rice
1 (about 17-oz.) can whole kernel corn, drained
1 (about 4-oz.) can chopped **or** *diced green chilies, drained*
2 cups (16-oz.) chunky, mild salsa sauce (use medium for hotter flavor)

1 *cup grated cheese (fat free)*
~ *corn **or** tortilla chips from page 171.*

Combine the cooked wild rice with the corn and chilies and spread in a lightly oiled 7" x 11" casserole. Spread the salsa sauce over this and sprinkle with the cheese. Cover and heat at 350° F about 30 minutes. Serve with a basket of baked corn or tortilla chips. Serves 4 as a main dish casserole.

To serve individual servings, heat the casserole ingredients without the cheese and spoon over corn or tortilla chips on individual plates; sprinkle cheese on top and, if desired, heat either under a broiler or in a microwave to melt cheese.

LEMON WILD RICE CONSOMMÉ

This simple beef consommé with the light lemony taste and the filling, nutritious grains of wild rice could be just for you!

4 *cups clear beef broth*
4 *teaspoons fresh lemon juice*
1 *cup shredded leaf lettuce*
2 *cups cooked wild rice*
*8-12 slivers of lemon peel **or** 4 thin lemon slices (2 or 3 slivers or 1 slice per serving)*

Heat beef broth and lemon juice until very hot or just to a boil, but do not allow to boil for any amount of time. Place 1/4 cup shredded lettuce and 1/2 cup wild rice in each of 4 soup cups or bowls. Divide slivers of lemon peel and/or lemon slices in each bowl. Dividing evenly, pour hot beef liquid over other soup ingredients and serve immediately. Serves 4.

NOTE: *Soup can be served cold or at room temperature, but beef broth and lemon juice should be heated together and allowed to cool to room temperature. If serving soup this way, do not combine lettuce and broth until broth is cooled to room temperature.*

WILD RICE MEDITERRANEAN WITH TUNA

Fresh herbs, garlic, onion, and fresh fish are some of the earthy flavors of Provence, a part of southern France that touches the Mediterranean Sea. In this recipe, these country and seaside flavors are combined with one of the most unique American foods, wild rice. Complement this main dish with fresh sliced tomatoes, and good French bread.

2 *cups cooked wild rice*
1 *cup unpeeled zucchini, cut into 1/4-inch slices*
1/2 *cup coarsely chopped red onion*

1/4 *cup chicken broth (defatted)*
4 *garlic cloves, pressed* **or** *very finely chopped*
1/2 *teaspoon mixed dried herbs, such as thyme, parsley, summer savory* **or** *oregano (or 1/2 cup mixed fresh summer herbs, bruised and very finely chopped)*
1/2 *teaspoon salt*
2 *fresh grilled or broiled tuna steaks, or 1 (6 1/2 oz, packed in water) can chunk tuna, drained.*

Prepare wild rice, zucchini, and red onion. Heat chicken broth with the garlic, salt, and herbs, pressing with the back of a wooden spoon to extract flavors. Add zucchini and onion and sauté about 1 minute, turning gently once. Add cooked wild rice and sauté until heated through. Do not overcook vegetables. Serve hot as a side dish with fresh tuna steaks, using fresh parsley and herbs to garnish. Serves 2.

If fresh tuna is not available, drain the can of tuna and reserve the nicest whole chunks. Divide the remaining pieces of tuna on two individual serving plates or a platter and top with hot wild rice and zucchini mixture. Arrange the reserved chunks of tuna on top and garnish with fresh parsley and/or herbs. Serves 2.

WILD RICE & SPINACH SALAD

With a hearty bread and fruit for dessert, this main dish salad can be a lunch or dinner entree that is low in fat and high in nutrition. The soy-flavored salad dressing adds an Oriental flavor.

2 *cups cooked wild rice, drained well and cooled*
2 *cups fresh spinach, torn into bite-sized pieces*
1/2 *cup thinly sliced green onion*
1/2 *cup cooked crisp, crumbled turkey bacon with grease pressed out with a paper towel*
2 *skinless, defatted chicken breasts, poached and cooled*
1/2 *cup Italian salad dressing (fat free)*
1 *tablespoon soy sauce*
1/2 *tablespoon sugar*

Prepare the wild rice, spinach, green onion, and bacon. Remove meat from chicken breasts in large chunks or "shreds." Combine salad dressing, soy sauce, and sugar, stirring to dissolve sugar. If doing salad preparations ahead of time, package and refrigerate each ingredient and dressing separately. When ready to serve, toss all ingredients in a serving bowl adding the dressing during the final tossing.
Serves 4.

NOTE: ***to make a "wilted" salad, heat the dressing before tossing with the ingredients.***

WILD RICE & CARROT MUFFINS

When cooking wild rice, cook some extra to try these carrot and wild rice muffins. With carrots, whole wheat flour and wild rice, these muffins can be a healthy addition to any mealtime or snack occasion. For sweeter muffins, frost cooled muffins with sweetened cream cheese frosting. (page 249)

- 1 *cup cooked wild rice*
- 1 *cup grated carrots*
- 3/4 *cup all-purpose flour*
- 3/4 *cup whole wheat flour*
- 2 *teaspoon baking powder*
- 1/2 *teaspoon salt*
- 1 *teaspoon cinnamon*
- 1/2 *teaspoon nutmeg*
- 1/2 *cup brown sugar*
- 2 *egg whites, lightly beaten*
- 3/4 *cup milk, skimmed*
- 1/2 *cup raisins puréed in 1/4 cup water*
- ~ *vegetable spray*

FOR TOPPING:

- 1 *tablespoon sugar*
- 1/4 *teaspoon cinnamon*

Preheat oven to 400° F. Prepare wild rice and carrots and set aside. Combine flours, baking powder, salt, cinnamon, nutmeg and brown sugar together in a mixing bowl, stirring to blend. Add the cooked wild rice to the dry ingredients and toss to coat wild rice.

In another bowl, combine the egg whites with the milk and raisins, add the grated carrots, then stir these wet ingredients into the dry ingredients, mixing just enough to blend well. Do not overmix. Divide batter evenly between 12 veggie-sprayed and floured (or paper muffin cup-lined) 2 1/2 inch muffin cups. Mix 1 tablespoon sugar with 1/4 teaspoon cinnamon for topping and sprinkle this over muffin batter. Bake at 400°, 20 to 25 minutes. Remove muffins from pans and cool on wire racks. Makes 12 muffins.

PASTA

Pasta is generally flour, water, and some nutrient-enriching additives. NEVER use egg noodles or pasta exceeding 1 gram of fat per 2-oz. (dry weight) portion. Observe the 1 gram of fat per 2-oz. portion and anything goes. ❋ In preparing your pasta, never use oil or fat in the cooking process; otherwise follow manufacturer's directions.

AMERICAN CLASSIC SPAGHETTI

1 *can (27¼ oz) Hunt's® Chunky Style Spaghetti Sauce*
½ *cup onions, chopped*
½ *cup bell pepper, diced*
1 *cup fresh whole mushrooms, small to medium size*
~ *pasta, your choice*

In saucepan simmer spaghetti sauce, onions, and peppers for 5 minutes. Add mushrooms and simmer for 15 minutes. Spoon onto pasta and serve. ❋

MACARONI & CHEESE

2 *cups dry elbow macaroni*
1 *batch cheese sauce (page 162)*
4 *slices fat-free cheese*

Preheat oven to 375° F. Prepare dry macaroni as per package instructions. Remove from stove and drain. Add cheese sauce and put mixture into a 2-quart casserole dish. Cover top with fat-free cheese and bake uncovered until top is slightly browned and sauce is bubbling, about 25 minutes. ❋

SEAFOOD MEDLEY WITH FETTUCINE

~ *cooked fettucine for 4*
½ *cup water*
¼ *cup crab meat* **or** *crab blend*
1 *tablespoon parsley, minced*
¼ *cup green onion tops, chopped*
1 *tablespoon dry powdered milk, no-fat*
1 *tablespoon flour*
1 *can chicken broth, defatted*
1 *cup mixed seafood, cooked*
~ *salt and white pepper to taste*

In blender add 1/2 cup water and crab meat and reduce to puree. Pour into a medium saucepan; add parsley, onion, and powdered non fat milk. Simmer on medium heat for 3 minutes. In bowl mix flour and chicken broth. Add to saucepan and simmer gently for 4 minutes. Stir to keep from burning. Remove from heat and add mixed seafood. Serve on fettucine.

MACARONI SALAD

- 2 *cups uncooked elbow macaroni*
- 1 *tablespoon Thousand Island dressing, fat free*
- 1 *tablespoon pickle relish*
- 1 *tablespoon mayonnaise, fat free*
- 2 *boiled eggs, chopped (discard yolks)*
- ~ *garnish with sweet pickle slices* ***or*** *pickled green tomato slices*

Cook macaroni, wash with cold water. Mix in the dressing, relish, mayonnaise, and eggs. Garnish top of dish with sweet pickle or pickled tomato slices.

SMOKED TURKEY FETTUCINE

- ~ *fettucine cooked for 4*
- 1 *cup skimmed milk*
- 1 *can chicken broth, defatted*
- 2 *cups hickory-smoked skinned turkey breast, cubed*
- 1 *cup whole mushrooms, small to medium size*
- 2 *tablespoons flour*
- 3 *slices fat-free cheese*
- ~ *salt and white pepper to taste*
- ~ *parsley sprigs*

In medium saucepan on medium heat, add milk, 1/2-can chicken broth and turkey. Simmer for 5 minutes. Add mushrooms and simmer for 5 minutes. Mix thoroughly, flour and 1/2 can chicken broth, add to saucepan along with the cheese. Simmer for 3 minutes. Season to taste and serve on top of fettucine. Garnish with parsley.

TOMATO & CHEESE FETTUCINE

- ~ *cooked fettucine*
- ~ *cheese sauce (page 162)*
- 1/2 *cup green onion tops, chopped*
- 1 *cup fresh tomatoes, bite-size pieces*
- ~ *salt and pepper to taste*

In medium saucepan on medium heat, combine cheese sauce, onion, and tomato. Heat to simmer, remove from heat. Season to taste and serve on top of fettucine. ❖

PASTA FIESTA

- 8 *oz. dry, multicolored spiral pasta*
- 1 *cup whole mushrooms cooked and marinated*
- 2 *tomatoes, ripe and cut into bite-size pieces*
- 1/2 *onion, sliced (sweet onion is best)*
- 1/2 *bell pepper, bite-size pieces*
- 1 *tablespoon red wine vinegar or your favorite non-fat dressing*
- 1 *fresh jalapeno pepper, seeded and sliced*
- 1 *teaspoon dry basil*

Cook pasta, wash, and chill. Boil mushrooms for 5 minutes. Remove and place in your favorite marinade sauce overnight. If you don't have a favorite, try balsamic vinegar, sliced onion rings and baby beets. Use the beet-colored onion rings for your salad. Next day, drain mushrooms and combine all ingredients. Toss and serve. ❖

DRIED BEANS (LEGUMES)

Beans have been, and continue to be, an absolute staple in many parts of the world. When coupled with rice or corn it is the protein source of choice for many peoples. In the orient, the soybean is almost never eaten as a bean, but is consumed as soy sauce, tofu, and many other variations. In our Southwest the pinto bean is preferred; in the Southeast, the black-eyed pea; in Boston, the navy bean, and if you see a lot of black beans, you are probably in South America or the Caribbean.

PREPARATION

Choose your favorite bean. Clean and wash. Soak beans overnight and do ***not*** *discard the soaking water but add to it so as to cover the beans. Gently simmer the beans until tender. Keep the beans adequately covered with water while cooking. Season with flavors you desire. No-fat bacon flavor or smoked salt works well, onions, peppers (all kinds), tomatoes, salt, and molasses continue to be used as traditional seasonings for different beans.*

SOUTH-WESTERN PINTO BEANS

YIELDS 4 CUPS

1 *cup dried pinto beans*
1/2 *medium onion, diced*
1/2 *cup salsa, thick and chunky*
1 *fresh jalapeno pepper, sliced (optional)*
~ *salt to taste*

Soak beans overnight. Mix ingredients together and simmer until tender.

MEXICAN PINTO BEANS

MAKES 3 OR 4 SERVINGS

1 *cup pinto beans, cleaned and washed*
2 1/2 *cups hot water*
1/2 *teaspoon salt*
1/2 *cup onions, diced*
1 *teaspoon garlic, minced*
1/8 *teaspoon black pepper*
1 *tomato, chopped*
1/4 *cup green chilies, chopped*
1 *teaspoon bacon flavoring*

Soak beans overnight, covered with water in a slow electric cooker. Next morning add all ingredients to pot and set cooker to cook all day. Serve with warm corn tortillas, rice and green salad.

NEW ORLEANS RED BEANS AND RICE

2 *cups red kidney beans, cleaned and soaked overnight*
1/4 *lb. lean ham, diced pork, or turkey ham*
1 *tablespoon flour*
1 *medium onion, chopped*
1 *small carrot, sliced*
6 *cups chicken stock* **or**
6 *cups water with 3 bouillon cubes*
1 *bay leaf*
1/8 *teaspoon thyme*
1/8 *teaspoon sage*
1 *teaspoon parsley*
1 *stalk celery, chopped*
~ *salt, pepper, and cayenne pepper to taste*

In Dutch oven brown flour, add onions brown also for 2 or 3 minutes. Add other ingredients and simmer until beans are tender and juice is thick and dark. Correct seasoning and serve over rice.

BOSTON BAKED BEANS

MAKES 3 OR 4 SERVINGS

1 *cup small white beans, cleaned and washed*
2 1/2 *cups hot water*
1/2 *teaspoon salt*
1/2 *cup diced onions*

1 *teaspoon minced garlic*
1 *tablespoon dark molasses*
1 *tablespoon Dijon-style prepared mustard*
1/4 *teaspoon thyme*
1 *bay leaf*
1/2 *teaspoon ginger, powdered*
1/8 *teaspoon black pepper*

Soak beans at least 4 hours then place all ingredients in electric slow cooker set to low or in oven set to 275° F. Cook overnight or 12-14 hours. Serve with cole slaw (page 95) and fresh bread.

NAVY BEANS & ONIONS

YIELDS 4 CUPS

1 *cup dried navy beans, washed and soaked*
1 *medium onion, chopped*
~ *salt and black pepper to taste*

Soak beans overnight, add onion, salt, and black pepper. Simmer until done. Balance seasonings.

CHILI BEANS

2 *cups dried pinto beans, washed and soaked*
1 *medium onion, chopped*
2 *tablespoons chili powder*
1 *cup salsa, thick and chunky*
1 *tablespoon garlic, minced*
1 *cup tomatoes, diced*
1/4 *cup Textured Vegetable Protein (TVP®)**
1/8 *teaspoon cayenne pepper*
~ *salt and pepper to taste*

Soak beans overnight. Combine ingredients and simmer until tender and water just covers the beans.

NOTE: *Textured Vegetable Protein (TVP®) takes on the appearance of ground meat, and can be purchased at most health food and specialty stores or by calling 1-800-8-FLAVOR.

BACHELOR'S (REALLY QUICK) MEXICAN BEANS & RICE

MAIN COURSE FOR TWO

1 *15-oz. can pinto beans*
1/2 *bean can of your favorite mexican salsa* **or** *taco sauce*
1 *tablespoon onion soup mix*
1/4 *bean can of water*
1 *bean can of instant rice*
1/2 *bean can of chopped sweet onions*
1/2 *bean can of chopped tomatoes*
~ *jalapeno pepper slices*

Mix first four ingredients in 2 quart or bigger saucepan and bring to a careful boil. (Don't burn the beans.) When mixture boils, add instant rice. Remove from burner and let sit for five minutes. Then add onions and tomatoes. Garnish with jalapeno peppers and serve with steamed or baked corn tortillas.

HOT DOG CHILI

1 can chili beans
1/2 medium onion, chopped
1/2 cup chicken broth, defatted
1/4 cup thick salsa
~ Hormel® Light & Lean® frankfurters

Simmer onion in chicken broth until tender. Add beans, salsa, and frankfurters cut into bite-sizes. Heat but don't burn. Goes great in a hot dog bun topped with fat-free cheese.

SAUCES

In France they say that the sauce is everything. Well, it may not be "everything," but a good sauce can turn an ordinary dish into an elegant dish. Sauces can be part of the heart and soul of good food. Sliced cold breast of turkey when served on a bed of purple kale and topped with cranberry wine sauce transcends the ordinary. ❦ *To a midwesterner it might be called "cream gravy"; in France, they would call it Béchamel sauce. Add curry powder and it becomes a cream curry sauce. Whatever the name, the sauce is the game.*

BUTTER SAUCE

1 *envelope Butter Buds® butter-flavored granules*
1/2 *cup water*
1 *teaspoon cornstarch*

Heat in saucepan or microwave until just boiling. Remove from heat and stir. Will keep covered for 3 days in refrigerator.

Brush on corn-on-the-cob, toast, bread, or vegetables. For garlic butter sauce add 1 teaspoon minced garlic.

I. WHITE SAUCE OR BÉCHAMEL SAUCE

(CREAM GRAVY)

2 *tablespoons flour*
1 1/2 *cups non fat milk*
1 *teaspoon dry Butter Buds® butter-flavored granules*
~ *salt and white pepper to taste*

Mix ingredients in blender or whisk in a bowl until mixture is thoroughly blended. Simmer for 5 minutes over low heat.

CURRY SAUCE *Add 1 teaspoon curry powder.*

CHEESE SAUCE *While sauce is hot, stir in 4 slices of fat-free cheese and allow to melt.*

EGG SAUCE *Add the chopped whites from 2 hard-boiled eggs.*

II. WHITE SAUCE

(BÉCHAMEL)

2 *teaspoons imitation butter flavoring*
2 *tablespoons flour*
1 *can evaporated skim milk*
~ *salt and pepper to taste*

Combine ingredients in saucepan and whisk briskly in order to thoroughly mix. Heat over medium heat, stirring all the time until sauce is thick and smooth. Simmer for 2 or 3 minutes and remove from heat.

HOT MUSTARD SAUCE *Stir in 2 teaspoons of hot Chinese mustard powder.*

TAME MUSTARD SAUCE *Stir in 2 tablespoons mustard of your choice.*

CHEESE SAUCE *While sauce is hot, stir in 2 slices of fat-free cheese and allow to melt.*

EGG SAUCE *Add the chopped whites from 2 hard-boiled eggs.*

PARSLEY SAUCE *Add 1/4 cup finely chopped parsley after sauce is done.*

CAPER SAUCE *Add capers to suit your taste to the finished sauce.*

WHITE WINE SAUCE
When cooking sauce, add 1/4 cup white wine.

CHAMPAGNE SAUCE *Sauté one medium onion (chopped fine) and 1/2 bell pepper in 1/4 cup champagne for 10 minutes. Add white sauce. Strain if desired.*

TOMATO-BASIL CREAM SAUCE *Add ½ cup chopped tomato pulp from canned Italian plum tomatoes and 1 tablespoon fresh basil (or 1 teaspoon dried basil) to white sauce.*
TARRAGON SAUCE *Add 2 teaspoons dried tarragon and 1 tablespoon white wine. Serve over broiled breast of chicken.*
WHITE CLAM SAUCE *Add cooked, chopped clams to taste. Add reduced clam broth if desired.*

BROWN SAUCE

- 1 *teaspoon flour*
- 4 *oz. sliced ham, diced*
- 1 *medium onion, diced*
- 1 *carrot, thinly sliced*
- 2 *cups beef broth*
- 1 *teaspoon imitation butter flavoring*
- ½ *bay leaf*
- ⅛ *teaspoon dried thyme*
- ¼ *cup tomato sauce*
- ¼ *cup red wine*
- ~ *salt and pepper to taste*

In cast iron skillet brown flour and ham over medium heat. Add onions, carrots, and a little beef broth and cook until onions are brown. Add the rest of the beef broth, bay leaf, butter flavor, and thyme and simmer for 1 hour. Add tomato sauce, wine and simmer for another half hour. Salt and pepper to taste and strain through a sieve. If sauce isn't thick enough, continue to simmer until it is.

MADEIRA BROWN SAUCE

Add Madeira to Brown Sauce.

MUSHROOM BROWN SAUCE

Sauté desired amount and type of sliced mushrooms in a little water. Boil off water and add to Madeira Brown Sauce.

SAUCE DIABLO

To one cup Brown Sauce, add 1 teaspoon hot Chinese mustard powder, 1 teaspoon Tabasco, ¼ teaspoon black pepper and 1 teaspoon fresh lemon juice. Simmer for a few minutes to mix flavors.

BORDELAISE SAUCE

Reduce 1 cup of red wine to ½ cup, add six chopped green onions and 1 cup of brown sauce. *Goes great on a Buffalo steak!*

LEMON BUTTER SAUCE

- ~ *grated rind of 1/2 lemon*
- 2 *tablespoons fresh lemon juice*
- 1/4 *cup chicken broth*
- 1/2 *cup Butter Buds® butter-flavor liquid mixture*
- 1 *teaspoon cornstarch*
- 1 *teaspoon chopped herbs such as parsley, dill **or** chives*

Bring lemon rind, juice, and chicken broth to a boil and simmer until reduced to about 3 tablespoons of liquid. Combine Butter Buds® liquid and cornstarch thoroughly then add to juice and simmer for a minute or so. Add herbs and serve over fish.

ONION BUTTER SAUCE

- 1 *cup water*
- 1/2 *envelope onion soup mix*
- 1 *envelope (1/2-oz.) Butter Buds® butter-flavored granules*
- 2 *teaspoons cornstarch*

Mix and simmer in saucepan for 5 minutes. Store covered in refrigerator. May be used as topping for toasted French bread, on baked or mashed potatoes or on pasta.

HORSERADISH SAUCE

- 1 *cup no-fat sour cream*
- 1/4 *cup horseradish*

Mix and chill
Great with roast beef.

FLUFFY HORSERADISH SAUCE

- 1/2 *cup no-fat sour cream*
- 2 *tablespoons no-fat milk powder*
- 4 *tablespoons prepared horseradish*
- 1/4 *teaspoon salt*
- ~ *pepper to taste*

Whip sour cream and milk powder until stiff; fold in horseradish, salt and pepper.
Goes great with a medium-rare prime rib of buffalo.

SOUR CREAM MUSTARD SAUCE

- 1 *cup no-fat sour cream*
- 1 *teaspoon prepared mustard*
- 2 *tablespoons green onion tops, minced **or** 1 tablespoon regular onion*
- ~ *salt and pepper to taste*

Mix, chill and serve.
Goes well with fish, fowl, or veggies.

TARTAR SAUCE

1 *cup fat-free mayonnaise*
2 *tablespoon minced onion*
1/2 *cup dill pickle, finely minced*
1 *teaspoon capers, minced*
1/8 *teaspoon cayenne pepper*

Mix and chill. *Great with fish.* ※

CUCUMBER CREAM SAUCE

1 *cup no-fat sour cream*
1/4 *cup cucumber*
1/8 *cup water*
1 *tablespoon vinegar*
~ *salt to taste*

In blender, purée cucumber and water. Remove to bowl and add sour cream, vinegar, and salt to taste. ※

HEAVY CREAM DESSERT SAUCE

~ *Simple Pleasures® Light Frozen Vanilla Dairy Dessert made with the all-natural fat substitute, Simplesse®*

Allow desired amount to thaw in refrigerator or hurry along in the microwave. Serve on desserts such as shortcakes, cake, berries, or parfaits. ※

MUSHROOM SAUCE

~ *white sauce (page 162)*
1 *cup mushrooms, sliced*
1 *teaspoon chicken bouillon powder*
1/4 *cup water*

Simmer mushrooms, water and bouillon until water is almost boiled away. Add to white sauce and serve. ※

HOLLANDAISE SAUCE

- $^1/_2$ cup Egg Beaters® egg substitute
- 2 tablespoons lemon juice
- 3 tablespoons Butter Buds® butter-flavored granules
- $^3/_4$ cup evaporated skim milk
- 2 teaspoons cornstarch
- 1 tablespoon parsley
- ~ salt and cayenne pepper to taste

In mixing bowl mix thoroughly with whisk or mixer. Pour into saucepan and bring to simmer over medium heat stirring continuously with whisk. Remove and serve.

COLE SLAW DRESSING

- $^1/_2$ cup fat-free mayonnaise
- 1 tablespoon cider vinegar
- 1 tablespoon sugar
- 1 teaspoon non fat dry milk solids
- 1 teaspoon Butter Buds® butter-flavored granules

Mix ingredients well.

CRANBERRY-WINE SAUCE

- $^1/_8$ cup burgundy wine
- 1 16-oz. can cranberry sauce
- 2 tablespoons light brown sugar
- 1 tablespoon prepared mustard
- $^1/_8$ teaspoon onion salt

Combine all ingredients and simmer for 3 minutes. Serve with sliced breast of turkey or chicken. May be served chilled.

BASIC GRAVY

- 1 cup liquid
- $1^1/_4$ tablespoon flour
- ~ seasonings

Combine in skillet beef broth, chicken broth, or other liquid with flour and mix thoroughly. Heat to boil and simmer for three or four minutes. Season to taste. For thicker gravy use more flour. To thicken any boiling hot liquid just add Wondra® flour from Gold Medal® and stir. Continue to add flour and stir until desired thickness is obtained. Allow to simmer for two or three minutes after desired thickness is obtained.

SANDWICHES, TACOS, BURRITOS & PIZZA

Sandwiches are the mainstay of our society. Both standard sandwiches and Latin varieties make our country functional. Without sandwiches, many people would become disoriented, confused, and unable to perform routine tasks. Some would probably starve. For these reasons, we include this life-saving section.

SANDWICHES

Always purchase fat-free bread! There are many brands and styles of fat-free bread to choose from; and, of course, homemade fat-free bread adds something special to any sandwich.

HOT TURKEY TOMATO MELT

~ *breast of turkey, sliced*
~ *tomato*
~ *fat-free cheese*
~ *English muffins*

Pile turkey onto muffin, add tomato, top with cheese, and broil until cheese melts. Serve hot. ※

BACON CHEESE BURGER

FOR TWO

2 *1/4 lb. patties Healthy Choice® extra lean ground beef*
4 *strips turkey bacon*
2 *slices fat-free cheese*
~ *salt and pepper*

Cook bacon crisp and place on paper towel. Press to remove fat. In skillet, fry beef patties. Season to taste. Place a slice of cheese on each patty, cover and allow to just melt. Remove from skillet to bun and top dress with two strips of bacon for each patty. (See page 78) ※

MUSHROOM CHEESEBURGER

2 *cooked Healthy Choice® beef patties, extra lean*
2 *cups sliced fresh mushrooms*
1 *teaspoon beef bouillon powder*
2 *slices fat-free cheese*
~ *salt and pepper*

In heavy skillet in which patties have been cooked, place small amount of water and add mushrooms. Sprinkle with beef bouillon. Place beef patties on top of mushrooms and simmer until mushrooms are done. Arrange mushrooms on tops of patties, season to taste, and cover with cheese slices. Cover skillet in order to melt cheese. Serve on homemade bread slices or buns. ※

PHILLY BEEF AND CHEESE

1/4 *lb. defatted roast beef*
1/2 *cup defatted beef broth*
2 *slices of large onion*
1/2 *sliced bell pepper*
1/2 *cup fat-free mozzarella cheese*
~ *salt and pepper*

Slice roast beef wafer thin. In heavy skillet, add broth, beef, onions, and peppers and simmer five minutes or until peppers are as you like them. Add cheese and mix thoroughly. Spoon on to toasted buns. Makes 2 sandwiches.

BARBECUE BEEF SANDWICH

2 *cups shredded beef (page 104)*
1/2 *cup defatted beef broth*
1 *cup your favorite barbecue sauce*

In saucepan, heat beef and beef broth. Add barbecue sauce and lower heat to just warm. Allow to warm for 5 to 10 minutes. Spoon mixture onto buns and serve.

HOT BEEF SANDWICH

~ *roast beef and gravy from page 103, sliced very thin*
~ *Mashed potatoes from page 137*

Heat and assemble "open-face" style.

SLOPPY JOES

1 *packet of Midland Harvest Burger Mix® (to obtain Midland Harvest Burger Mix®, see Chapter 13)*
1 *can **or** jar Sloppy Joe sauce*

Reconstitute burger mix and brown in skillet. Add sauce and serve.

CHILI DOGS

~ *hot dogs, Hormel® Light & Lean® Frankfurters*
~ *chili beans from can **or** chili from page 159*
~ *hot dog buns*

Place beans and hot dogs in saucepan and heat. Place hot dog in bun and top with chili. For slaw dogs substitute cole slaw from page 95 for chili.

HOT DOGS & SAUERKRAUT

- *Hormel® Light & Lean® hot dogs*
- *canned sauerkraut*
- *hot dog buns*
- *mustard*

In large skillet, heat sauerkraut and hot dogs. Place a plate of hot dog buns in the center of skillet, cover and allow buns to warm. Serve with mustard.

HOT TURKEY SANDWICH

- *turkey and gravy from page 103*
- *mashed potatoes from page 137*
- *cranberry sauce*

Heat and assemble "open-face" style.

BACON, LETTUCE & TOMATO (BLT)

- *turkey bacon*
- *lettuce*
- *tomato*
- *fat-free mayonnaise*

Fry bacon crisp and remove all visible grease from bacon with paper towels. Assemble sandwich.

FISH SANDWICH

- *fish fillet, baked with Shake 'n Bake® seasoning and coating original recipe for fish*
- *fat-free cheese*
- *tartar sauce, page 165*

Top fish with cheese, spread on tartar sauce.

FRIED HAM & CHEESE

- *turkey ham slices*
- *dill pickle slices*
- *lettuce*
- *tomato*
- *fat-free mayonnaise*

Fry ham and press with paper towel to remove fat. Assemble sandwich.

FRIED HAM & EGG

- *sliced turkey ham*
- *Egg Beaters® egg substitute*
- *lettuce*
- *tomato*
- *pickle*
- *fat-free mayonnaise*

Fry ham and press with paper towel to remove fat. Fry egg and assemble.

TACOS

Do not purchase prepared taco shells unless they are clearly marked "fat free." Purchase corn tortillas and form and bake your own. If simplicity is desired, lay tortillas flat on cookie sheet and bake for 20 minutes at 325°. These will make open-face tacos or tostadas.

BEAN TACOS

- *refried beans, page 84*
- *baked tortillas*
- *shredded lettuce*
- *chopped tomatoes*
- *chopped onions*
- *shredded fat-free mozzarella cheese*

Spread hot refried beans on tortilla. Top with other ingredients.

NOTE: ***For chicken or turkey tacos, use meat from page 103 or low-fat deli slices. For meat tacos, use meat from page 104 or 1-fat-gram-per-slice deli beef luncheon meat.***

SOFT TACOS

Use fat-free flour tortillas or quick flour tortillas from page 211; assemble as for corn tortilla tacos and fold in half.

BURRITOS

Traditionally in Mexico and parts of the Southwest, the burrito, for lunch, is nothing more than unleavened bread wrapped around last night's leftovers. It might be filled with beans, rice, corn, liver, meat, poultry, tripe, cheese, fish, or combinations of leftovers. Potatoes are often cooked, diced, and mixed with eggs and chilies and used as a filling for a burrito. When wrapped in aluminum foil and taken to work in the lunch bucket, a construction worker can have a hot lunch by placing the wrapped burrito on top of a hot engine. Americanized versions show up as deep fried or baked with various toppings. So, let your imagination go to work and just exclude any fatty ingredients.

BEAN BURRITO WITH CHILIES & CHEESE

- *fat-free flour tortillas* **or** *from page 211*
- *refried beans from page 84*
- *fat-free cheese*
- *salsa* **or** *taco sauce*
- *green chilies*

Spread beans on tortilla, add cheese, chilies, and salsa. Roll up and wrap in aluminum foil. Place in warm oven and allow cheese to melt. May be prepared well in advance. Any extra can go to work the next day in the lunch box.

SCRAMBLED EGG & POTATO BURRITO

- *Egg Beaters® egg substitute*
- *fat-free flour tortilla* **or** *from page 211*
- *diced onions*
- *diced potatoes*
- *beef broth*
- *green chilies*
- *salsa*
- *salt and pepper to taste*

Simmer onions, potatoes, green chilies, and beef broth until potatoes are done and beef broth is completely reduced. Scramble Egg Beaters® and assemble burrito. Wrap in aluminum foil if desired.

GREEN PEON BURRITO

- ~ *fat-free frozen* **or** *fresh hash-brown potatoes*
- 1 *4-oz. can chopped green chilies*
- ~ *thick salsa* **or** *taco sauce*
- ~ *salt and pepper to taste*
- ~ *fat-free flour tortillas* **or** *from page 211*

In large veggie-sprayed skillet, place desired amount of potatoes and brown over medium heat. When browned, add green chilies and stir while warming chilies. Remove from heat and place tortillas on top of mixture in order to warm. Cover skillet and allow to sit for a few minutes. Place skillet in the center of dining table and let people make their own burritos. Serve with salsa or taco sauce.

RED CHILI VEGGIE BURGER BURRITO

- 1/2 *lb. Midland Harvest Burger® Mix, reconstituted*
- 1/2 *medium sliced onion*
- 1/4 *cup thick salsa* **or** *taco sauce*
- 2 *slices fat-free cheese*
- 4 *teaspoons enchilada sauce mix*
- ~ *fat-free flour tortillas* **or** *from page 211*

On medium heat, veggie spray a cast-iron skillet and spoon veggie burger into center of skillet. Place onion slices around outer edges. sprinkle enchilada sauce mix onto top of burger mix. Brown burger, mix, and turn over adding salsa or taco sauce. Cover and allow to steam for a few minutes. Add more onions into the mixture if desired and allow to cook through. Break cheese into pieces and add to mixture so it doesn't stick to the tortillas; place tortillas on top and cover. Remove from heat and allow time for tortillas to warm.

RED CHILI CHICKEN BURRITOS

FOR TWO

- ~ *hash-brown potatoes for two (fresh* **or** *frozen, but fat free)*
- ~ *enchilada sauce mix powder*
- 1/2 *chicken breast cut into strips*
- 1 *small chopped tomato*
- 4 *fat-free flour tortillas* **or** *from page 211*
- ~ *salt and pepper to taste*
- ~ *vegetable spray*
- 1 *small chopped onion*

In large veggie-sprayed cast-iron skillet, spread hash browns over half of skillet. Coat chicken liberally with enchilada sauce mix and place on the other half of skillet and cook over medium heat. Top chicken with tomatoes as you turn chicken. Add onions to skillet when desired, but keep separate. Salt and pepper hash browns. When done, remove from heat and place tortillas on top and cover skillet. Allow to sit while tortillas warm. Set skillet on dining table and enjoy.

BAKED BURRITO

- ~ *fat-free flour tortillas* ***or*** *from page 211*
- ~ *filling of your choice (i.e. meat, poultry, beans, etc.)*
- ~ *chili beans from page 159* ***or*** *canned*

Assemble burritos and place on cookie sheet. Bake in 400-degree oven for 30 minutes or until brown and crispy. Remove and top with chili beans just before serving. Serve with fresh, chopped jalapeno peppers, no-fat sour cream, and shredded lettuce.

CHICKEN OR TURKEY BURRITO

- 1 *cup breast meat, cooked and shredded*
- 1/4 *cup chopped onions*
- 1 *cup sliced long green chilies*
- 1/4 *cup salsa of your choice*
- 6 *slices fat-free cheese singles*
- 6 *fat-free flour tortillas* ***or*** *from page 211*

In cast iron skillet place meat, onions, chilies and salsa. Brown and heat. Place cheese on top of mixtures and allow to melt. Serve on tortillas.

DOGGIE BURRITOS

- 6 *corn* ***or*** *flour tortillas, your choice*
- 6 *frankfurters, Hormel® Light & Lean®*
- 3 *slices fat-free cheese*
- 1 *can chili beans*

Preheat oven to 400° F.
Place frank and 1/2 slice cheese in a tortilla; roll up and hold together with a toothpick. Repeat. Place in oven-proof pan and top with beans. Bake for 20 minutes. Serve with shredded lettuce.
NOTE: *Beans may be replaced with your favorite salsa and topped with additional slices of cheese.*

PIZZAS

From the crust up, pizzas are a fine source of eating contentment. Starting with the crust, "store bought" pizza doughs are fine if they do not contain oil, hydrogenated oils, shortening, or lard. Read the ingredient label carefully. If you can't find fat-free dough in your supermarket, then use any fat-free homemade yeast bread recipe. Just form into pizza crust after the second rising. ❦ Fat-free cheese toppings are fine. If you have an absolute craving for pepperoni, then purchase the wafer thin slices and boil the fat out of them for about 30 minutes. Another meat topping might be smoked sausage from Healthy Choice®, sliced wafer thin, or sausage from page 114. ADM Midland Harvest Burger® mix also makes a fine topping. The pizza sauce should comply with the 1 fat-gram-per-serving rule. Hunt's® Chunky Style Spaghetti Sauce with tomato chunks is a fine sauce for pizzas. Molly McButter® Cheese Flavor adds a lot of good flavor to any pizza. The basic rule for fat-free pizza is: Buy proper ingredients and use your imagination.

OUR FAVORITE QUICK PIZZA

- ~ *Patmos brand prepared pizza dough*
- ~ *Hunt's® Chunky Style Spaghetti Sauce*
- 6 *slices ripe tomato*
- 2 *cups sliced mushroom*
- 1 *cup sliced bell pepper*
- 1 *large sweet onion, sliced*
- ~ *Molly McButter® cheese flavor to taste*
- ~ *fat-free mozzarella cheese*

Except for the cheese, assemble and bake at 400° for 15 minutes. Remove from oven and add cheeses. Place back in oven and add water to bottom of oven to make steam (see next recipe) and bake for another 5-10 minutes until edges are brown and crusty. ❦

This second pizza recipe is a very thick-crust pizza. I'm talking 1½ - 2 inches on the outer crust and much thinner towards the center. This is a substantial meal for two big eaters and clearly demonstrates what fabulous fat-free foods should be.

OUR MOST FAVORITE THICK CRUST PIZZA

- ~ *basic French bread dough from page 194*
- ¾ *cup cheddar cheese, no-fat, shredded*
- 1 *tablespoon fresh oregano, chopped (or 1 teaspoon dried)*
- 1 *cup Hunts® light no-fat spaghetti sauce*
- 6 *slices ripe tomato*
- 1 *4-oz. can mushrooms, sliced and drained*
- 1 *cup bell pepper, chopped*
- 1 *large sweet onion*
- ½ *lb. Italian sausage, fried from page 114*
- 1 *cup mozzarella cheese, no-fat, shredded*

Preheat oven to 400° F with an empty cookie sheet placed in the bottom of oven.

Prepare French bread dough from page 194 adding to it the Cheddar cheese and fresh oregano. Allow to rise until double in size, punch down, cover, and allow to rise another 15 minutes. Place dough into a 12-inch cast iron skillet and line the bottom and up the sides forming a deep dish for the toppings.

Spread the spaghetti sauce all over the dough and add the other toppings *except* for the mozzarella cheese.

Place pizza in the oven and bake for 30 minutes. Remove and add mozzarella cheese. Return pizza to the oven and splash ¼ cup water onto the cookie sheet that you placed in the bottom of the oven. This will steam and melt the mozzarella cheese. Remove pizza after 5 minutes and serve.

VEGETABLES

The cook said to the King, "This bowl of peppers will go well with your leg of venison." Now the King was not knowledgeable of the nature of red and green cayenne peppers, so unknowingly he did partake of the venison and did dip handily into the bowl of peppers. His temples did throb, he perspired profusely, his lips and mouth were afire, his eyes watered and his throat allowed him not to speak. ❧ *When the King finally did recover he had the cook's head lopped off. The moral of this story is – present your vegetables as they are perceived to be. That is, French fried potatoes should be crisp and brown, buttered carrots should be buttery, sauces should be flavorful and creamy, and so on.* ❧ *To accomplish these ends, learn to use those "flavor tools" at your disposal that are fat free. As an addition to your vegetables, consider the bacon and cheese sprinkles, the cheddar cheeses, Butter Buds® butter-flavored granules, mozzarella cheese, American cheese, dry soup mixes (especially onion and vegetable soup), along with the always available fresh mushrooms and onions.* ❧ *Don't be afraid to experiment, just don't shock the King.*

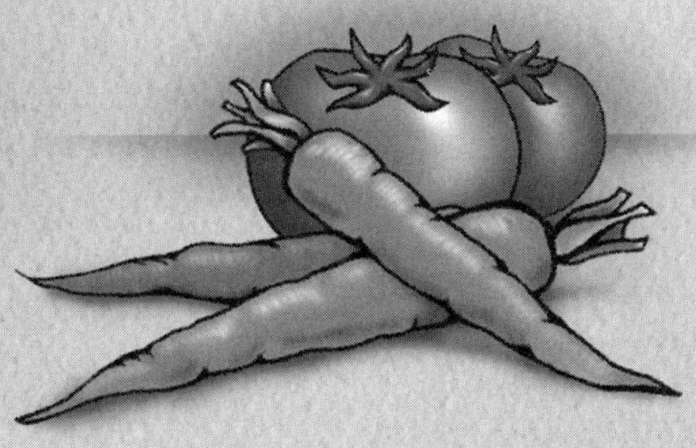

PEAS AND MUSHROOMS

2 *cups frozen **or** fresh peas*
1 *cup sliced mushrooms*
1/4 *cup baby onions **or** chopped onions*
1 *teaspoon Butter Buds® butter-flavor granules*
1 *teaspoon sugar*
1 *tablespoon chopped red bell pepper*
1/4 *cup water*

Cook peas as directed or until tender and drain. Cook onions, mushrooms, and red bell pepper in 1/4 cup water until tender. Mix all ingredients together, cover and heat through.

CREAMED PEAS

1 *package frozen peas, cooked and drained*
~ *White Sauce from page 162*

Combine, warm, and serve.

GREEN KALE & DUMPLINGS

2 *tablespoons beef bouillon granules*
2 *lbs. kale*
3 *slices turkey ham cut in strips*
1 *lb. potatoes, diced in one-inch cubes*
2 *ears of sweet corn cut into thirds*
10 *cups water*
~ *dumpling batter (page 228)*
~ *salt and pepper to taste*

Remove stems from kale, and in a large Dutch oven or kettle bring water to boil, add kale, potatoes, ham, corn, and simmer for 20 minutes. Spoon in large tablespoons of dumpling batter so as to make about a dozen dumplings. Cover and simmer for an additional 30 minutes or until dumplings are done. Serve greens and broth in bowl topped with dumplings. Serve corn on the side brushed with Butter Sauce (page 162).

BROCCOLI-CAULIFLOWER SOUFFLÉ

2 *cups water with 2 teaspoons salt added*
1 *cup chopped broccoli*
1 *cup chopped cauliflower*
1 *teaspoon Butter Buds® butter-flavored granules*
2 *tablespoons flour*
1/2 *cup non-fat milk*
6 *slices fat-free cheese*
1 *cup Egg Beaters® egg substitute*

Preheat oven to 350° F. In salted water, cook broccoli and cauliflower 10 minutes, drain well. Blend Butter Buds®, flour, and milk. Cook and stir until bubbly; remove from heat. Add cheese and stir until blended; then add broccoli and cauliflower. Beat eggs at high speed for 4 minutes, and add to veggies. Spoon into an ungreased 1 quart soufflé dish. Bake for 35 minutes until a knife inserted comes out clean. Serve immediately.

REFRIED BEAN CASSEROLE

- ~ *pinto beans*
- ~ *fat-free cheese*
- ~ *salt and pepper to taste*

Mash beans and season. Spoon into casserole dish and cover top with cheese slices. Cover with aluminum foil and bake in 350° F oven until beans are hot and cheese is bubbly (about 20 minutes).

CORN POPOVERS

- 1 *cup canned corn, whole kernel drained*
- 1 *popover recipe page 210*

Add corn to Popover batter and spoon into veggie-sprayed muffin tins. Bake as per popover recipe.

CANDIED-RAISIN SWEET POTATOES

- ~ *sweet potatoes, as desired*
- ~ *raisins*
- ~ *brown sugar*

Place desired amount of sweet potatoes in casserole dish with raisins, sprinkle liberally with brown sugar, and bake at 350° F for 60 minutes or until done.

TOMATO-MUSHROOM QUICHE

- 4 *strips turkey bacon, cooked crisp, drained of fat, and broken into small pieces*
- 1 *cup fresh ripe tomatoes, chopped*
- 1 *cup fresh mushrooms, sliced*
- 1 *cup Egg Beaters® egg substitute*
- 2 *cups evaporated skimmed milk*
- 1/2 *teaspoon salt*
- 1/8 *teaspoon nutmeg*
- ~ *dash cayenne pepper*
- 1 *cup grated mozzarella cheese (non fat)*
- 4 *slices fat-free American cheese*
- 2 *pie shells (page 222), uncooked*

Heat oven to 425° F. Place tomatoes, pieces of bacon, and mushrooms into 2 pie shells. Heat milk with salt, nutmeg, pepper, and cheese until cheese melts. *Do not burn!* Beat eggs for 1 minute; then add to milk mixture. Pour over tomatoes and mushrooms and bake for 15 minutes. Then lower heat to 350° F and continue to bake for 30 minutes or until knife inserted in center comes out clean. Serve hot or cold.

NOTE: *These quiches are as variable as your imagination. You might try:*

- **SMOKED TURKEY & MUSHROOMS**
- **BACON-SPINACH**
- **CRAB & RED BELL PEPPER**
- **TUNA-ONION**
- **HAM & FRESH GREEN BEANS**
- **ASPARAGUS & LOBSTER BLEND**

Just pour the milk, egg and cheese liquid on top of other choice ingredients.

GREEN BEAN CASSEROLE

1 Cheese Sauce from page 162
1 tablespoon beef bouillon granules
1 teaspoon soy sauce
2 green onions, chopped
1 29-oz. package frozen green beans, cooked and drained

Combine ingredients and spoon into casserole dish. Bake at 350° F for 30 minutes.

SNAPPY THREE-PEPPER CORN

1 can whole kernel corn
1/4 cup green bell peppers, chopped
1 tablespoon pimento pepper, chopped (or red bell pepper)
3-4 slices jalapeno pepper
salt and pepper to taste

Combine ingredients in saucepan and simmer for 5 minutes.

CABBAGE & SAUERKRAUT

For ages, cabbage has been the winter green vegetable of choice. The reason being that cabbage keeps well in the root cellar. It also keeps well if you shred it into a barrel and allow it to ferment, as in sauerkraut. An eastern European person probably couldn't exist without cabbage. Almost every day, cabbage shows up in soup, stews, slaws, salads, and in sandwiches. How about sauerkraut and sausage, cabbage and pork, sauerkraut and pork, and in Poland, sauerkraut, cabbage, and pork. The combinations and uses found for cabbage are apparently endless. ❧ *I like to keep a bag of shredded cabbage in the refrigerator. It keeps really well and it is easy to grab a handful when making a fast soup or stew. Or throw a couple of handfuls into a skillet, splash on some liquid, add some vinegar and sugar and you have a tangy addition to many meat dinners.* ❧ *One tip on cabbage you might remember is that it gets stronger in flavor the longer it cooks and some people find this objectionable. When steaming cabbage, cook it until it is just tender, maybe just not quite tender.*

SWEET CABBAGE & SOUR BEETS

- 3 *handfuls shredded cabbage*
- 1 *can whole beets*
- 3 *tablespoons vinegar*
- 3 *tablespoons sugar*
- 1 *tablespoon cornstarch mixed with 1/4 cup water*

In skillet boil cabbage, beets, beet juice, vinegar, and sugar until cabbage is just tender. Don't overcook! Pour in cornstarch and water mixture and continue heating until liquid thickens.

STEAMED CABBAGE WEDGES

- ~ *cabbage wedges*
- ~ *chicken broth, defatted*
- ~ *black pepper*
- ~ *Butter Buds® butter-flavor sprinkles*
- ~ *chopped parsley*

Place cabbage in saucepan with enough broth to steam. Sprinkle with pepper, butter-flavor granules, and parsley. Simmer until tender.

TERIYAKI CABBAGE

FOR TWO

- 2 *handfuls shredded cabbage*
- 2 *tablespoons teriyaki sauce*
- 1/4 *cup chicken broth*
- 1/2 *cup broccoli florets*
- 1 *handful bean sprouts*
- ~ *teriyaki glaze (bought in supermarket)*

In hot skillet or wok, steam cabbage, broccoli, teriyaki sauce, and chicken broth. Add bean sprouts at the end of the process to just warm good. Remove from heat. Serve over rice topped with teriyaki glaze to taste.

STEAMED SHREDDED CABBAGE

- ~ *shredded cabbage, (desired amount)*
- ~ *chicken broth to steam*
- ~ *salt and pepper to taste*

In skillet over medium heat, add cabbage and broth. Cover and steam until desired doneness is achieved. Salt and pepper after it is cooked.

NOTE: ***Pre-shredded cabbage or cole slaw mix in a plastic bag available at most produce departments works well and saves time.***

SPINACH CASSEROLE SUPREME

- 1/2 *cup Egg Beaters® egg substitute*
- 1 *15-oz. can spinach (drained)*
- 1 *cup fat-free ricotta cheese*
- 4 *slices fat-free cheese*
- 1 *tablespoon minced garlic*
- 1/8 *teaspoon white pepper*
- 1 *teaspoon chicken bouillon granules*
- 1/4 *cup chopped onions*
- 1/2 *cup chopped fresh tomatoes*

Preheat oven to 400° F. Except for cheese slices, combine ingredients and place in a 2-quart casserole dish. Top with cheese slices and bake for 35 minutes.

ROASTED GREEN CHILIES

Place long green chilies (Anaheim's) under broiler and broil until brown and puffy. Turn and brown the other side. Remove and cool. Peel skin from peppers and remove seeds. Skin should peel off easily. If not, you probably didn't brown them enough.

LEEKS

I call leeks the lonely vegetable because I never see anybody buy them. I didn't buy them because my mother didn't buy them, and I didn't eat them and my friends didn't eat them. Maybe your mother didn't buy them either and you don't. Here's a reason to give them a try. ✻ *Leeks have a wonderful onion-family flavor that accentuates the flavor of potatoes and sour cream. If that sounds like a peculiar combination of flavors, I ask you to consider your baked potato with sour cream and chives. Leeks are giant chives, or chives are midget leeks, I think. Anyhow, when you simmer leeks and potatoes together you end up with a wonderful soup that is about as simple as simple gets. Ladled up fresh from the soup pot, topped with a spoon of sour cream, and served with fresh homemade bread, you have true gourmet fare that is elegant and easy.*

LEEK & POTATO SOUP

3 TO 4 SERVINGS

- 2 *cups leeks, sliced, including some tender green part*
- 2 *cups potatoes, diced*
- 3 *cups water*
- 1/2 *teaspoon salt*
- 1/4 *cup evaporated skim milk, (optional)*
- ~ *sour cream*

In a heavy saucepan, bring leeks, potatoes, water, and salt to a boil, cover and simmer for 30 minutes. Add milk and remove from heat. Correct seasoning. Serve hot with a spoonful of sour cream on top.

NOTE: *For Vichyssoise, serve chilled.*

SAVORY SPINACH

2 *packages frozen spinach, chopped*
1/4 *cup Healthy Choice® fat-free cream cheese*
1 *cup fresh mushrooms, sliced*
1 *tablespoon flour*
1/2 *cup evaporated skim milk*
1/2 *medium onion, diced*
1/4 *cup chicken broth*
~ *salt and pepper to taste*

In a large saucepan gently simmer onions and broth until onions are tender. Add spinach and mushrooms and simmer until tender. Combine milk and flour and add to pan. Remove when thickened and add cream cheese cut into small pieces. Stir but don't boil. Season to taste and serve.

LEMON BABY CARROTS

2 *cups baby carrots*
~ *juice from 1/2 lemon*
1 *teaspoon Butter Buds® butter-flavor sprinkles*
~ *water to boil* **or** *chicken broth*

In a saucepan add carrots, lemon juice, and enough water to cover carrots. Boil until tender, sprinkle with Butter Buds® and serve.

GLAZED CARROTS

Remove carrots from previous recipe to oven-proof serving dish. Add 1/4-cup brown sugar, toss, and place under broiler until brown and bubbly.

QUICK CHILI (NO MEAT)

1/2 *lb. Midland Harvest Burger®* **or** *3 tablespoons TVP® (see Chapter 6)*
1/2 *can chicken broth*
1 *can chili beans*
2 *teaspoons chili powder (or more to taste)*
1 *small can tomatoes*
~ *vegetable spray*

In veggie-sprayed skillet, brown reconstituted veggie burger. Add other ingredients and simmer for 10 minutes.

COLE SLAW II

FOR TWO

2 *cups shredded cabbage*
4 *tablespoons fat-free mayonnaise*
4 *tablespoons canned evaporated skim milk*
3 *teaspoons vinegar (red wine vinegar is fine)*
1 *packet artificial sweetener or sugar to taste*

Combine and refrigerate.

BREADS

Anybody can make bread, but why would anyone want to? The task of bread-making probably originated in our pre-agricultural history, while we were still hunting and gathering. Smooth river stones were used to grind and pulverize gathered seeds, grain, and nuts. The resultant meal was then mixed with water and wild seasonings, placed on a hot rack, and allowed to steam and bake. This cooking process rendered the ingredients more digestible and unwittingly created stronger bonds among family members. The act of "breaking bread" together was, and is, a celebration of humanity's victory over the elements. To gather, to prepare, and to share. Each family member had an important responsibility in the act of survival, and one of those responsibilities was the making of bread. ❧ *Turn-of-the-century farm life was entirely dependent upon homemade breads. Oftentimes it was Grandma, arising at 4:30 - 5:00 a.m., who slipped deftly into the quiet kitchen to coax the*

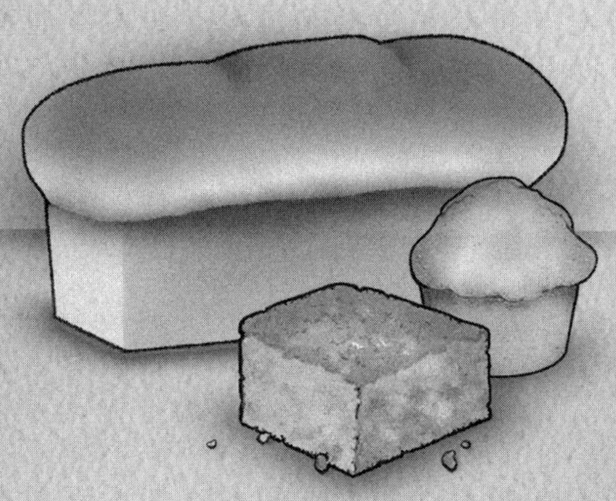

wood cookstove back to life using kindling brought in the night before by one of the young men. Soon the "quick breads" in the form of biscuits, pancakes, griddle cakes, and waffles were mixed and cooking. ❧ As the coffee began to boil, the household sprang to life. The older boys followed Dad to milk the cows. The older girls helped the younger children get dressed for school. When those tasks were accomplished, everyone filed into the kitchen to assist in different ways with the preparation of the day's food. The sorghum molasses pot was refilled, a new jar of apple butter was retrieved from the cellar, along with a jar of spiced peaches, and everyone sat down to break the night-long fast by partaking of and giving thanks for the daily bread. ❧ After the kitchen was cleaned, it was Mom's turn to shine in the bread-making department. The "sponge" that was prepared the night before was uncovered and, sure enough, the mixture consisting of a yeast starter, flour, molasses, and water had created a large bowlful of a bubbling, aerated, growing mass of yeast and flour. More water was added along with salt, leftover mashed potatoes, and flour. Mixed, kneaded, and allowed to rise, this bread dough would be turned into hot rolls for tonight and loaves of bread for three days. ❧ This type of hot roll was almost always still warm about the time school was out. When matched with slices of vine-ripened tomatoes and nothing more than salt and pepper, these rolls, the odors and tastes, would create childhood memories that would be remembered over and over again, silenced only by the grave. ❧ Make bread for someone you love and give them something to remember, especially a child!

COMMON ERRORS IN BREAD-MAKING

DEAD YEAST (BREAD WON'T RISE)

If warm water is good, then hot water must be better. Right?—Wrong! You just killed the yeast! Warm water means about the temperature of baby's milk (85-95° F).

TOO MUCH FLOUR

The bread was kneaded too much and it just kept absorbing flour and more flour. The texture is course and the crust is hard.

OVER-RISING

The dough was allowed to triple in size, resulting in big air pockets and really irregular texture.

UNDER-RISING

Bread that got cooked in the squat. As it was squatting to rise, you cooked it.

LOW OVEN TEMPERATURE

Very porous in center and upper half.

HIGH OVEN TEMPERATURE

Crust becomes very brown before bread has had a chance to cook.

KNEADING

Some recipes that follow are marked "easy to knead" and some are marked "hard to knead." The difference is entirely based upon the ratio of flour to liquid called for in the recipe. ❧ Traditionally, three cups of flour when mixed with one cup of liquid will yield a dough that will not stick to your hands but is difficult for some people to knead into a fine loaf of bread. When the flour content is lowered to two cups, it takes well-floured hands to keep it from sticking. By lowering the amount of flour initially mixed with the liquid and adding flour around the sides, bottom and top of the dough, it can be more easily turned into fine bread by a person who does not possess great strength and stamina. ❧ Kneading is the act of pressing, stretching, and folding the dough, thereby separating the gluten and starch so that the bread will more readily hold its "rise" during the baking stage. A well-kneaded loaf will be more uniform in size and texture. When the dough ball becomes smooth and elastic and I'm tired of kneading, I stop. The dough always turns into bread and I always enjoy it, so don't worry if you have kneaded it long enough.

CARE OF BREAD JUST OUT OF THE OVEN

Remove bread from pans immediately after baking. Allow air to circulate all around the loaves. This will retain moisture. Allow to thoroughly cool before wrapping in plastic wrap. For a tender crust, cover hot bread with cloth.

YEAST BREADS

The yeast breads are broken down into three categories according to the type of yeast used: first, standard yeast bread; second, salt-rising bread; third, sourdough bread.

THE STARTERS

STANDARD YEAST STARTER

1 *packet rapid-rise yeast*
1 *cup warm (85–95°F) water*
1 *teaspoon sugar*

Combine and allow yeast to dissolve for 5 or 10 minutes. *This yeast is a commercial strain available in any supermarket.*

SALT-RISING BREAD STARTER #1

1 *medium potato, grated*
1½ *cups boiling water*
3 *tablespoons cornmeal*
2 *teaspoons sugar or honey*
1 *teaspoon salt*
~ *random yeast or 1 packet rapid-rise yeast. (If you want to try random yeast, just mix, cover, and wait to ferment; if you want the flavor, but just can't wait, then add rapid-rise yeast.)*

Peel and grate potato, and in a medium bowl, add to the boiling water cornmeal, oatmeal, sugar, and salt. Allow to cool and stir in yeast. Cover and allow to set overnight. Warning: Do not add yeast to hot water!

SOURDOUGH STARTER

Purchase a commercial starter or use the following recipe and allow to "sour" over time. It won't be San Francisco, but it works.

1 *packet yeast (lager beer yeast preferred) (see note below)*
2½ *cups lukewarm (85-95°F) water*
2 *cups flour*
¼ *cup sugar*

Dissolve yeast in water, add sugar and flour, stir well, and allow to sit for at least 24 hours. Stir every day. Note: Brewer "lager" yeast was probably originally used and can be purchased from a local home-brew store.

NOTE: *All three of these starters can be maintained over a period of years simply by replacing original ingredients as they are used. For example, if you use a cup of sourdough starter, put a cupful of flour/water/sugar mixture back into your starter pot. Some strains, in fact, have been maintained for hundreds of years.*

THE SPONGE

After you have a starter and you want to make bread, the most reliable method is to create a sponge. All you are really doing is allowing the yeast in your starter to multiply in an anaerobic environment (as in under water). This usually is accomplished overnight and results in a bowl of flour and water that has the appearance of a sponge. If it isn't frothing and full of holes (except for sourdough), then your yeast probably isn't any good and you will have to start over. The holes in the batter are caused by the rising and escaping carbon dioxide gas. This will provide "leaven" for your bread. This gas, along with alcohol, are by-products formed by the single-celled yeast fungi as they devour, through fermentation, the sugars present in the act of multiplying. Alcohol you say! Yes, alcohol. Look at the ingredient lists for beer and for bread.

BEER	BREAD
Grain	Grain
Water	Water
Yeast	Yeast

BY- PRODUCTS

BEER	BREAD
Carbon Dioxide Gas	Carbon Dioxide Gas
Alcohol	Alcohol

They are identical. In beer, the carbon dioxide gas provides the carbonation, whereas in bread, it provides bubbles that cause the bread to rise. ❀ *The alcohol in beer acts as a preservative and makes you tipsy. In bread, the alcohol is boiled off during baking and provides, in part, the distinctive odor of baking bread. If you were to capture the boiled-off alcohol and cool it (or distill it), you would have grain alcohol.*

THE FLOURS

ALL-PURPOSE FLOUR

A white flour which contains satisfactory gluten for all types of baking. Gluten in wheat flour possesses properties which enable the dough to stretch and hold its shape during "leavening."

ENRICHED FLOUR

Vitamins and minerals added to all-purpose flour.

BLEACHED FLOUR

Processed by bleaching in order to have a whiter product. This changes the color of the flour, but adds nothing to the quality.

WHOLE WHEAT OR GRAHAM FLOUR

Made from the whole kernel of wheat containing varying amounts of bran and wheat germ. Makes for a coarser bread. Almost always used in conjunction with white flour.

RYE FLOUR

Rye is a hardy annual cereal grass, the flour of which is also almost always used in conjunction with white flour.

SELF-RISING FLOUR

An all-purpose flour containing baking powder and salt. This flour provides its own leavening.

BREAD FLOUR

A white flour with a high gluten content; i.e. high protein.

CORNMEAL FLOUR

Ground corn containing no gluten.

STANDARD RECIPE FOR WHITE BREAD

HARD TO KNEAD - MAKES TWO 1-POUND LOAVES

- 1 *packet rapid-rise yeast*
- 1/4 *cup lukewarm (85-95°F) water*
- 2 *tablespoons sugar*
- 1 *teaspoon salt*
- 2 *cups non-fat skim milk (canned evaporated is okay)*
- 6 *cups unbleached flour*
- ~ *vegetable spray*
- ~ *cornmeal*

Add yeast, water, sugar, and allow to dissolve for 5 to 10 minutes. Yeast should become active and bubbly the longer it sits. Pour into a large mixing pan along with the milk and salt. Stir and add 3 cups of flour. Add enough of the remaining flour to form into a soft dough ball. Knead, using remaining flour to keep dough from becoming sticky, until dough is firm and elastic. Place dough in veggie-sprayed bowl and allow to rise to about double its original size. Punch down, deflate and form into two loaves. Place in veggie-sprayed, corn-meal-dusted loaf pans or medium Dutch oven. Cover and allow to rise to double original size. Preheat oven to 375° F. Bake for 45 minutes. Remove and cool.

BASIC FRENCH BREAD OR ROLLS

HARD TO KNEAD - MAKES TWO SMALL LOAVES

- 1 *package rapid-rise yeast*
- 1/4 *cup warm (85-95°F) water*
- 1/2 *teaspoon sugar*
- 3 *cups flour for bread* ***or*** *unbleached all-purpose flour*
- 2 *teaspoons salt*
- 3/4 *cup tap water*
- ~ *vegetable spray*
- ~ *cornmeal*

Dissolve yeast in 1/4 cup warm water with sugar and let sit for 5 minutes. Add salt to liquid. In large mixing pan, mix with the rest of the water and combine with flour. Work into a dough ball and knead. Add more flour to bottom and sides of pan to keep dough from sticking. Knead for 5 to 10 minutes or until dough ball becomes elastic; that is, it resists being flattened out and folded over. Remove dough to a veggie-sprayed bowl that will hold dough after it has risen to twice its size. Cover bowl and allow to rise to double its size (about 50 to 60 minutes). This rising should take place in a warm (room temperature) place. After dough has risen, remove from bowl and punch it down or deflate it. Fold dough over end to end, put it back in veggie-sprayed bowl to rise again to double its original size. On floured counter top, press dough out into a 1/2-inch thick rectangle and with a knife, cut dough in half lengthwise. Fold sides of dough together, press inward and roll into a cigar-shaped loaf with your hands, and rotate "cigar" back and forth to firm loaf, pinching the ends to seal loaf. Place on a veggie-sprayed, cornmeal-dusted cookie sheet, cover with clean towel and allow to rise to double its original size. Preheat oven to 450° F. With a razor blade or sharp knife, make three diagonal slashes across top of loaves. Place loaves in oven and toss in five or six ice cubes into the bottom of the oven. This will create steam for a crunchy crust. Add four more ice cubes after five minutes. Lower temperature to 400° F and bake for 30 minutes. Remove and allow to cool where air can get to all sides of the bread. ❖

QUICK YEASTY DINNER BISCUITS

EASY TO KNEAD - MAKES ONE PIE PAN FULL

2/3 *cup warm water*
1 *package rapid-rise yeast (1/4 oz)*
1 1/2 *cups flour*
1 *teaspoon salt*

Preheat oven to 400° F. In large mixing bowl, dissolve yeast in warm water (85-95° F). Add flour, salt and mix and form into a ball. Add more flour to the bottom of the pan to keep dough from being sticky and knead dough for five minutes. In bottom of mixing pan, press dough into a circle 1/4 inch thick. Using a small cookie cutter, cut dough into biscuits and place into a veggie-sprayed cake or pie pan. Cover pan with a clean dish towel and place on back of stove for 30 minutes. Uncover rolls and place in oven on medium-high shelf and bake for 25 minutes. ❖

POTATO-OATMEAL BREAD

EASY TO KNEAD - MAKES TWO LOAVES

1 *package yeast dissolved in*
1/4 *cup warm water and*
1 *tablespoon sugar and allowed to sit for 10 minutes*
2 *cups hot non-fat milk*
2 *teaspoons salt*
2 *tablespoons sugar*
1/2 *cup instant mashed potato granules*
1 *cup regular oats*
5 *cups flour, approximately*
~ *cornmeal*

Mix yeast, water, and sugar and allow to sit for ten minutes. Mix hot milk, salt, sugar, potatoes, and oats. Allow to cool to room temperature. Add the yeast solution and mix well. Add three cups of flour and mix; add one more cup and mix. Turn dough out onto a well-floured board or counter top and knead for a couple of minutes. Let dough rest for ten minutes. Knead dough until smooth and elastic, adding flour as needed to keep dough from being sticky. Place dough in large veggie-sprayed pan, cover and allow to rise to about double its original size. Punch down and form into two loaves and place in veggie-sprayed loaf pans that have been dusted with cornmeal. Cover and allow to rise until double in bulk. Bake in preheated 425° F oven for ten minutes, reduce heat to 375° F and bake for 35 minutes more. Remove from pans and allow to cool.

NOTE: ***For Pearl Barley bread, add two cups of barley that has been boiled for 15 minutes, and add another cup of flour.***

WHOLE WHEAT BATTER BREAD

NO KNEADING REQUIRED - MAKES TWO SMALL LOAVES

2 *cups lukewarm non-fat milk*
1/4 *cup molasses*
1 1/2 *teaspoon salt*
1 *package dry yeast*
1/4 *cup lukewarm water*
4 1/3 *cups whole wheat flour*

Stir the yeast into the 1/4-cup lukewarm water and let it stand for five minutes to dissolve. Mix the milk, molasses, and salt in a large mixing bowl. Add the dissolved yeast and flour and beat well. Cover mixture with a clean towel and let rise in a warm place until double in size. Beat again briefly and put mixture into veggie-sprayed loaf pans. Cover and let rise to just less than double size. Preheat oven to 375° F. Bake bread for about 45 minutes. Remove from pan and cool.

SINGLE-RISE WHITE BREAD

EASY TO KNEAD - MAKES TWO LOAVES

1 *teaspoon salt*
1/2 *cup sugar*
2 1/4 *cups lukewarm non-fat milk*
1 *package dry yeast*
6 *cups white flour*

Mix everything but the flour in large mixing bowl and let sit for five minutes. Add three cups flour and beat until well blended. Add two more cups flour, mix, and place on well-floured board or counter top. Add flour so dough is not sticky. Knead for five minutes, then let dough sit for ten minutes. Form dough into two loaves and place in two veggie-sprayed loaf pans. Cover and let rise in warm place until dough doubles in size. Preheat oven to 425° F. Bake bread for ten minutes, reduce heat to 375° for 25 minutes more. Remove from pans and cool.

WHOLE WHEAT BREAD

EASY TO KNEAD - MAKES TWO LOAVES

2 *cups lukewarm non-fat milk*
1 *package dry yeast*
1/4 *cup sugar*
2 *teaspoons salt*
2 *cups whole wheat flour*
4 *cups white flour*
~ *vegetable spray*

Mix yeast and warm milk together and let stand for five minutes. Add sugar and salt and mix. Add two cups whole wheat flour and two cups white flour. Mix thoroughly and pour out onto well-floured board or counter top, adding enough flour so that the dough isn't sticky. Knead for three or four minutes and then let sit for ten minutes. Resume kneading for about ten minutes, adding more white flour if dough is sticky. Place in veggie-sprayed bowl. Cover and let rise in a warm place until double in size. Poke down dough and form into two loaves or one loaf and a pan of rolls. Cover and let double in size. Preheat oven to 375° F and bake for about 40 minutes. Remove and cool on racks.

HONEY GRAHAM BREAD

EASY TO KNEAD - MAKES TWO SMALL LOAVES

- 1 *cup salt-rising **or** yeast starter from page 191*
- 1 *cup graham flour*
- 1 *tablespoon sugar*
- $3^1/_2$ *cups unbleached white flour*
- 1 *teaspoon imitation butter flavor*
- 1 *cup warm water (85-95°F)*
- 1 *teaspoon salt*
- $^1/_4$ *cup honey*
- ~ *vegetable spray*
- ~ *cornmeal*

The night before, in mixing bowl, combine starter, graham flour, one cup white flour, butter flavor, warm water, sugar, honey, and salt. Stir, cover, and set in warm spot. The next day, combine with two cups white flour and form into dough ball. Use the rest of the flour when kneading bread for ten minutes to keep dough from sticking. Use more flour if necessary. Place dough in veggie-sprayed dish or pan, cover, and allow to rise to double in size. Punch down and place in veggie-sprayed Dutch oven or baking pan that has been dusted with cornmeal. Bake in 350° F preheated oven for 45 minutes. Remove and cool. ❖

OATMEAL RAISIN GRAHAM BREAD

EASY TO KNEAD - MAKES ONE ROUND LOAF

- 1 *cup starter (sourdough or salt-rising from page 191)*
- 1 *cup uncooked oatmeal*
- $^1/_2$ *cup raisins*
- 2 *tablespoons molasses **or** brown sugar*
- 1 *cup warm water (85-95°F)*
- 1 *cup unbleached white bread flour*
- $1^1/_2$ *cups graham flour*
- ~ *cornmeal*
- ~ *vegetable spray*

The night before, except for the graham flour, combine all ingredients, cover, and allow to sit all night. The next day, in large mixing bowl, combine with graham flour, form into a dough ball, and knead for ten minutes. Sprinkle on more graham flour in order to manage dough while kneading. Place dough in veggie-sprayed bowl, cover, and allow to rise to double its size in a warm (not hot) spot. Punch down and place in round 8-inch oven pan that has been veggie-sprayed and cornmeal dusted. Dust top of bread with cornmeal. Preheat oven to 375° F and bake for 45 minutes. ❖

SWEDISH LIMPA BREAD

MODERATE KNEAD - MAKES ONE LOAF

1 *cup rye flour*
2 *cups unbleached bread flour*
1 *teaspoon anise seeds*
1 *package rapid-rise yeast*
2 *tablespoons sugar*
1 *can evaporated skim milk*
1 *tablespoon molasses*
2 *tablespoons imitation butter flavoring*
~ *veggie spray*
1 *egg white, beaten slightly*

In large mixing bowl, combine rye flour, bread flour, and anise seeds, and mix. In small bowl, combine yeast, sugar, salt, milk, molasses, and butter flavoring. Mix thoroughly and pour into flour mixture. Form into a ball, add more bread flour around ball in order to facilitate kneading for ten minutes. Veggie spray another bowl or pan and place the round ball of dough in, cover, and allow to rise until double in size (about one hour). Punch down dough and form into a 14-inch long loaf with tapering ends. Place on veggie-sprayed cookie sheet, cover, and let rise again to double its size. Preheat oven to 400° F. With a sharp knife or razor, make 5 slashes across loaf about 1/4 inch deep and brush loaf with egg white. Place in oven, reduce temperature to 375° F, and bake for 30 minutes until loaf sounds hollow when tapped. ❖

SURE-FIRE SALT-RISIN' BREAD #2

This bread is yet another effort to put air bubbles in bread dough. Without a rising agent, flour dough ends up hard, gloppy, and unappetizing. ❧ *Originally, this starter relied on luck in finding a random, wandering yeast culture, whether airborne or coexisting with the potato, cornmeal, or sugar. Probably, unpasteurized wild honey would have been more useful than the sugar in providing a source of random yeast.* ❧ *Once the random yeast is combined with the sugar, potato, and cornmeal, it begins to devour the sugars and multiply.* ❧ *This form of spontaneous fermentation was at best unreliable. To ensure a reliable rising agent, we simply add to our starter a packet of rapid-rise dry yeast. Incidentally, the salt was thought to improve and guarantee results.* ❧ *This recipe makes two 8-inch loaves.*

SALT-RISIN' STARTER #2

1 medium **or** *2 small potatoes*
1 1/2 cup boiling water
3 tablespoons cornmeal
2 teaspoons sugar **or** *honey*
1 teaspoon salt
1 packet rapid-rise yeast

Peel and shred the potato and in a medium bowl, add to the water, cornmeal, sugar, and salt. Allow to cool and stir in the yeast. Cover and allow to sit overnight.

Now this mixture is going to begin to ferment, forming by-products of carbon dioxide gas and alcohol. As this occurs, the yeast multiplies. The next day, you have a soupy, gloppy mixture which is very rich in yeast and alcohol. For those whose lips never touch alcohol, not to fear, it will all boil off during the baking process. This alcohol occurs during the making of all yeast breads. Stir and strain off one cup of the liquid, putting the solids back into the bowl.

Now let's make some of the most delicious bread you have ever tasted. ❧

THE SALT-RISIN' BREAD DOUGH

MODERATE KNEAD - MAKES TWO LOAVES

1 *cup starter liquid from previous page*
1 *packet rapid-rise yeast*
6 *cups all-purpose flour*
1/4 *teaspoon baking soda*
1 *cup non-fat, evaporated skim milk*
1 *egg white*

Mix yeast into starter liquid and allow to dissolve. In a large mixing bowl, combine flour, baking soda, milk, and starter liquid. Stir until well mixed, knead for five to ten minutes until smooth. Add more flour if necessary to manage. Using veggie spray, lightly grease two 8-inch loaf pans. Divide dough into two parts, shape into loaves, and place in loaf pans. With sharp knife, make several diagonal cuts across tops of loaves—about 1/4-inch deep. Set loaves on top of stove, cover with a dish towel, and allow to rise to double their size (about one hour). Preheat oven to 375° F. After bread has risen, brush tops with egg white and place on medium rack in oven and bake for 35 minutes until golden brown and loaf sounds hollow when tapped. Remove from oven and allow to cool on top of stove for 10 minutes; remove from pans and allow to cool somewhat. While still warm, slice off one end piece and with a very fresh cup of coffee, sit down, kick back, and enjoy the fruits of your honest labor.

SALT-RISIN' OATMEAL BREAD

EASY TO KNEAD - MAKES ONE 9-INCH ROUND, 4-INCH HIGH LOAF

1 *cup liquid starter from previous page*
1 *cup uncooked oatmeal*
2 1/2 *cups flour for bread*
1 *cup warm water*
~ *vegetable spray*
~ *cornmeal*

The night before, combine starter, oatmeal, one cup flour, and warm water. Stir, cover with plastic wrap, and let rest overnight. The next day, add one cup flour and stir to form into a dough ball. Sprinkle a part of the remaining flour on top of and around dough. Knead for five minutes and place in veggie-sprayed dish or pan. Cover and allow to rise to double its size. Punch down, form into a loaf, and place in a veggie-sprayed pan that has been dusted with cornmeal. Brush or sprinkle top of dough with warm water and sprinkle cornmeal on top. Preheat oven to 375°. When dough has almost risen to double its original size, bake for 45 minutes. Remove from pan and allow to cool. ※

SALT-RISIN' BREAKFAST BISCUITS (WHITE FLOUR)

EASY TO KNEAD - MAKES ONE 10-INCH PAN OF BISCUITS

Prepare the night before use:

- 1/2 *cup starter liquid from page 191*
- 1/2 *cup evaporated skim milk or reconstituted non-fat powdered milk*
- 1/2 *teaspoon salt*
- 2 *cups all-purpose flour*

In a large, stainless steel mixing pan, combine ingredients and form into a ball. Add more flour as needed in order to manage the dough. It shouldn't stick to your hands as you knead the dough for 5 to 7 minutes. In the bottom of the mixing pan, press out the dough until the size of a 9- or 10-inch cake pan. Cut biscuits and place in veggie-sprayed cake pan or other oven-proof pan. Cover with plastic wrap and sit on top of stove overnight. The next morning, preheat oven to 400° F and bake for 20 minutes until golden brown. ※

BREAKFAST SALT-RISIN' CINNAMON RAISIN ROLLS

- 1/2 *cup starter liquid from page 191*
- 1/2 *cup evaporated skim milk*
- 1 *teaspoon vanilla, butter, nut flavoring*
- 1/2 *teaspoon salt (optional)*
- 2 *cups all-purpose flour*
- 1/2 *cup raisins*
- 1/2 *cup brown sugar (loosely packed)*
- 1 *teaspoon cinnamon*
- ~ *vegetable spray*

The night before, in a large stainless steel mixing pan, combine and mix starter liquid, milk, flavoring, salt, and flour. Mix well into a ball and knead for 5 to 10 minutes adding more flour as needed to manage. Turn dough onto a floured surface and roll into a 1/8-inch thick rectangular shape. Sprinkle cinnamon, sugar, and raisins evenly over the entire surface. Roll dough up into a giant burrito-like shape. Cut roll into 1/2 to 3/4 inch thick sections and place flat side down in a veggie-sprayed 9-inch cake pan or equivalent. Cover well and let sit overnight. The next morning, place in 400° F preheated oven for 20 minutes until golden brown. Serve warm. Freeze leftovers. ※

SALT-RISING WAFFLES OR GRIDDLE CAKES

FOR TWO

- 1/2 *cup salt-rising starter liquid from page 191*
- 1 *cup all-purpose flour*
- 1 *teaspoon baking powder*
- 1 *tablespoon sugar (optional)*
- 2 *moderately beaten egg whites*
- ~ *vegetable spray*

In mixing bowl, combine flour, sugar, and baking powder. Mix thoroughly. Add beaten eggs and starter liquid and beat gently until batter is smooth. Pour batter into hot veggie-sprayed waffle iron or griddle. Enjoy. ※

SALT-RISIN' TEA BREAD

MAKES SIX HAMBURGER BUN-SIZE ROLLS

- 1 *packet rapid-rise yeast*
- 1 *cup starter liquid from page 191*
- 1 *teaspoon imitation butter flavoring*
- 1 *tablespoon sugar (optional)*
- 2 *cups unbleached all-purpose bread flour*
- ~ *vegetable spray*

Preheat oven to 425° F. Combine starter liquid, butter flavoring, yeast, and sugar. Dissolve yeast, then combine with flour. Form into a ball and knead for 5 to 10 minutes until dough is springy and elastic. Divide dough into 3-x 3/4-inch biscuits and place on a veggie-sprayed cookie sheet. Cover and in a warm spot, allow to rise until double in size. Put in oven and bake for 20 minutes until golden brown. Allow to cool, then slice very thin and serve with jam or preserves. ※

SALT-RISIN' BUTTER COCONUT STICKY BUNS

MAKES TWELVE

- 2 *cups unbleached flour*
- 2 *tablespoons sugar*
- 1 *cup salt-risin' starter liquid from page 191*
- 2 *teaspoons liquid imitation butter flavoring*
- 1 *teaspoon imitation coconut extract*
- 1/2 *cup raisins*
- 1 *cup brown sugar*
- 2 *teaspoons cinnamon*
- ~ *vegetable spray*

Prepare the night before. Mix starter liquid with coconut flavor and butter flavor. In a mixing bowl, combine flour and sugar, then add starter/flavor mixture. Form into a ball and knead for 10 minutes, adding more flour to make dough manageable. Roll out dough to rectangle about 3/4-inch thick. Spread on brown sugar, raisins, and cinnamon. Roll up in a tight pin wheel, cut 1/2-inch thick slices and place each in veggie-sprayed muffin tin. Cover and allow to rise all night. the next morning, preheat oven to 400° F and bake for 15 to 20 minutes. Remove and serve warm.

SALT-RISIN' PUMPKIN BREAD

MAKES ONE 9-INCH LOAF

- 1/2 *cup salt-risin' liquid from page 191*
- 1 *cup canned pumpkin*
- 1 *teaspoon pumpkin pie spice*
- 4 *tablespoons sugar*
- 1/2 *cup raisins*
- 2 *cups unbleached bread flour*
- ~ *vegetable spray*

In the evening, in a large mixing bowl combine salt-risin' liquid, pumpkin, spice, sugar, and raisins. Mix well, then add flour and form into a ball. Add more flour around ball of dough and knead for 7 to 10 minutes. Form into a loaf and place into a 9-inch loaf pan. Cover with dish towel and allow to rise all night. The next morning, preheat oven to 350° F and bake loaf for 40 to 45 minutes until loaf is golden brown and sounds hollow when tapped on top. Slice warm for a nice breakfast, brunch, or tea bread.

SALT-RISIN' SIMPLE BREAKFAST MUFFINS

MAKES TWELVE MUFFINS

- 2 *cups unbleached flour*
- 1 *cup starter liquid from page 191*
- 1/2 *cup evaporated milk*
- 2 *tablespoons sugar*
- 1/2 *cup raisins*
- 2 *tablespoons oat bran*
- ~ *vegetable spray*

The night before, mix ingredients until smooth and spoon into a veggie-sprayed muffin tin. Cover and allow to rise overnight. The next morning, preheat oven to 400° F and bake for 25 minutes.

SALT-RISIN' EGG BREAD

EASY TO KNEAD - MAKES TWO ROUND 6-INCH LOAVES 3 INCHES HIGH

1 *cup starter liquid from page 191*
1 *packet rapid-rise yeast*
1/2 *cup Egg Beaters® egg substitute*
2 1/2 *cups unbleached flour*
1 *tablespoon oat bran (optional but recommended)*
1 *slightly beaten egg white*
~ *vegetable spray*

Preheat oven to 400° F. Dissolve yeast in starter liquid and mix in bowl with the flour, oat bran, and egg substitute. Form into a ball, pour more flour around dough, and knead for 5 to 10 minutes. Divide dough in half and form into round balls. Place separated on a veggie-sprayed cookie sheet. Cover loaves, place on top of stove, and allow to rise until double in size (about 1 hour). Using a sharp knife or razor blade slash each loaf 2 or 3 times about 1/4 inch deep. Brush completely with egg whites and place in oven. Lower heat to 375° F and bake for 30 minutes.

SALT-RISIN' BAGELS

Preheat oven to 375° F. Use dough from Salt-Risin' Bread on page 201 or other bread dough recipe and one beaten egg white. After dough has risen to double its size, punch down and form into 3-inch disks (about the size of a donut). Poke a 1-inch hole in middle and form into bagel. Place on veggie-sprayed cookie sheet, cover, and allow to rise again to about double size (30 to 40 minutes). Bring a pan of water to a boil and immerse a bagel into water and turn over immediately. Immediately remove bagel with a slotted spoon or spatula and place on veggie-sprayed surface to drain. Place bagels on veggie-sprayed cookie sheet, brush with egg white, and bake for 20 minutes until golden brown. Freeze leftover bagels.

SOURDOUGH BREAD

Sourdough and beans have been almost inseparable ever since there has been sourdough. So for that reason, I have left them together here in the "Bread" chapter. It might seem a little weird to find a bean recipe in amongst the breads, but I assure you that they really are partners.

SMOKY RANCH BEANS & SOURDOUGH BISCUITS

A hundred years ago, on a western cattle drive, you could always count on the blackened bean pot (usually cast iron) to be filled in the morning with beans and water and allowed to slush around aboard the chuck wagon all day long. After the evening meal, the bean pot was placed next to the campfire and allowed to simmer most of the night. Chopped up bits and pieces of leftover fire-grilled beef, along with a little sugar and salt, were added to the pot and perhaps some onions or molasses if available. Wild onions were and are readily available over much of the old western cattle drive country. After the beans were beginning their all-night affair with the campfire, the sourdough starter was opened and a portion of this liquid starter was poured into the biscuit-making pan. Warm water from the water barrel strapped to the side of the chuck wagon and some flour was added to the starter so as to make a thick liquid. This liquid was allowed to sit while clean-up chores were attended to. What happened in the bread pan during the next several hours largely determined the overall success or failure of the cook. Should the sourdough fail, then baking powder biscuits would be the back-up bread; however, yeast bread was always preferred. If a good cook could make good bread, everything else was second fiddle. ❧ *The first step in the sourdough biscuit process was simply to add more flour, some salt, knead, and form into biscuit balls. These dough balls were placed in a big Dutch oven, covered, and set aside to begin their all-night rising effort. The next morning, when placed next to the campfire, these rolls were soon baked into golden goodness, and when matched with the bubbly, beefy beans, they provided really substantial food. This low-fat fare, when washed down with plenty of hot cowboy coffee, would keep a person going all day long.*

SMOKY RANCH BEANS

- 2 *cups small dry white beans*
- 1 *cup burnt end pieces of beef (well-browned trimmings)* **or** *meat from 1 Pit Barbecue Beef sandwich*
- 4 *cups water*
- 1/2 *cup brown sugar*
- 1/3 *cup molasses*

Clean and soak beans all night, drain water prior to combining ingredients. Remove all visible fat from beef and chop into small pieces. Place beef in a Dutch oven (or big pot) along with four cups of water and boil vigorously for a half hour or so. Remove from heat and skim off any surface grease. Add onion, salt, sugar, and beans, and simmer until beans are tender and the juice is thick. Add more hot water to cooking beans as needed. Remove from heat and serve. Beans are more flavorful the second and third day.

NOTE: ***Some would add 1/4 cup of barbecue sauce or plain tomato sauce. I believe this alters the authenticity, but it also tastes good.*** ❧

SOURDOUGH BISCUITS

- 1 *cup sourdough starter from page 191*
- 5 *cups flour*
- 1 *cup water*
- 1 *teaspoon salt*
- ~ *vegetable spray*

Preheat oven to 375° F. In a large mixing bowl, combine starter, water, salt, and one cup of flour. Stir this soupy mixture well, cover, and allow to rest and rise in a warm place (but not hot!). After a couple of hours, the mixture should be an active, bubbly beehive of yeasty proliferation. Add rest of flour, stir, and form into a ball. Add more flour over dough, as needed, and knead for 10 minutes. Divide dough into golf-ball–size pieces and place side by side in a veggie-sprayed Dutch oven or cast iron skillet. Cover and allow to rise until the biscuits double in size. Bake for 40 minutes or until golden brown and hollow sounding when thumped. Serve hot from the oven.

BASIC SOURDOUGH BREAD

HARD TO KNEAD - MAKES 1 BIG ROUND OR 2 SMALL LOAVES

1 *cup starter from page 191*
1 *cup water*
2 *teaspoons salt*
2 *tablespoons sugar*
5 1/2 *cups flour*
~ *vegetable spray*
~ *cornmeal*

The night before, mix starter, water, one cup flour, salt, and sugar. Stir well, cover, and allow to sit all night. The next day, in a large mixing pan, combine frothy, foamy starter mixture that has been sitting all night with 4 1/2 cups of flour. Stir, forming into a ball of dough, knead for 10 minutes or until dough is smooth and elastic. Place dough in a veggie-sprayed pan or bowl that will allow sufficient room for the dough to rise to double its size. After doubling in size, punch down, and form into loaf or loaves and place in veggie-sprayed, cornmeal-dusted baking pan or pans. Preheat oven to 375° F. After dough has risen to double its original size, place in oven and bake for 40 minutes or until loaf is browned, sounds hollow when tapped, and has shrunk away from the sides of the pan. Remove and cool on wire rack.

SOURDOUGH OATMEAL RAISIN BREAD

EASY TO KNEAD - MAKES TWO SMALL LOAVES

1 *cup sourdough starter from page 191*
1 *cup warm water (85-95°F)*
1 *cup dry, rolled oats, regular or quick*
2 1/2 *cups unbleached flour*
1 *cup raisins*
1 *teaspoon salt*
~ *vegetable spray*
1 *tablespoon cornmeal*

The night before, combine starter, water, rolled oats, one cup flour, raisins, and salt. Stir well, cover with plastic wrap, and allow to rest all night. The next day, add and mix one cup flour and knead for five minutes. Use remaining 1/2 cup flour to dust on and around dough to keep it from sticking. Place in a veggie-sprayed Dutch oven or other oven-proof cookware, cover, and allow to rise to double its size. Punch down and dust top with cornmeal; allow to rise again to almost double its original size. Preheat oven to 375° F and bake for 45 minutes. Remove and allow to cool somewhat.

LAGER BREAD

HARD TO KNEAD - MAKES ONE LARGE ROUND OR TWO SMALL LOAVES

1 *cup sourdough lager starter from page 191 (sourdough starter made with lager yeast)*
1 *cup water*
2 *teaspoons salt*
1 *tablespoon sugar*
5 1/2 *cups flour*
~ *vegetable spray*
~ *cornmeal*

The night before, in a mixing bowl, combine and stir thoroughly starter, water, salt, sugar, and one cup flour. Cover with plastic wrap and allow to sit overnight. The next day, in a large mixing pan, add 4 1/2 cups of flour and starter mixture. Form into a ball and knead until smooth and elastic. Place in veggie-sprayed pan, cover with plastic wrap, and allow to rise to double its original size in a warm (75 to 80° F) spot. Punch down and form into a loaf or loaves and place in a veggie-sprayed, cornmeal-dusted pan. Preheat oven to 375° F. When dough has risen to double its original size, place in oven and bake for 40-45 minutes until brown, hollow sounding when thumped, and somewhat shrunken away from sides of the pan. Remove from oven and take bread immediately from pans and allow to cool on a wire rack where air can get to all sides of the bread.

QUICK BREADS

As the name implies, these breads require much less time to prepare. They do not use yeast as a leavening agent, instead they rely upon a chemical reaction to create carbon dioxide gas, the built-in air from beaten eggs or steam. They include biscuits, muffins, crumpets, cornbread, steamed breads, popovers, griddle cakes, waffles, and Irish soda bread. With the exception of Irish soda bread, they are almost always served hot.

BAKING POWDER - BAKING SODA

When you combine an acid with bicarbonate of soda, you produce a large quantity of carbon dioxide gas which makes your dough fluff up or rise. Baking soda is a bicarbonate of soda, which is the main ingredient of baking powder. Sour cream, yogurt, vinegar, or sour milk are very acid and react quickly with baking soda.

POPOVERS

MAKES SIX

- 1/2 *cup no-fat skim milk*
- 1/4 *cup Egg Beaters® egg substitute*
- 1/2 *cup flour*
- 1 *tablespoon Butter Buds® butter-flavor granules*
- 1/8 *teaspoon salt*
- ~ *vegetable spray*

Preheat oven to 450° F. Spray non-stick muffin tin with butter-flavored vegetable spray. Beat eggs for a minute or two, add rest of ingredients and mix thoroughly. Spoon mixture into six muffins and place in oven. After 15 minutes, lower temperature to 350° F. DO NOT OPEN OVEN UNTIL 15 MORE MINUTES HAVE ELAPSED. Serve immediately with your favorite topping or use as bread. To make 12 popovers, just double the ingredients.

QUICK FAT-FREE FLOUR TORTILLAS

1 *package of generic biscuit dough (1 gram of fat per 2 biscuits)* ***or***
1 *package of French bread dough (1 gram of fat per slice or less)*

On well-floured board or counter top, combine 2 biscuits into a ball. roll in flour, then roll out to the size of a tortilla. Turn dough, adding flour to top frequently. Place tortilla into medium hot skillet. Turn when dough starts to puff up. Remove when tortilla is spotted with dark brown spots. Don't over-cook. Remove to plate and cover with plastic wrap. ❋

SOUR CREAM BISCUITS

2 *cups self-rising flour*
1 *tablespoon Butter Buds® butter-flavor granules*
1 *teaspoon cheddar cheese sprinkles (optional)*
1 *cup no-fat sour cream*
~ *vegetable spray*

Preheat oven to 425° F. In mixing bowl combine and mix the flour, butter flavor, and cheese sprinkles. Add sour cream, mix, and form into a ball. Add more flour around ball and knead for 2 or 3 minutes. Press into a 1/2-inch thick oval and then, using a cookie cutter or glass, cut dough into biscuits and place on a veggie-sprayed pan, keeping them separated. Bake for 20 minutes until done. ❋

VARIATIONS OF SOUR CREAM BISCUITS

CHEESE SANDWICH BISCUIT
Roll or press dough to 1/4 inch thickness; cut into biscuits, place slightly smaller piece of fat-free cheese on bottom piece, and place another biscuit on top and press edges together. You now have a 1/2-inch thick biscuit with a piece of cheese in the middle.

HAM AND CHEESE BISCUIT
Add sliced ham pieces to cheese middle.

PINEAPPLE BISCUIT
Place one biscuit on bottom; cut a 1-inch hole in another biscuit and place on top. Fill hole with pineapple jelly. Other flavors optional.

MEAT AND POULTRY FILLING
Make bottom biscuit thinner, cut 1-inch hole in thicker top biscuit and leave empty. After cooking, fill with a favorite spread.

FRESH FRUIT FILLING
Prepare as per meat and poultry filling except substitute fresh fruit and top with cheesecake topping from page 253. ※

BUTTER PECAN CINNAMON ROLLS

2 1/4 cups self-rising flour
1 cup skim milk
1/4 cup brown sugar
1/2 cup raisins
3 teaspoons cinnamon
2 tablespoons TVP® For the bottom of pan (see note)
1/4 cup brown sugar
1 oz. (1 packet) Butter Buds® Butter Flavored Granules
4 tablespoons evaporated skim milk
1 oz. praline pecan liquor (or 2 tablespoons vanilla, butter, nut flavoring)

Preheat oven to 400° F. In large mixing bowl combine flour and skim milk and form into a dough ball. Add flour to keep from sticking to your hands if needed. Remove dough ball from bowl and place on floured board or counter top. Roll and form dough into a 6- x 12- x 1/4-inch thick shape. Sprinkle on 1/4 cup brown sugar, raisins, and cinnamon. Roll up in pinwheel fashion and set aside.

Prepare the bottom of a 9-inch cake pan (preferably one with a rotating removal arm). Evenly spread the brown sugar, Butter Buds® butter-flavored granules, and the TVP® on the bottom of pan. In a small bowl mix the evaporated skim milk and the praline liquor (or the vanilla, butter, or nut flavoring). Pour liquid evenly over bottom of pan. When cooked, this bottom will become the top of your rolls. Now slice your rolls one inch thick and place on top of sugar-liquid mixture. Bake for 22 minutes until golden brown. Remove from oven, place a plate over top of pan and turn pan upside-down in order to remove rolls from pan. This must be accomplished while rolls are hot. Don't burn yourself!
NOTE: *TVP® is textured vegetable protein and can be obtained from most health food stores. Here, after cooking, TVP® takes on the appearance of nut meats.* ※

QUICK IRISH SODA BREAD

4 cups self-rising flour
2 tablespoons sugar
1 cup raisins
2 cups buttermilk (reconstituted powdered buttermilk is fine)
~ vegetable spray

Preheat oven to 375° F. In mixing bowl, thoroughly mix

flour and sugar. Add raisins and buttermilk, mix, and form into a ball. Knead for 5 minutes, form into a round loaf, and place on a veggie-sprayed baking sheet (or pan). Make two 1/2-inch deep cuts across loaf to form a cross and bake for 40 to 45 minutes until brown and sounds hollow when thumped on top. Remove from oven and allow to cool. Slice very thin, NEVER THICK. Makes great toast.

CHEESY IRISH SODA BREAD

- ~ *Irish soda bread from preceding recipe*
- 2 *tablespoons cheese flavored sprinkles*

Omit raisins and one tablespoon of sugar from recipe and add two tablespoons of cheese-flavored sprinkles. Prepare and bake as indicated.

IRISH SODA CINNAMON ROLLS

MAKES ONE 9-INCH CAKE-PAN FULL

- 2 *cups all-purpose unbleached flour*
- 1/2 *teaspoon baking soda*
- 1/2 *teaspoon baking powder*
- 1/2 *teaspoon salt*
- 1 *tablespoon sugar*
- 1/2 *cup raisins*
- 1 *cup buttermilk*
- 1 *teaspoon vanilla flavoring*
- 1 *teaspoon butter flavoring*

THE FILLING

- 1 *teaspoon cinnamon*
- 1/2 *cup brown sugar*
- ~ *vegetable spray*

Preheat oven to 400° F. In mixing bowl, mix thoroughly flour, soda, raisins, baking powder, salt, and sugar. Add flavorings to buttermilk (reconstituted powdered buttermilk works well); then combine buttermilk with flour mixture. Form into a ball, add more flour to manage dough, and knead for 5 minutes. Turn out onto floured surface, and press down into a 12- x 6- x 3/8-inch form. Sprinkle dough with brown sugar and cinnamon and roll up into a pinwheel. slice into 3/4-inch thick rolls and place in a veggie-sprayed 9-inch cake pan. Bake for 20 minutes until golden brown. Serve warm.

IRISH SODA BREAD

- 4 *cups all-purpose flour (unbleached if available)*
- 1 *teaspoon baking soda*
- 1 *teaspoon baking powder*
- 1 *teaspoon salt*
- 2 *tablespoons sugar*
- 1 *cup raisins*
- 2 *cups buttermilk*
- \- *vegetable spray*

Preheat oven to 375° F. In large mixing bowl, mix thoroughly the flour, soda, baking powder, salt, and sugar. Then add raisins and buttermilk. Form into a ball and knead for 5 minutes or so until smooth. Form into a round loaf and place on a veggie-sprayed sheet pan. With a sharp knife, cut a 1/2-inch deep cross on top of loaf. Bake for 40 to 45 minutes until nicely brown and sounds hollow when tapped on top. The cross will have spread into the characteristic trademark of Irish soda bread. Cool and slice thin. Makes wonderful toast. ※

STEWED IRISH SODA BREAD

Use the recipe for Irish soda bread substituting 1 1/2 cups (1 can) lite beer and 1/2 cup buttermilk for the 2 cups of buttermilk. ※

CHEDDAR CORNBREAD

MAKES ONE 9-INCH CAKE PAN

- 1 *cup self-rising flour*
- 1/2 *cup cornmeal*
- 2 *teaspoons cheddar-flavored sprinkles*
- 1 *cup liquid buttermilk (reconstituted powder is okay)*
- ~ *vegetable spray*

Preheat oven to 400° F. In mixing bowl, mix thoroughly flour, cornmeal, and cheddar sprinkles. Add buttermilk and mix well. Spoon out into cornbread molds or a veggie-sprayed 9-inch cake pan. Bake for 20 to 25 minutes. Serve warm. ※

CAJUN CORNBREAD

Cajuns like their cornbread sweet, so we've added sugar to buttermilk cornbread. Coincidentally, they also like their stuffing sweet, so we use our sweetened cornbread to make Cajun cornbread stuffing.

- 1/4 *cup sugar*
- 1 *cup self-rising flour*
- 1/2 *cup cornmeal*
- 2 *teaspoons imitation butter flavoring*
- 3 *egg whites*
- 1 *cup buttermilk (reconstituted powder is okay)*

Preheat oven to 400° F. In mixing bowl, mix sugar, flour, and cornmeal. In another bowl, lightly beat egg whites; then mix with butter flavoring and buttermilk. Combine the two bowls, mix, and pour into cornbread molds or a veggie-sprayed 9-inch cake pan. Bake for 22 minutes or until a toothpick inserted into the center of cornbread comes out clean. Serve warm.

HERBED CHEESE BISCUITS

2 *cups self-rising flour*
1/4 *teaspoon each of dried parsley, oregano, thyme, and marjorum*
1 *tablespoon Molly McButter® all-natural cheese-flavored sprinkles*
2 *teaspoons imitation butter flavor*
1 *cup evaporated skim milk*
~ *vegetable spray*

Preheat oven to 450° F. In a large mixing bowl, mix flour, herbs, and cheese sprinkles. In measuring cup, mix butter flavor and milk, then pour into flour. Stir and form into a ball. Add more flour around ball of dough and knead for 3 or 4 minutes. Press out into a 1/2- to 3/4-inch thick circle. Using cookie cutter, cut into biscuits and place apart on veggie-sprayed cookie sheet. Bake for 12 to 15 minutes.

VERY QUICK YEAST ROLLS

1 *cup warm water (85-95°)*
1 *package rapid-rise yeast*
1/4 *cup sugar*
2 *cups self-rising flour*
1/4 *cup no-fat milk powder*
2 *teaspoons vinegar*
1 *tablespoon skim milk*
~ *non-fat grated Parmesan* ***or*** *Romano cheese*
~ *vegetable spray*

Combine water, yeast, sugar and allow to sit at room temperature for at least 1/4 hour or until 1/2 inch of foam forms on top of liquid. Preheat oven to 400° F. In large mixing pan combine flour and milk powder. Add vinegar to yeast liquid, stir well, and pour into the flour. Mix into a dough ball and knead for 4 or 5 minutes. Sprinkle with more flour to facilitate kneading. Cut into biscuits and place in veggie-sprayed 9-inch cake pan. Brush tops with skim milk and sprinkle with cheese. Allow to sit on top of stove for 10 minutes; then bake for 20 minutes.

NOTE: ***For a butter-cheese–flavored roll add 2 teaspoons imitation butter flavoring and 1 tablespoon Molly McButter® natural cheese-flavor sprinkles. Your rolls will be a golden yellow color.***

SOUR CREAM OR BUTTERMILK SCONES

2 *cups self-rising flour*
1 *cup no-fat sour cream* **or** *buttermilk*
1 *teaspoon vanilla, butter, nut flavoring*
2 *tablespoons sugar*
1/2 *cup raisins*
~ *vegetable spray*

Preheat oven to 450° F. Combine ingredients, stir, and form into a ball. Add more flour around dough so it doesn't stick to your hands as you knead the dough for 3 or 4 minutes. Flatten into a circle of dough about 1/2- to 3/4-inch thick. With biscuit or cookie cutter, cut into biscuits and place separated in a veggie-sprayed pan or cookie sheet. Bake for 15 to 20 minutes until golden brown and done. Serve warm for tea time with raspberry jam (grape will do).

SCONES

2 *cups all-purpose flour (unbleached is best)*
1 *tablespoon baking powder*
1/2 *teaspoon salt*
1 *tablespoon sugar*
1 *cup evaporated skim milk*
~ *vegetable spray*

Preheat oven to 450° F. Combine and mix thoroughly flour, baking powder, salt, and sugar. Add milk and quickly stir mixture and form into a ball. Knead dough for 3 to 5 minutes, then pat out to a thickness of 1/2-inch. Cut into biscuits and place on veggie-sprayed cookie sheet or pan. Bake 12 to 15 minutes until golden brown.

BUTTERMILK PANCAKES

2 1/2 *cups buttermilk, either fresh* **or** *reconstituted dry buttermilk*
1/2 *cup Egg Beaters® egg substitute*
1/2 *teaspoon salt*
1 *teaspoon baking soda*
3 *cupfuls flour*

Mix buttermilk, eggs, salt, and baking soda thoroughly. Add flour and beat until smooth. Do not overbeat. Spoon onto veggie-sprayed hot griddle or pan and cook until top is full of holes and the underside is brown. Turn and brown other side. Batter should be used immediately after mixing. **NOTE:** ***Leftover batter may be mixed with raisins and spooned into veggie-sprayed muffin tin and baked at 350° F for 20 minutes or until done.***

SWEET MILK PANCAKES

2 *egg whites, slightly beaten*
2 *cups skim milk*
1 *teaspoon imitation butter flavoring*
3 *cups self-rising flour*

Combine ingredients and beat until smooth. Do not overbeat. Spoon onto hot griddle and cook. For a smaller batch, reduce amounts of milk and flour while maintaining desired thickness of batter.
NOTE: ***For blueberry pancakes just add fresh, washed blueberries to suit your taste.***

FRENCH TOAST

Thick slices of homemade bread are best for French toast. Thick slices of other bread are second best.

1/4 *cup Egg Beaters® egg substitute*
1 *cup non-fat milk*
~ *dash nutmeg*
~ *dash cinnamon*
1 *tablespoon sugar*

Mix well. Dip bread slices into mixture. Do not soak. Fry on hot veggie-sprayed griddle or skillet. Brown both sides, remove and sprinkle with powdered sugar.

FILLED FRENCH TOAST

With an unsliced loaf of bread, slice a 1/4- to 3/8-inch thick slice partially through the loaf (close to the bottom). Move knife over 1/4- to 3/8-inch and make another slice completely through the loaf. You should now have a thick slice of bread hinged at the bottom. Spread inside of slice (or pocket) with your favorite jam or jelly, dip in French toast batter and fry.

DESSERTS

When the sweet tooth craving strikes and you feel it has to be satisfied, at least do it without fat. This chapter will show you how. ❧ *The average American consumes approximately 150 pounds of sugar each year. The standard argument among lay people has always been that sugar has been shown to only cause cavities in your teeth and otherwise is not detrimental to your health. Right? Wrong!* ❧ *As long ago as 1986, it has been shown that elevated levels of triglycerides are a highly significant independent risk factor for coronary heart disease in women, according to William P. Castelli, M.D., Director of the famous Framingham Heart Study. (AM Heart Journal, Vol. 112, page 432, 1986). In addition, they appear important in men with low HDL cholesterol (the good guys). Individuals with elevated triglycerides should be considered at risk for coronary heart disease unless the total cholesterol/HDL ratio is under 3.5 (refer to Chapter 5). More recently, this same conclusion was reached by a group of Finnish researchers (See: Joint Effects of Serum Triglyceride and LDL cholesterol and HDL cholesterol concentration on coronary heart disease risk in*

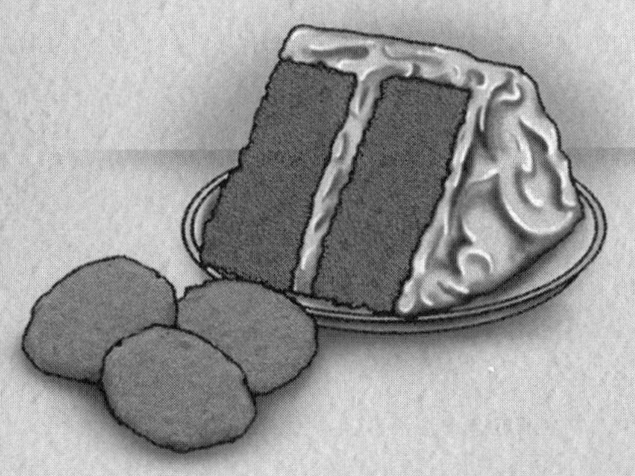

the Helsinki Heart Study; January 1992 issue of Circulation, *85: 37-45, published by the American Heart Association: The Helsinki summary is, "The present data suggests that elevated serum triglyceride concentration is a marker of elevated coronary heart disease risk, especially in subjects with a high LDL/HDL ratio."* ✽ *So what does all this have to do with sugar? Your liver converts excess calories from carbohydrates (as in sugar) first into fatty acids and then into triglycerides. The more excess sugar, the more elevated serum triglycerides.* ✽ *Recently, I took advantage of a free cholesterol screening at the Lipid and Arteriosclerosis Prevention Clinic, Department of Medicine, Division of Clinical Pharmacology, University of Kansas Medical Center, located in Kansas City. Here are the results:*

Total Cholesterol: 183 (good)

Triglycerides: 394 (terrible)

HDL: 25 (That's bad)

LDL: 79 (That's good)

Ratio LDL/HDL: 3.71 (good)

Since my triglycerides should have been less than 200, I was asked to come in for a second screening and was told, "By the way, I know you are writing the chapter in your book about desserts, so why don't you refrain from consuming excessive amounts of sugar for two weeks prior to the second screening?" I gave up sugar and the results were as follows:

Total cholesterol: 188

Triglycerides: 153

HDL: 29

LDL: 128

Ratio LDL/HDL: 4.43

❧ *I had always been a big sugar eater with elevated triglyceride levels hovering around 400 and no one had ever proclaimed me at risk for coronary heart disease until the Lipid Clinic at the University of Kansas. Fortunately, they also prescribed a simple remedy, "Don't eat so much sugar," and it brought my triglyceride levels down where they belonged.* ❧ *The moral of this story is MODERATION. Be moderate in your consumption of sugar and always take the fat out. Remember: There isn't a dime's worth of difference between sugars. If it's sweet, it's probably sugar, and you can't rationalize a difference between juice concentrate, honey, brown sugar, or molasses. It is all sugar!* ❧ *For your Thanksgiving Day dessert table, I recommend some or all of the following items with 1 gram of fat or less per serving (with the exception of chocolate fudge cheesecake which has approximately 1.5 grams per serving):* ***Pumpkin Pie, page 226, Lemon Meringue Pie, page 225, Cream Cheese, Maraschino Cherry Spread, page 86, with Mini Loaves of Pumpkin Bread, page 204, Raspberry Shortcake, page 240, Pineapple Upside-down Cake, page 238, Olde, Olde Fashioned Cake, page 232, and Chocolate Fudge Cheesecake, page 242.*** ❧ *For your Christmas cookie selection, why not try some of the following with less than 1 gram of fat per cookie:* ***Brownie Oatmeal, page 246, Brown Sugar Raisin, page 245, Brownies, page 242, Chocolate Raisin, page 245, and Chocolate-Covered Cherry Cookies, page 245.*** ❧ *Remember the key word when it comes to sugary desserts—MODERATION—and minimal fat. Good luck.*

PIE CRUSTS & PIES

BISCUIT PIE CRUST (REGULAR OR BUTTERMILK)

A traditional fat-laden pie crust has approximately 10 to 15 grams of fat per serving. This recipe, using a whole can of generic biscuits (10), will contain just 5 grams for the entire crust!

1 *can biscuits (1 gram of fat per 2 biscuits)*
2 *tablespoons sugar*
~ *flour*
~ *vegetable spray*

Remove biscuits to mixing bowl and sprinkle with sugar. Press in sugar and form biscuits into a dough ball. Remove to floured surface and roll into a 12- to 14-inch circle. Place into a veggie-sprayed pie pan.
NOTE: *The recipe for scones on page 216 makes a wonderful pie crust or use any biscuit recipe in this book.*

CAKE CRUMB PIE CRUST

One cup of graham cracker crumbs has approximately 14 grams of fat. Using two cups per pie would amount to about 5 grams of fat per serving in the crust alone. The following crusts yield 0 grams of fat per serving:

CHOCOLATE CAKE CRUMB CRUST

2 *cups non-fat chocolate cake*
~ *water to moisten, if needed*

In mixing bowl, crumble cake and sprinkle lightly with water if needed. in veggie-sprayed pie pan, press crumbs to sides and bottom.

YELLOW CAKE CRUMB PIE CRUST

~ *non-fat yellow cake* ***or*** *pound cake*
~ *water to moisten if needed.*

Crumble cake and sprinkle lightly with water, if needed. In veggie-sprayed pie pan, press crumbs to the sides and bottom.

CORNFLAKE CRUMB CRUST

- 1 *cup cornflake crumbs (buy them in a box* **or** *make them yourself)*
- 2 *tablespoons sugar*
- 2 *tablespoons water*
- ~ *vegetable spray*

Thoroughly mix ingredients in a mixing bowl. Pour into a veggie-sprayed pie pan. Press and form to shape pie crust. Chill well before filling. Use where graham cracker crusts are called for. Chill before serving. ❖

FLOUR TORTILLA PIE CRUST

Perhaps the easiest pie crust ever is accomplished by taking a large flour tortilla, holding it under the hot water faucet for a few moments, laying it on a towel to dry a little, and then placing it in a pie pan. Each large tortilla generally has less than 5 grams of fat so it will provide a very low-fat crust. If baking this crust empty, be sure to poke a few holes in the bottom and around the sides to keep large bubbles of air from forming. Use as you would any pie crust. ❖

TWO-CRUST PIE CRUST

- 2 *cups self-rising flour*
- 3/4 *cup buttermilk*
- 1/4 *cup apple juice concentrate*
- 1 *teaspoon imitation butter flavoring*
- 1 *teaspoon vanilla flavoring*
- ~ *vegetable spray*
- 1 *egg white, beaten slightly*

Combine buttermilk, apple juice concentrate, and flavorings. Pour into flour and form into a moist ball. Pour more self-rising flour around dough, then knead for 5 minutes. On a smooth, floured surface, roll out 2/3 of dough into circle about 1/8-inch thick. Place in a veggie-sprayed pie pan. Trim edges, poke fork holes in the bottom, and place in a 350° F preheated oven for 10 minutes. While crust is baking, roll out remaining dough for the top and beat the egg white. Remove crust from oven and pour in boiling hot filling. Place dough on top, trim around edges, brush with egg white, cut several slits in top, and put back in oven for 20 minutes. ❖

As another option, I offer a giant crepe placed in a pie dish, then filled with your favorite pie filling. It's wonderful and easy.

PIE CREPE BATTER

- 1 *cup egg whites*
- 1 *cup all purpose flour*
- 1/4 *cup non-fat milk powder*
- 3/4 *cup water*
- 1/8 *teaspoon salt*
- 1 *teaspoon butter flavoring*

Combine ingredients and mix until smooth. Let stand for one hour at room temperature before use so as to allow air bubbles to escape. Makes approximately one dozen crepes.

CREPUS GIANTICUS (BIG CREPE FOR PIE CRUST)

- 3/4 *cup crepe batter from preceding recipe*
- ~ *veggie spray*

Preheat oven to 400° F. Place a veggie-sprayed 12-inch cast iron skillet in oven and heat for 15 minutes or longer. Using insulated gloves remove skillet and pour in crepe batter and rotate skillet to cover bottom of skillet and 3/4 inch up the sides of skillet. Return to oven and bake for an additional 5 minutes. Remove from oven and place crepe in a 9 inch pie dish. Fill crepe with your desired cooked or fresh filling.

BRANDIED BLACKBERRY CREPE FILLING

FOR USE WITH LEFTOVER CREPE BATTER

- 1 *cup frozen blackberries*
- 1 *tablespoon sugar*
- 1/2 *teaspoon butter flavoring*
- 1/2 *oz. brandy*

In a small skillet over a medium heat, mix and heat ingredients until blackberries are fully thawed. Remove from heat and serve.

MERINGUE FOR PIE

Use standard meringue recipe or purchase a box of fluffy white frosting mix, making sure that it is fat free and made from egg whites. Prepare as per instructions and pile on top of your pie. Place in a preheated 500° F oven for just a minute or so until browned to suit you.

NOTE: ***For cold refrigerated pies you may use the whipped yogurt cream topping on page 250***

LEMON MERINGUE PIE

- ~ *Jell-O® brand lemon pie filling mix prepared with Egg Beaters® eggs substitute*
- 1 *package fluffy white frosting mix (fat free and made with egg whites)*
- 1 *pie crust baked to light brown, page 222*

Prepare filling and spoon into pie shell. Top with frosting mix and place in preheated 500° oven for 1 minute to brown the meringue.

BANANA CREME PIE

- 1 *package Jell-O® brand banana cream (cook and serve) pudding and pie-filling*
- 1 *package fluffy white frosting mix (fat free)*
- 1 *large banana, sliced*

Prepare filling using non-fat milk; add banana, and spoon into cool pie shell. Cover with fluffy white meringue and place in preheated 500° oven for one minute to brown meringue.

BOURBON PIE OR MOCK PECAN PIE (MADE BY OMITTING THE BOURBON)

This is a very fine replacement for pecan pie. These pies come in at about one-plus gram of fat per slice, whereas traditional pecan pie will average 32 grams of fat per slice. You would have to eat about 5 whole bourbon pies to equal just one slice of regular pecan pie. So, kick back and enjoy.

BOURBON PIE

- 1 *buttermilk biscuit pie dough, uncooked, page 222*
- 1 *cup dark corn syrup*
- 1 *cup sugar*
- 2 *tablespoons Butter Buds® butter-flavor granules*
- 2 *tablespoons bourbon whiskey*
- 1 *teaspoon vanilla*
- 1/2 *cup oatmeal, regular and uncooked*
- 1/2 *cup cooked rice*
- 1/2 *cup Egg Beaters® egg substitute*

Except for rice and oats beat other ingredients for 2 or 3 minutes. Add rice and oats and mix. Pour into uncooked pie shell and in a 350° F preheated oven, bake for 60 minutes until center is set. There will be some liquid but filling will be firm. **NOTE: *For mock pecan pie just omit the bourbon whiskey. You'll fool a lot of people.***

CRUSTLESS PUMPKIN PIE

- 1 *16-oz. can pumpkin*
- 1 *can evaporated skimmed milk*
- 3/4 *cup Egg Beaters® egg substitute*
- 3/4 *cup sugar*
- 1/2 *cup flour*
- 1 1/2 *teaspoon pumpkin pie spice*
- 3/4 *teaspoon baking powder*
- 1/8 *teaspoon salt*
- 1/2 *cup regular rolled oats*

Except for the oats, beat and thoroughly mix all ingredients. Fold in oats and spoon into a round deep casserole dish. This makes one big pie or two small ones. Bake in preheated 350° oven for 50 minutes or until toothpick or knife inserted in center comes out clean. Sprinkle powdered sugar on top and serve when cool.

APPLE OR CHERRY PIE

- 1 *16-oz. can pie filling (fat free)*
- ~ *pie shell, uncooked (page 222)* ***or*** *use 2-crust recipe (page 223)*

Spoon pie filling into cooked pie shell. If desired use additional pie dough cut in strips to make a lattice top for the pie. Bake in preheated 375° F oven for 25 minutes. To prevent overbrowning of crust, cover with aluminum foil.

KEY LIME PIE

- 1/4 *cup water*
- 1 *envelope unflavored gelatin*
- 1/2 *cup fresh lime juice grated rind of one lime*
- 1 *package fluffy white frosting mix (fat free and made with egg whites)*
- 1 *cup evaporated skimmed milk*
- 1 *cup Egg Beaters® egg substitute*
- ~ *green food coloring*
- ~ *9-inch chocolate cake crumb pie crust from page 222*

Dissolve gelatin in 1/4 cup hot water, add milk, eggs, lime juice, and lime rind. Bring to simmer over medium heat, stirring constantly. Simmer for 2 or 3 minutes and remove from heat. Prepare frosting mix as per directions, adding one or two drops of food coloring while beating. Add one drop of food coloring to egg mixture, also. Gently fold frosting mix into egg mixture. Spoon out into pie crust and chill. Garnish with wafer thin slices of fresh lime prior to serving.

NO-SUGAR SOUR CREAM APPLE RAISIN PIE

THE FILLING

- 1/2 *cup water*
- 3 *cups sliced Granny Smith apples*
- 1 *cup apple juice concentrate*
- 1 *tablespoon cornstarch*
- 1 *teaspoon apple pie spice*
- 1 *cup no-fat sour cream*
- ~ *Artificial sweetener to taste*
- ~ *two-crust pie crust from page 223*

In a saucepan, bring apples and water to a boil and simmer for 5 minutes. Meanwhile, combine in a bowl the apple juice concentrate, cornstarch, and apple pie spice. Then pour into the apples and simmer for another 5 minutes. Remove from heat and fold in sour cream. Add artificial sweetener, if desired. Pour into pie crust and follow pie crust directions.

SOUR CREAM APPLE PIE

- 6 *medium apples, peeled, cored, and sliced thin*
- 2/3 *cup brown sugar*
- 1/4 *teaspoon cinnamon*
- 1/8 *teaspoon nutmeg*
- 1/8 *teaspoon salt*
- 1 *tablespoon cornstarch*
- 1 *cup no-fat sour cream*
- 1 *egg white, lightly beaten*

Preheat oven to 400° F. In mixing bowl combine everything but the sour cream. Make sure apples are well coated. Place in biscuit pie crust from page 222. Pour sour cream over top of apples, fold over pie crust. Then brush pie crust with egg white and dust with sugar and/or cinnamon if desired.

CINNAMON PEACH PIE

- 1 *29-oz. can sliced peaches in heavy syrup*
- 1 *teaspoon cinnamon*
- 2 *tablespoons cornstarch*

Mix ingredients in saucepan and bring to a boil, being careful not to burn. Pour out into biscuit pie crust from page 222 and fold excess pie crust over to center of pie and sprinkle crust with sugar and cinnamon. Bake in a preheated 400° F oven for 10 minutes. Reduce temperature to 350° F and continue baking for 20 minutes more. Remove pie from oven and allow to cool.

BASIC COBBLER BATTER

This batter can be spooned into all sorts of combinations to make delicious cobblers.

2 *cups flour*
3 *teaspoons baking powder*
1 *tablespoon sugar (omit for veggie cobblers)*
$^1/_2$ *cup non-fat milk powder*
~ *Water and fruit juice* **or** *nectar as needed*

Mix dry ingredients together, then add liquid to make a spoonable batter.
NOTE: ***For vegetable cobblers, omit sugar and fruit juice.***

COBBLERS

When making these fruit cobblers, a basic rule to follow is that for every 16-oz. can of fruit (about 2 cups) or equivalent fresh fruit and juice, add $1^1/_2$ tablespoon of cornstarch. This will thicken your cobbler juice to a nice consistency. Also, add sugar to suit your tastes if using fresh tart fruit. Fill baking dish only half full, as dough will rise.

PEACH & RASPBERRY COBBLER

2 *cups sliced canned peaches in heavy syrup*
2 *cups frozen raspberries with sugar added to taste*
3 *tablespoons cornstarch*

Combine ingredients and spoon one half into baking dish. Spoon cobbler batter from this page onto fruit. Cover batter with remaining fruit and bake in 350° F preheated oven for about 45 minutes until toothpick stuck into dough comes out clean.

BLACKBERRY COBBLER

4 *cups canned blackberries and juice, sweetened to taste*
3 *tablespoons cornstarch*
~ *cobbler batter from this page*

Combine berries and cornstarch and spoon one half into baking dish. Spoon batter onto fruit. Pour remaining berries on top of batter and bake in preheated 350° F oven for 45 minutes or until toothpick stuck in batter dough comes out clean.

FRESH STRAWBERRY COBBLER

1 pint fresh strawberries, sliced, sweetened to taste
1 cup cranberry-raspberry juice
1 1/2 tablespoons cornstarch
~ cobbler batter from page 228

Combine fruit, juice, and cornstarch, spoon one half into baking dish. Spoon batter onto fruit. Spoon rest of fruit on top of batter. Bake in preheated 350° F oven for 45 minutes or until a toothpick stuck into dough comes out clean.

PUDDINGS

Pudding mixes are fine to use as long as they contain no fat. Just use non-fat ingredients in preparing the mix. That is, use Egg Beaters® if eggs are called for, and non-fat milk if milk is called for. Your puddings should be very near fat free.

BANANA ANGEL PUDDING

- 2 *cups angelfood cake, broken into small, bite-size pieces*
- 1 *box vanilla pudding cooked with non-fat milk*
- 1 *sliced large banana*

Mix ingredients and chill.

RICE PUDDING

- 2 *cups water*
- 1 *cup raisins*
- 2 *cups instant rice*
- 2 *tablespoons sugar*
- 1/2 *cup non-fat frozen yogurt, thawed*

Bring water, raisins, and sugar to a boil. Add rice and remove from heat. After 5 minutes, add yogurt to rice and serve.

WHISKEY BREAD PUDDING

- 1 *cup Egg Beaters® egg substitute*
- 2 *cups non-fat milk*
- 1/4 *cup sugar*
- 1/2 *oz. your favorite whiskey*
- 1/2 *teaspoon cinnamon*
- 1/2 *teaspoon vanilla*
- 1/8 *teaspoon salt*
- 2 1/2 *cups dry non-fat bread cubes*
- 1/3 *cup raisins*

In mixing bowl, lightly beat Egg Beaters,® milk, sugar, whiskey, cinnamon, vanilla, and salt. Place bread in baking dish, sprinkle raisins on top, and pour egg mixture over all. Bake in preheated 350° F oven for 30 to 40 minutes until toothpick inserted in center comes out clean.

BAKED CUSTARD CRUSTS

2 or 3 slices of homemade bread (Irish Soda Bread from page 212 **or** *Salt-Risin' Pumpkin Bread from page 204 are just excellent breads for this recipe)*
1 can evaporated skim milk
1/4 cup sugar
2 egg whites, slightly beaten
1/4 teaspoon nutmeg syrup (maple is great, too)

Preheat oven to 400° F. Beat egg whites for 2 or 3 minutes, add milk, sugar, and nutmeg. Place bread slices in a pie dish or pan and pour milk/egg mixture on top. Turn bread over to coat, then place in oven for 20 minutes. Remove and serve hot, topped with a splash of syrup.

BOURBON BREAD PUDDING

~ crusty bread
1/2 cup raisins
2 egg whites, slightly beaten
1/4 cup sugar
1 can evaporated skimmed milk
1/4 teaspoon nutmeg
1 oz. bourbon

Preheat oven to 350° F. Slice bread, preferably homemade, 1/2- to 3/4-inch thick and place in the bottom of an ovenproof pie dish or pan. Mix raisins in with bread. Beat egg white for a minute or so, add sugar, milk, nutmeg, and bourbon, mix thoroughly, and pour over bread. Sprinkle with nutmeg and bake for 30 minutes. When serving, splash on a bit of maple syrup, and enjoy.

NOTE: ***For*** **LEMON BREAD PUDDING,** ***replace bourbon with grated rind of 1/2 lemon and juice from 1/2 lemon.***

For **RUM PUDDING,** ***replace bourbon with 2 teaspoons rum flavoring.***

For **VANILLA PUDDING,** ***replace bourbon with 1 teaspoon vanilla extract.***

CAKES & FROSTINGS

Most cakes today are loaded with fat, within the cake itself, the frosting, or both. However, it wasn't always this way. Eggs (with their fat yolks) were not readily available to city folks in days gone by, and believe it or not, animal fat was also in short supply. Consequently, the celebratory cakes were often crafted without the use of eggs or fat.

OLDE, OLDE FASHIONED CAKE

Circa 1710

In 1835, when great-great grandfather Zebulon Rose and his wife Sarah pulled up stakes and left Boston Town, it was an event filled with fear and great apprehensions. A trip like that today can be made in a day, while it took them, literally, years. You see, they were headed west to the Kentucky territory. Neatly tucked into the hand-made, dove-tailed recipe box, among other things, were Sarah's notes on how to make a simple brown-sugar–raisin cake.

The recipe hadn't always contained brown sugar and raisins. In fact, it had been passed down to her as an old English recipe that used wild honey for a sweetener and dried local berries instead of the Mediterranean raisins (sometimes called currants) she was used to. Wild honey in Boston Town was rare, whereas brown sugar from the West Indies was plentiful. In Kentucky, the recipe would revert back to the use of wild honey and prunes made from an abundant supply of wild plums.

The leavening agent also changed from brewer's yeast to what we now call baking powder. What has remained constant is the Dutch oven to cook it in, the whole grain flour, skimmed milk, and the apple butter used in the self-contained icing.

This is a robust, rich, moist cake in the old world country tradition, vastly different from present day "air" cake. The consumption of this cake carries with it an obligatory requirement, which is: as you sit down with your cake in front of you, fork in hand, pause for just a moment and imagine how your ancestors of 1835 would have received this special treat. Enjoy!

THE CAKE

4 *egg whites, beaten stiff*
2$^1/_4$ *cups whole wheat flour*
1$^1/_2$ *cups brown sugar*
3 *teaspoons baking powder*
1 *teaspoon salt*
1 *cup raisins*
1 *cup cooked and drained whole grain barley* **or** *wheat berries*
1 *cup skimmed milk*

THE ICING

1 *cup brown sugar*
1 *cup apple butter*

Preheat oven to 375° F. In 10-inch Dutch oven or 10-inch deep cake pan spread evenly on bottom, one cup brown sugar. Using a teaspoon, spoon 1 cup apple butter on top of brown sugar. Set aside. Beat egg whites stiff and set aside. In mixing bowl combine and mix thoroughly: 2$^1/_4$ cups whole wheat flour, 1$^1/_2$ cups brown sugar, 3 teaspoons baking powder, 1 teaspoon salt. Add to mixing bowl and mix well: 1 cup raisins, 1 cup cooked and drained whole grain barley or wheat berries, 1 cup skimmed milk. Fold in egg whites and pour mixture into Dutch oven on top of brown sugar and apple butter.

Bake for 50 minutes or until inserted toothpick comes out clean. Remove from oven, run a knife around cake to loosen, place a plate on top of the cake and turn upside down, thereby removing cake from Dutch oven. In the bottom of the Dutch oven is your icing for this cake. Spoon icing onto cake and serve hot or cold with a cup of hot fresh coffee. ❖

LEMON ANGEL CAKE

1 *angelfood cake, already cooked*
1 *package Jell-O® lemon pudding mix (not instant)*
~ *thin lemon slices*
~ *fresh mint sprigs*

Prepare pudding using Egg Beaters® egg substitute instead of regular eggs. Place cake on large cake dish and cover with lemon pudding. Garnish around base of cake with lemon slices and mint sprigs alternating. This is an elegant, yet quite simple dessert. ❖

FAT-FREE CHOCOLATE CAKE

1$^1/_4$ *cups flour*
1 *cup sugar*
$^1/_2$ *cup unsweetened cocoa*
$^1/_4$ *cup cornstarch*
$^1/_2$ *teaspoon baking soda*
$^1/_2$ *teaspoon salt*
$^1/_2$ *cup Egg Beaters® egg substitute*
1 *cup water*
$^1/_2$ *cup corn syrup*

In large bowl combine dry ingredients. Mix well. In smaller bowl, mix eggs, water, and corn syrup. Stir into dry ingredients until smooth. Pour into non-stick Teflon cake pan. Bake 30 minutes in preheated 350° F oven, or until toothpick test is passed. Remove to wire rack and cool thoroughly before icing. Ice with fluffy white frosting mix or Creole mocha frosting from page 248.

BLACK WALNUT CREAM CAKE OR TRIFLE

In the wonderful world of no-fat fare all nuts are an absolute no-no. However, the cravings sometimes surface and cry to be placated, such as it was with black walnut cake like mom used to make in the old wood cook stove. Black walnuts weighing in at 64 grams of fat per 4 ounces represents nearly 5 times the daily fat requirement for an average person. So real black walnuts were eliminated from all consideration, immediately. However, thanks to modern technology, you can obtain all the flavor and texture of black walnuts and yet do it fat-free. You'll need to take a trip to a local health food or specialty store and pick up some TVP® (Textured Vegetable Protein), and from your local grocer pick up a bottle of imitation black walnut extract.

Place 1/4 cup of TVP® into a cup or glass and pour 1 tablespoon of walnut extract on top. Mix well, cover, and set aside for at least an hour. Now you have the flavor and texture to make a wonderful cream-filled black walnut cake or black walnut raspberry cream trifle without the fat.

BLACK WALNUT CAKE

- 1 *tablespoon imitation black walnut extract*
- 1/4 *cup TVP® mixed with imitation black walnut extract and allowed to sit for at least one hour*
- 3/4 *cup Egg Beaters® egg substitute*
- 1 1/2 *cups sugar*
- 1/2 *cup cold water*
- 2 *teaspoons baking powder*
- 1/8 *teaspoon salt*
- 1 *teaspoon vanilla extract*
- 1 1/2 *cups flour*

In mixing bowl, beat Egg Beaters® for 3 or 4 minutes. Mix in water, sugar, baking powder, salt, and vanilla. Mix thoroughly but do not beat. Mix in flour to smooth consistency, then mix in

TVP®. *(Note: Reserve a small portion of flavored TVP® to sprinkle on top of the finished cake.)* Pour into two 8-inch sure-release cake pans and bake in 350° F preheated oven for 20 minutes or until toothpick placed in center of cake comes out clean.

VANILLA, BUTTER & NUT CREAM FILLING FOR BLACK WALNUT CAKE

- 2 *cups skimmed milk*
- 1 *tablespoon Butter Buds® butter-flavored granules*
- 1/4 *cup Egg Beaters® egg substitute*
- 1/2 *cup sugar*
- 2 *tablespoons cornstarch*
- 1 *teaspoon vanilla, butter, and nut extract*

Mix ingredients in saucepan and bring to boil on medium heat, stirring constantly. Remove from heat and allow to cool. Spread between layers of cake.

THE ICING
1 package fluffy white frosting (no-fat) or use your own beaten egg white and sugar frosting recipe. Prepare as per instructions.

THE MECHANICS

Your cake pans should be the type that have a rotating removal device that extends from the center of your cake pans to the outside. If you don't have this type of pan and your cake won't come free except in pieces, then proceed on to the "Contingency Trifle." Wax-paper–lined cake pans work well, as do springform cake pans. Assuming your cake does come out intact, place one layer in a regular plate so that the rounded top is on the bottom. Insert a tablespoon into this layer and twirl, making openings so that the filling can seep down into the bottom layer. Ten or twelve such openings should be enough. Spoon on cooled filling and spread. Place top layer on filling and hold in place by inserting four or five toothpicks through both layers. Spoon on fluffy white frosting and sprinkle with leftover TVP®.

THE CONTINGENCY BLACK WALNUT-RASPBERRY TRIFLE

If your cake comes out in pieces, or if you just want to make a trifle, then assemble six tall, narrow glasses (Parfait, ice cream soda, or Tom Collins glasses will work) and one package of frozen whole unsweetened raspberries. Next. fold fluffy white icing into filling. Spoon into each glass alternating layers of filling/icing mixture, cake pieces (bite-size), and raspberries. Make sure filling/icing ends up topping your trifle. Sprinkle on TVP®, garnish with a sprig of mint, and enjoy—fat free!

PINEAPPLE MAYONNAISE CAKE
WITH CREAM FILLING

$2^1/_4$ cups all-purpose flour
1 cup sugar
1 teaspoon baking powder
2 teaspoons baking soda
1 cup cold water
1 teaspoon vanilla
1 cup fat-free mayonnaise
2 cups pineapple, crushed and drained
1 teaspoon imitation butter flavoring
~ vegetable spray

Preheat oven to 350° F. In a large mixing bowl, combine and mix thoroughly the flour, sugar, baking powder, and baking soda. In another bowl, combine and mix thoroughly the water, vanilla, mayonnaise, pineapple, and butter-flavoring. Combine the two bowls and mix well—QUICKLY! Pour into a 10-inch springform pan and bake for 50 minutes or until toothpick inserted into cake comes out clean. Remove, cool, and split into 2 layers. Onto the first layer, spoon the following filling. Place the remaining layer on top and use several toothpicks to hold the layers together. Then ice with fluffy white frosting mix.

PINEAPPLE FILLING

1 can $5^1/_2$-oz. crushed pineapple with juice
1 teaspoon imitation butter flavor
1 cup water
$^1/_3$ cup non-fat milk powder
$^1/_4$ cup Egg Beaters® egg substitute
$^1/_2$ cup sugar
2 tablespoons cornstarch

Mix ingredients in large saucepan and bring to a boil. Remove from heat, allow to cool somewhat, and use for cake filling.

PINEAPPLE RUM CAKE

$1^1/_4$ cups flour
1 cup sugar
$^1/_4$ cup cornstarch
$^1/_2$ teaspoon baking soda
$^1/_2$ teaspoon salt
$^1/_2$ cup Egg Beaters® egg beaters
$^1/_4$ cup pineapple juice from can of pineapple
$^3/_4$ cup water
$^1/_2$ cup corn syrup
1 cup pineapple chunks
1 cup dark brown sugar
2 teaspoons rum flavoring

Preheat oven to 350° F. Except for dark brown sugar, combine all ingredients, but do not beat. Place dark brown sugar in bottom of 9-inch springform cake pan. Spoon cake mixture on top and bake for 45 minutes or until toothpick in center comes out clean. Remove and cool. Serve upside down.

PINEAPPLE UPSIDE-DOWN CAKE

1 cup Egg Beaters® egg substitute
1 1/2 teaspoon vanilla
1 1/2 cups sugar
2 1/2 cup flour
3 teaspoons baking powder
1 teaspoon salt
1 cup skimmed milk
1 cup dark brown sugar
1 20-oz. can pineapple slices
~ maraschino cherries

Preheat oven to 350° F. In mixing bowl, beat Egg Beaters® for 3 or 4 minutes until frothy and add vanilla. In bottom of 10-inch springform cake pan, spread dark brown sugar and space pineapple slices uniformly with cherries in centers of each slice. In separate mixing bowl, mix rest of ingredients thoroughly. Fold in eggs and mix well. Pour into cake pan on top of pineapple. Bake for 50 minutes or until toothpick in center of cake comes out clean.

DARK SWEET CHERRY UPSIDE-DOWN CAKE

Use previous pineapple upside-down cake recipe, substituting a 17-oz. can of dark, sweet, pitted cherries for the pineapple.

CINNAMON-PEACH UPSIDE-DOWN CAKE

Using previous pineapple upside-down cake recipe, substituting a 17- to 20-oz. can of sliced peaches for the pineapple. Sprinkle one teaspoon of cinnamon on top of the peaches.

CRANBERRY-RAISIN CAKE

1 1/2 cups all-purpose flour
1/8 teaspoon salt
2 teaspoons baking soda
1 cup sugar
1/2 cup cold water
1 teaspoon vanilla
1 cup canned whole cranberries
1/2 cup raisins
~ vegetable spray

Preheat oven to 350° F. In a large mixing bowl, combine and mix thoroughly the flour, salt, soda, and sugar. In a separate bowl, combine and mix thoroughly the water, vanilla, cranberries, and raisins. Combine the two bowls and mix—QUICKLY! Pour into a 9- or 10-inch springform pan that has been veggie-sprayed and flour dusted. Bake for 45 minutes or until toothpick inserted in cake comes out clean. ❖

APPLE BUTTER RAISIN CAKE

1 1/4 cup self-rising flour
1 cup dark sugar
1/4 cup cornstarch
1/2 cup Egg Beaters® egg substitute
1 teaspoon imitation butter flavoring
1/2 teaspoon vanilla extract
1 1/4 cup apple butter
1/2 cup dark corn syrup
1/2 cup raisins
~ vegetable spray

Preheat oven to 350° F. In a large mixing bowl, combine and mix thoroughly the flour, sugar, and cornstarch. In another bowl, beat eggs for 3 to 4 minutes, then add butter-flavoring, vanilla, apple butter, corn syrup, and raisins, mixing well. Combine the two bowls, mix thoroughly but quickly, and pour into a 9- or 10-inch springform, veggie-sprayed cake pan. Bake for 40 to 45 minutes until toothpick inserted in center of cake comes out clean. ❖

COCONUT CAKE

1 1/2 cup self-rising flour
1 cup sugar
1/4 cup cornstarch
1/2 cup Egg Beaters® egg substitute
1 teaspoon imitation butter flavor
1 cup cold water
1/2 cup corn syrup
1 tablespoon imitation coconut extract
~ vegetable spray

Preheat oven to 350° F. In a large mixing bowl, combine and mix thoroughly the flour, sugar, and cornstarch. In another bowl, beat eggs for 3 or 4 minutes. Add and mix the butter-flavor, water, corn syrup, and coconut flavoring to eggs. Combine the two bowls, mix thoroughly but quickly, and pour into a veggie-sprayed 9- or 10-inch springform cake pan. Bake for 40- to 45 minutes or until toothpick inserted in center of cake comes out clean. ❖

BOURBON CARROT CAKE

2 *cups all-purpose flour*
1½ *cups granulated sugar*
1 *teaspoon baking soda*
1 *teaspoon baking powder*
1 *teaspoon cinnamon*
½ *cup whole raisins*
1 *oz. bourbon (optional)*
¾ *cup pureed raisins in ½ cup cold water*
1 *cup Egg Beaters® egg substitute*
3 *cups shredded carrots*
~ *veggie spray*

Preheat oven to 325° F. Combine flour, sugar, soda, baking powder, cinnamon, and mix well. In a blender or food processor, puree ¾-cup raisins with water and bourbon. Combine all ingredients and mix until moist. Beat at medium speed for two minutes. Pour into a 12 x 9 x 2 inch veggie-sprayed and floured baking pan. Bake for 50 minutes until toothpick inserted comes out clean. If possible, allow this cake to sit around for a day or so. It ages very well. As an option, consider sprinkling cake with liqueur syrup from page 250 prior to aging. Frost cake with fluffy yogurt frosting from page 248 or fluffy white frosting.

STRAWBERRY SHORTCAKE

SHORTCAKE BATTER

~ *sour cream biscuit dough from page 216*
¼ *cup sugar*
2 *teaspoons imitation butter flavoring*
1 *teaspoon vanilla flavoring*
¼ *cup water (to make consistency of cake batter)*

FRUIT FILLING

4 *cups fresh sliced strawberries*
½ *cup strawberry glaze*
~ *sugar* ***or*** *sweetener to taste*
~ *whipped yogurt cream topping from page 250*

Preheat oven to 375° F. To biscuit dough, add ¼ cup sugar, butter flavoring, and vanilla flavoring. Mix well to consistency of cake batter. Bake in veggie-sprayed 9-inch cake pan (springform works best) for 45 minutes. Remove and cool. Split cake into 2 layers using a good knife. Invert rounded top layer of cake and place on a plate. Combine strawberries, glaze, and sweetener and spoon ½ onto bottom layer. Place other layer on top of strawberries, secure with several toothpicks, then spoon on remaining strawberries. Prepare whipped yogurt cream topping and spoon generously and decoratively onto top of cake. Chill and serve.

NOTE: ***Just change the selection of fruit for other delicious shortcakes for instance use fresh raspberries in season or pineapple anytime.***

WHIPPED CREAM CAKE

- 3 *egg whites*
- 3/4 *cup no-fat yogurt*
- 1/2 *cup no-fat milk powder*
- 1/2 *cup cold water*
- 1 *teaspoon almond flavoring*
- 2 *cups self-rising flour*
- 1 1/2 *cups sugar*

Preheat oven to 325° F. Beat egg whites until stiff and set aside. Combine yogurt and milk powder and beat until stiff; then gently fold into egg whites. Gradually fold in the cold water and almond flavoring. Fold flour and sugar into creamy mixture. Pour into two 8-inch layer pans lined in the bottom with wax paper. Top one layer with bake-on icing from page 249. Bake for 35 minutes until done. Remove and cool. Use your favorite filling in between layers or use fresh fruit or jam or a mixture of the two, or just ice cake as desired.

NOTE: *For a really simple and quick filling, cover bottom layer with slices of pineapple and spoon on 4 or 5 tablespoons of pineapple juice or use peaches and peach juice or cherries and cherry juice or whatever you like.*

5-STAR CREAM CHEESECAKE

(LESS THAN 1 GRAM PER 1/16 OF CAKE)

- 3 *8 oz. packages Healthy Choice® fat-free cream cheese product* **or**
- 3 *cups cream cheese from page 256*
- 3/4 *cup sugar*
- 1/2 *cup evaporated skim milk*
- 8 *egg whites from grade A large eggs*
- 4 *tablespoons flour*
- 1 *teaspoon vanilla flavoring*
- 1 *teaspoon lemon flavoring*
- 1 *teaspoon imitation butter flavoring*
- 1/2 *cup non-fat sour cream*
- ~ *vegetable spray*
- ~ *cornflake crumbs*

Preheat oven to 350° F. Mix cheese, sugar, and milk in a large mixing bowl. In another mixing bowl, lightly beat egg whites and mix in flour, vanilla, butter, and lemon flavoring. Make sure flour is evenly blended, then combine the two bowls. Mix and pour into a veggie-sprayed, cornflake crumb dusted, 9-inch, springform cake pan. Place a sheet pan containing about 1/2 inch water in the bottom of the oven. Place cake in middle of oven, and after 15 minutes, reduce heat to 200° F. Bake for two hours. Turn off heat and slightly open the oven door and allow

cake to sit in oven for one more hour. Remove and chill for at least 2 hours (preferably overnight) before serving.
NOTE: ***Make a special effort NOT to beat a lot of air into the batter. After cooling, spread sour cream on top. Then cake may be topped with fresh strawberries, pineapple chunks, blueberries, or cherries along with the appropriate glaze.***

CHOCOLATE FUDGE CHEESECAKE

(1½ GRAMS OF FAT PER 1/16 OF CAKE)

- 1 *box "lite" brownie mix (1 gram fat per serving)*
- 4 *8 oz. packages Healthy Choice® fat-free cream cheese*
- 1 *cup sugar*
- 2/3 *cup evaporated skim milk*
- 4 *tablespoons flour*
- 8 *egg whites from Grade A large eggs*
- 1 *teaspoon vanilla flavoring*
- 1 *teaspoon imitation butter flavoring*
- 1 *teaspoon lemon flavoring*
- 1 *cup no-fat sour cream*
- 1 *17 oz. can cherry pie filling*

Preheat oven to 350° F. Prepare brownie mix as per directions. Pour ½ of the mix into a 9-inch springform cake pan and bake until done. While brownie mix is cooking combine and mix thoroughly the cream cheese, sugar, milk, and flour. Add egg whites, vanilla, butter and lemon flavorings. Mix well but do not beat! Remove brownie mix from oven when done and pour cheesecake mixture on top and put back into oven. After 15 minutes lower oven temperature to 200° F and cook for 2 hours. Turn oven off and slightly open oven door. After an hour remove cake and place in refrigerator to cool. Spoon sour cream on top of cake and spoon cherries onto sour cream. Enjoy.

MY FAVORITE BROWNIES

- 1 *package "lite" brownie mix (1 gram per serving)*
- 1 *cup raisins*
- 1/4 *cup "walnuts" from page 257 (optional)*

To brownie mix add raisins and "walnuts" and follow mix directions.

TRIFLES

A beautiful outrageous fat-free dessert.

- ~ *fruit, sweetened to taste*
- ~ *heavy dessert cream from page 250*
- ~ *cake, leftover (even a little stale is okay)*

In tall glass, pour a little heavy cream in the bottom, then add alternate layers of fruit and cake to fill. Top off with more heavy cream and garnish with a maraschino cherry and a sprig of fresh mint.

CREPES

These are French pancakes. They should be thin, yet fluffy —not gummy and chewy. Wrap them around your favorite sweetened fruit, sprinkle on some powdered sugar, top with a spoon of sweetened fat-free sour cream or heavy dessert cream (page 250) and you have a definite winner.

CREPE BATTER

- 1 *cup Krusteaz® brand oat bran lite complete pancake mix*
- 1 *cup Egg Beaters® egg substitute*
- ~ *water to make batter the consistency of heavy cream*

Veggie-spray a medium hot griddle or heavy skillet. Spoon on batter and brown on both sides. Fry a quantity, then assemble crepes. These crepes also go well with meat, seafood, and vegetable fillings.

SPECIALTY DESSERTS

These desserts work well in a long-stemmed margarita glass. The possible combinations are endless, so let your imagination rule the day: Non-fat cake, non-fat dairy frozen dessert, and fruit, sweetened to taste or pureed fruit or sauce. ✱ Place a small scoop of frozen dessert in bottom of glass. Place slice or small squares of cake on top. Spoon fruit or sauce or pureed fruit onto cake. Place another small scoop of frozen dessert beside cake. Garnish with sprig of fresh mint or some fruit. Another specialty dessert full of surprises is Baked Alaska.

INDIVIDUAL BAKED ALASKA

- ~ *fat-free pound cake*
- ~ *fat-free frozen dessert*
- ~ *fluffy white frosting mix (fat free), and made with egg whites. Prepare frosting as per directions.*

On baking sheet, arrange flat separated slices of pound cake. Top with a scoop of fat-free ice cream or other frozen dessert. Spoon on frosting mix to cover ice cream and cake. Place in preheated 500° oven for 3 minutes until brown. Serve immediately.

NOTE: *Spoon fresh or frozen raspberries onto cake before ice cream for a wonderful variation.*

COOKIES

The availability and variety of fat-free cookies and frozen desserts is rapidly increasing. Just be sure to purchase fat-free or non-fat products.

CHOCOLATE-COVERED CHERRY COOKIES

MAKES 20 COOKIES - 1/3 GRAM OF FAT PER COOKIE

1/3 *package "light" brownie mix (1 gram of fat per serving) with 1/3 required water*
20 *maraschino cherries, drained*

Preheat oven to 375° F. Dry cherries on a paper towel. Mix one-third brownie mix with one-third the required water. Add cherries and mix until covered with brownie mix. On veggie-sprayed cookie sheet, spoon cherries with approximately one tablespoon of brownie mix per cherry. Allow room for cookie to spread. Bake for 10 minutes. Allow to cool.

CHOCOLATE RAISIN COOKIES

MAKES 20 COOKIES, 1/2 GRAM OF FAT PER COOKIE

1/3 *package "lite" brownie mix (1 gram of fat per serving)*
1/3 *water required per brownie mix directions*
3/4 *cup raisins*
~ *vegetable spray*

Preheat oven to 375° F. Mix brownie mix according to directions. Add raisins and spoon onto veggie-sprayed cookie sheet in about one tablespoon portions. Bake for 10 minutes. Remove and cool.

BROWN SUGAR RAISIN COOKIES

2 1/4 cups whole wheat flour
1 1/2 cups light brown sugar
3 teaspoons baking powder
1 teaspoon salt
1 cup raisins
1 cup whole grain barley, cooked and drained
1 cup non-fat skimmed milk

Combine and mix thoroughly the flour, sugar, baking powder, and salt. Add raisins, barley, and milk. Spoon onto cookie sheet and bake in a preheated 375° F oven for 8 to 10 minutes until done. ❖

CHEWY CHOCOLATE COOKIES

MAKES TWO DOZEN

1 1/2 cups self-rising flour
1/2 cup sugar
1/2 cup cocoa powder
1/2 cup light ***or*** *dark corn syrup*
3 egg whites
~ vegetable spray

Preheat oven to 350° F. In large mixing bowl, combine flour, sugar, and cocoa. Stir in corn syrup and egg whites until blended. Drop full teaspoons onto cookie sheet and bake for about 8 minutes until firm yet soft. Do not overbake. Remove and cool. ❖

BROWNIE OATMEAL COOKIES

MAKES TWO DOZEN

2/3 cup self-rising flour
2/3 cup sugar
1 cup uncooked oatmeal
1/3 cup cocoa powder
2 egg whites
1/3 cup corn syrup (light ***or*** *dark)*
1 teaspoon vanilla
~ vegetable spray

Preheat oven to 350° F. In large mixing bowl, combine flour, sugar, oatmeal, and cocoa powder. Add syrup, egg whites, and vanilla. Stir until everything is just moistened. Drop full teaspoons onto a veggie-sprayed cookie sheet. Bake for 8 minutes or until cookies are just set. Remove and cool. ❖

OLD FASHIONED SUGAR COOKIES

- 1 *cup lite white* **or** *yellow cake mix*
- 1 *cup self-rising flour*
- 1/3 *cup sugar*
- 1 *egg white*
- 1/2 *teaspoon vanilla*
- 1 *teaspoon lemon juice*
- 1/4 *cup skimmed milk*
- ~ *vegetable spray*

Combine and mix cake mix, flour, and sugar. In another bowl, briefly whisk egg white, vanilla, lemon juice and skimmed milk. Combine liquid mixture with flour mixture, mix and form into ball, and chill in refrigerator for at least one hour. Preheat oven to 375° F. Roll out dough to about 1/4 inch thick on lightly floured board or pastry cloth. Sprinkle with granulated sugar and cut into cookies. Bake on veggie-sprayed sheet for 10 minutes. Ice with confectioner's glaze (page 248).

VARIETIES OF SUGAR COOKIE

SUGAR-RAISIN COOKIES
Add 1/2 cup raisins when mixing dough.

SUGAR CHERRY COOKIES
Add 1/2 cup chopped glazed cherries when mixing dough.

SUGAR CINNAMON TARTS
Roll out dough, cut with 2-inch cutter. Brush with lightly beaten egg white and sprinkle with sugar and cinnamon (2 tablespoons sugar and 1/4 teaspoon cinnamon).

SUGAR & SPICE COOKIES
Substitute brown for granulated sugar, omit vanilla, and add 1/4 teaspoon cinnamon, 1/8 teaspoon cloves, and 1/8 teaspoon nutmeg.

SUGAR RAISIN SPICE
Add 1/2 cup raisins to spice cookies above.

LEMON-SUGAR
Omit vanilla and add 1 teaspoon grated lemon rind and 1/2 teaspoon lemon flavoring.

MAPLE PECAN
Omit vanilla and add 1 teaspoon imitation vanilla, butter, and nut flavor, 1 tablespoon TVP®, and 1/4 teaspoon maple extract.

FRUIT STREUSEL MUFFINS

MAKES 12 MUFFINS

- 1 1/2 *cups self-rising flour*
- 3/4 *cup sugar*
- 1 *tablespoon oat bran (optional)*
- 2/3 *cup yogurt, plain, non-fat*
- 2/3 *cup evaporated skim milk*
- 1/2 *cup crushed pineapple, blueberries, apples, etc.*
- ~ *vegetable spray*

STREUSEL FILLING

- 1/3 *cup sugar*
- 1/2 *teaspoon cinnamon*

Preheat oven to 375° F. In mixing bowl, combine flour, sugar, oat bran, yogurt, milk, and fruit. Fill veggie-sprayed muffin tin one-half full. Place one teaspoon of filling on top, then add more batter to fill muffin tins three-fourths full. Bake for 30 minutes until browned. Serve warm.

PINEAPPLE FRITTERS

MAKES 12 MUFFINS

- 2 *cups self-rising flour*
- 1/4 *cup sugar*
- 1/2 *cup crushed pineapple with some juice*
- 2/3 *cup non-fat yogurt*
- ~ *vegetable spray*
- ~ *powdered sugar*

Preheat oven to 400° F.

Mix flour and sugar in mixing bowl. Quickly add pineapple and yogurt and stir. Spoon into veggie-sprayed muffin tin and pop into oven as quickly as possible. Bake for 30 minutes or until well browned. Remove and dust generously top and bottom and all parts in between with powdered sugar. Serve warm.

CONFECTIONER'S GLAZE OR ICING

- 3/4 *cup powered sugar*
- 1/4 *teaspoon vanilla*
- ~ *skim milk*

In a mixing bowl combine sugar, vanilla, and enough milk to make an icing of the desired consistency.

VARIATIONS: *Instead of vanilla, add orange, lemon, maple, black walnut, peppermint, or other desired flavor.*

FLUFFY YOGURT FROSTING

- 1 *package fluffy white frosting mix (no-fat made with egg whites)*
- 1/2 *cup plus 1 tablespoon non-fat yogurt*
- 2 *teaspoons imitation butter flavoring*

Prepare frosting mix as per directions, except use 1/2 cup no-fat yogurt for the 1/2 cup

water that is called for. When thick and stiff, add butter-flavoring and then spread on cooled cake.
NOTE: *Yogurt when boiled will separate and look yucky. Not to worry, the small curds will give texture to your icing.*

CREOLE MOCHA FROSTING

2 *cups powdered sugar*
4 *tablespoons cocoa*
2 *teaspoons instant coffee powder*
4 *tablespoons boiling water*
1 *teaspoon vanilla*
1 *teaspoon hot water (if needed)*

Mix sugar and cocoa, add instant coffee dissolved in boiling water and vanilla. Stir until smooth. Add some additional hot water to make a smooth, manageable frosting.

SUGAR-FREE LEMON CREAM FROSTING

1/2 *cup non-fat powdered milk powder*
3/4 *cup non-fat yogurt*
2 *tablespoons lemon juice*
artificial sweetener equal to 1/2 cup sugar or to taste

Beat milk powder and yogurt until somewhat fluffy (about 3 minutes). Pour in the lemon juice and continue beating until stiff. Fold in sweetener until mixed. Note: Substitute other flavors for the lemon juice to ensure variety.
Betty Crocker® offers an excellent fat-free fluffy white frosting mix that goes well with almost any cake. Use your favorite recipe for angelfood cake or sponge cakes.

CHOCOLATE FROSTING

1/2 *package light fudge brownie mix (1 gram of fat per serving)*
~ *water as called for*
~ *powdered sugar as needed*

Mix 1/2 package brownie mix as directed. Add powdered sugar and mix until consistency of thick frosting. For a more chocolaty taste add chocolate extract.

SWEETENED CREAM CHEESE FROSTING

1 *cup Healthy Choice® fat-free cream cheese*
½ *cup powdered sugar*

Blend, softened to room temperature cream cheese and sugar until creamy smooth.

BAKE-ON FROSTING

2 *egg whites*
¼ *teaspoon salt*
2 *cups brown sugar*

Add salt to egg whites and beat until stiff. Beat in brown sugar and set aside until cake batter is poured into cake pan, then spoon this frosting on top of cake batter and bake cake for at least 35 minutes.

NOTE: *Top of frosting may be lightly sprinkled with cornflake crumbs.*

FOR BURNT ORANGE FROSTING

Add 2 teaspoons orange flavoring.

FOR COCONUT FROSTING

Add one teaspoon coconut flavoring.

LIQUEUR SYRUP FOR CAKES

MAKES ABOUT ONE CUP

¾ *cup hot water*
¼ *cup sugar*
4 *tablespoons rum, orange liqueur, flavored brandies,* ***or*** *1 tablespoon vanilla extract*

Dissolve sugar in hot water, add flavoring and use by spooning or sprinkling onto layers of cake just prior to icing or onto shortcake just prior to the fruit.

WHIPPED YOGURT CREAM TOPPING

EXCELLENT WITH SHORTCAKES

½ *cup non-fat powdered milk powder*
¾ *cup non-fat yogurt*
2 *tablespoons lemon juice*
½ *cup sugar*

Beat milk powder and yogurt until somewhat fluffy (about 3 minutes). Pour in lemon juice and continue beating until stiff. Fold in sugar and serve as whipped cream topping.

HEAVY DESSERT CREAM

This "cream" pours well on cobblers, cake, fruit, shortcake, or pies.

- ~ *fat-free vanilla frozen dessert (Simple Pleasures® is excellent)*

Set out desired amount in refrigerator to thaw out. This also works as a fat-free creamer in coffee.

CHANTILLY CREAM

1 *cup frozen non-fat vanilla yogurt*
1 *teaspoon brandy*
1 *teaspoon triple sec*
2 *tablespoons fat-free sour cream*

Allow frozen yogurt to melt in the refrigerator, then add brandy, triple sec, and sour cream. Whisk briefly to mix, then serve.

CREME FRAÎCHE

- ~ *frozen vanilla non-fat yogurt, thawed*
- ~ *no-fat sour cream*

Combine equal parts of yogurt and sour cream. Whisk to mix thoroughly and then let set in refrigerator. (Overnight is okay) **NOTE: *For variations, use different flavors of frozen non-fat yogurt.***

WHIPPED CREAM

This recipe is accomplished quite well by simply reconstructing our cream minus the butterfat. Canned evaporated skim milk is a sweet and tasty product. It does not have the twang associated with evaporated whole milk. The flavor of butterfat is obtained by using a liquid butter flavor. Since the basic recipe contains 1/2 cup of evaporated skim milk and 4/10 of 1 gram of fat, the entire bowlful of whipped cream will contain only 4/10 of 1 gram of fat. A low-sugar version can be created by using artificial sweetener in place of sugar. However, it doesn't stay whipped as long. This whipped cream is so low in fat that you can generously ladle it onto your dessert and no one gets fat—and it tastes outrageous. ***NOTE: Guar gum can be purchased at most health food stores and will make your whipped cream stand tall, maintaining its stiff peaks for hours.***

BASIC WHIPPED CREAM DESSERT TOPPING

- 1 *teaspoon unflavored gelatin dissolved in*
- 3 *tablespoons of boiling water, then cooled*
- 1/2 *cup evaporated skim milk, chilled*
- 1/2 *tablespoon sugar* ***or*** *one packet artificial sweetener*
- 1/2 *teaspoon liquid butter flavor*

Combine and beat in a mixing bowl until cream holds its peak. Serve.

VARIATIONS OF WHIPPED CREAM:

BUTTER RUM CREAM
Add 1/2 teaspoon rum flavor

BRANDIED CREAM
Add 1/2 teaspoon brandy flavor

LEMON CREAM
Add 1/2 teaspoon lemon flavor

COCONUT BUTTER CREAM
Add 1/2 teaspoon coconut flavor

MOCHA CREAM
Add 1/2 teaspoon chocolate extract and 1/2 teaspoon instant coffee powder

SIMPLE WHIPPED CREAM TOPPING

- 3/4 *cup cold evaporated skimmed milk*
- 1/2 *cup no-fat milk powder*
- 1 *teaspoon lemon juice*
- 1 *teaspoon imitation butter flavoring*
- 1/2 *cup sugar*
- 1/2 *teaspoon guar gum*

Whip evaporated skimmed milk, milk powder, and guar gum until stiff; fold in lemon juice, butter flavoring and sugar. Serve cold. ※

NOTE: Milk powder and lemon juice can be eliminated and the recipe will more nearly resemble whipped cream. Modify the amount of butter flavor to suit your taste.

REALLY QUICK HOT CHOCOLATE SAUCE

Buy some chocolate-flavored syrup with no fat and heat it. ※

CHEESECAKE CREAM TOPPING

- 1 *teaspoon unflavored gelatin*
- 1/4 *cup sugar*
- 1/2 *cup hot water*
- 1 *teaspoon vanilla*
- 1 *cup no-fat sour cream*

Dissolve gelatin in hot water, then add sugar and dissolve, pour into mixing bowl and add sour cream and vanilla. Beat on high speed for 5 minutes. Chill and serve.

NOTE: ***Topping should be used fairly soon after beating as the gelatin tends to set up and it becomes firm.*** ※

XI.

SPECIAL FOODS

If you can't buy fat-free sour cream, then here is how to make your own. If your culture doesn't work, try another one.

FAT-FREE SOUR CREAM, CULTURED

MAKES TWO CUPS

- 1/2 *cup water*
- 12 *oz. can of evaporated non-fat milk*
- 1 *heaping teaspoon cultured "lite" sour cream (2 grams of fat per ounce or less)*

Combine and mix thoroughly in a glass bowl or large drinking glass. Cover with plastic wrap and set aside at room temperature for 24 hours. After 24 hours, if you have used sour cream with a living culture, your mixture should have the consistency of a very heavy, thick cream. If you have used a blend or heat-sterilized sour cream product containing a dead culture, then nothing will have happened and you'll have to find a different sour cream with a living culture. These cultures sometimes tend to grow in rope-like configurations and sometimes will appear stringy and goopy. Just stir briskly, thereby breaking down these strings. You now have essentially fat-free sour cream for use in most recipes.

The 12-oz. can of evaporated non-fat milk contains about 1.2 grams of fat, and the sour cream used as a culture contains about 1 gram of fat. That totals 2.2 grams per 2 cups or 1.1 grams of fat per cup.

NOTE: ***Two cups of reconstituted non-fat powdered milk may be used instead of canned milk and water. This will result in an even lower fat content and an equally good sour cream product.***

CREAM CHEESE

MAKES ABOUT EIGHT OUNCES OR ONE CUP
(This is an excellent cream cheese.)

- 1 *32-oz. container of fat-free yogurt*
- ~ *cheese cloth*
- ~ *tall plastic container with a press-on top*

In a bowl large enough to hold all of the yogurt, place cheese cloth at least 4 layers thick, allowing at least an extra 6 inches to lay over the side of the bowl. Spoon all of the yogurt into the cheese cloth, gather the cheese cloth around the top, and tie or twist at the top of the yogurt. Suspend yogurt inside plastic container at least 4 inches from the bottom so water may drain from yogurt. Allow to drain in refrigerator for at least 2 days. This cream cheese may be used in any recipe.

MOCK BLACK WALNUTS

- 1/4 *cup TVP®*
- 1 *tablespoon black walnut flavoring extract*

Combine, cover, and let sit for at least an hour. Use in recipes calling for black walnuts such as the brownies on page 242

NOTE: *For almonds, use almond flavoring extract.*

NOTE: *TVP® (Textured Vegetable Protein) can be purchased at most health food stores or from Harvest Direct at 1-800-8-FLAVOR.*

EPILOGUE

"It was a pleasant morning in September 1990. I had just completed a "routine" treadmill. The cardiologist called me into his office and stated matter-of-factly, "You are a walking time bomb. I would like you to check into the hospital this afternoon." Two days later the surgeon opened my chest and stitched in by-passes to six clogged arteries. ❧ That got my attention. Before my surgery my nutrition motto was "Life is uncertain... eat dessert first." And if I got the urge to exercise, I would lie down until it went away. Suddenly I became highly motivated to learn what food to put into my body to keep my arteries clear. I suddenly found the time to exercise, and I devoured every book I could find on exercise, nutrition and stress management. ❧ Within a few weeks I became more energetic, my endurance increased, I lost several pounds and even my mental capacity seemed sharper. At 60 years of age I felt 25 years younger. I became hooked on exercise and proper nutrition! ❧ In July 1992 I retired from 42 years of banking to open the Vital Life Center, which is dedicated to my new passion... helping people to stay well and feel great. I discovered Norm's first book, NO FAT PLEASE, while on vacation in Branson, Missouri, and I am making it "required reading" for my clients. It is chock-full of great recipes and common sense!"

GENE MILLEN, *President*
Vital Life Center
3184 Collins Drive
Merced, CA 95340

ACKNOWLEDGEMENTS & REFERENCES

Favorite Foods: No-Fat Cooking ***by Norman Rose sounds like I wrote the whole book. I would like to take full credit, but that would be foolish of me to do so. Several people, more than one professional association, various federal agencies, and the University of Kansas Medical Center have all contributed to this book.***

My thanks to Warren Walker for his strong editing that made sense out of a lot of varied thoughts in Chapter 3.

Chapter 5 is essentially a reprint of the National Institute of Health Publication *No. 89-2922 titled, "So You Have High Blood Cholesterol."*

Part of the information in Chapter 7, "Eating Out," was obtained from a Human Nutrition Information Service bulletin entitled "Eating Out."

Part of the information in Chapter 6, "Soy Bean and Soy Products - A Rich Source of Protein" was provided by ADM, Archer Daniels Midland Company, Decatur, Illinois, and is used with permission.

Part of the information in Chapter 9, "Venison", was provided by the New Zealand Farm Ranch Venison Council, Oakland, California, and is used with permission.

Thanks for the information provided in Chapter 10, by the American Bison Association, Denver, Colorado.

Other references include:

"The Triglyceride Issue: A View from Framingham," William P. Castelli, M.D. (American Heart Journal *112:432, 1986)*

"Joint Effects of Serum Triglyceride and LDL Cholesterol and HDL Cholesterol Concentration on Coronary Heart Disease Risk" in the Helsinki Heart Study, et al. (Circulation 1992; 85:37-45)

"Nutritive Value of Foods, USDA Home and Garden *Bulletin Number 72*

"Nutritive Value of American Food, Agriculture Handbook *Number 456*

"Composition of Foods," USDA Agriculture Handbook *Number 8*

"The Effect of Ethanol on Fat Storage in Healthy Subjects," by Paulo M. Suter, M.D., M.S., Yves Schutz, Ph.D., M.P.H., and Eric Jequier, M.D., New England Journal of Medicine, *Vol. 326, No. 15.*

COPYRIGHT & TRADEMARK ACKNOWLEDGMENTS

Krusteaz® is a registered trademark of Continental Mills, Inc.

Nabisco® and Egg Beaters® are registered trademarks of Nabisco, Inc.

*Betty Crocker® is a registered trademark of General Mills, Inc.
Used with permission.*

Jell-O® is a registered trademark of Kraft General Foods, Inc.

Kraft® and Free® are registered trademarks of Kraft General Foods, Inc.

Shake 'n Bake® is a registered trademark of Kraft General Foods, Inc.

*Simplesse® and Simple Pleasures® are registered trademarks of the
NutraSweet Company.*

*TVP®, Harvest Burger® and Midland Harvest® are registered trademarks of
Archer Daniels Midland Company.*

Lipton® and Golden Sauté™ are trademarks of Thomas J. Lipton, Inc.

Stove Top® is a registered trademark of Kraft General Foods, Inc.

Light & Lean® is a registered trademark of Geo. A. Hormel and Company.

Molly McButter® is a registered trademark of Alberto-Culver Company.

Butter Buds® is a registered trademark of Cumberland Packing Corporation.

Hunt's® is a registered trademark of Hunt-Wesson, Inc.

Grape-Nuts® is a registered trademark of Kraft General Foods, Inc.

Promise® is a registered trademark of Van Den Bergh Foods Company.

Healthy Choice® is a registered trademark of Con Agra.

*Wondra® and Gold Medal® are registered trademarks of General Mills, Inc.
Used with permission.*

Land O'Lakes® is a registered trademark of Land O'Lakes®, Inc.

APPENDIX

FAT CONTENT OF COMMON FOODS

ITEM	GRAMS OF FAT
[A]	
Almonds: whole, 1 ounce	15
Angel food cake: 1 piece	trace
Apple: 1 apple	trace
Apple juice: 1 cup	trace
Applesauce: 1 cup	trace
Apricots: 3 apricots	trace
Apricot nectar: 1 cup	trace
Artichoke: globe or French, 1 artichoke	trace
Asparagus: 4 spears	trace
Avocado: California, whole, 1 avocado	30
[B]	
Bacon: Canadian, cooked, 2 slices	4
Bacon: turkey, cooked crisp, 2 slices	1
Bacon: cooked, 3 medium slices	9
Bagel: water, 3½ inch diameter, 1 bagel	1
Baking powder: 1 teaspoon	0
Baking soda: 1 teaspoon	0
Banana: 1 banana	1
Barbecue sauce: 1 tablespoon	trace
Beans: chick pea, garbanzos, 1 cup	4
Beans: Pork 'n Beans, 1 cup	7
Beans: kidney, 1 cup	1
Beans: lentils, 1 cup	1
Beans: lima, 1 cup	1
Beans: pinto, 1 cup	1
Beans: black-eyed peas, 1 cup	1
Beans: green, 1 cup	trace
Beans: white, navy, great northern, 1 cup	1
Beans: yellow, 1 cup	trace
Beef: dried, 2.5 ounces	4
Beef: ground patty, regular, broiled, 3 ounces	18
Beef: ground, Healthy Choice® extra lean, 1 ounce	1
Beef: roast, relatively lean such as eye of round, baked lean only 2.6 ounces	5
Beef: steak, sirloin, broiled, lean only, 2.5 ounces	6

ITEM	GRAMS OF FAT
Beef: chuck blade, cooked, lean only, 3 ounces	13
Beer: 1 glass	0
Beets: 1 cup	trace
Biscuit: from mix, 1 biscuit	3
Biscuit: from home recipe, 1 biscuit	5
Blackberries: raw, 1 cup	1
Bologna: 1 ounce slice. 2 slices	16
Bouillon cube: 1 teaspoon	trace to 1 gram (check label)
Braunschweiger (liver sausage): 1 ounce per slice, 2 slices	18
Bread: Boston brown, 1 slice	1
Bread: cracked wheat, 1 slice	1
Bread: commercial French or Italian with oil added, 1 slice	1
Bread: regular French or Italian, no oil added, 1 slice	trace
Bread: mixed grain, 1 slice	1
Bread: pita, 1 pita	1
Bread: wheat bread, enriched with oil added, 1 piece	1
Bread: wheat bread, enriched, no oil added, 1 piece	trace
Bread: whole wheat, enriched, oil added, 1 slice	1
Broccoli: cooked, 1 cup	trace
Brussels sprouts: cooked, 1 cup	1
Buffalo, 1 oz. lean, broiled	less than 1
Butter: 1 tablespoon	11
Buttermilk: 1 cup	2
Buttermilk: from skimmed milk, 1 cup	1/4

[C]

ITEM	GRAMS OF FAT
Cabbage: raw, 1 cup	trace
Cake: angel food, 1 piece	trace
Cake: regular coffee cake, crumb, 1 piece	7
Cake: regular devil's food, 1 piece	8
Cake: regular carrot, with cream cheese frosting, 1 piece	21
Cake: regular yellow with chocolate frosting, 1 piece	8
Candy: caramels, plain or chocolate, 1 ounce	3
Candy: chocolate, milk, 1 ounce	9
Candy: gum drops	trace
Candy: jelly beans, 1 ounce	trace
Candy: marshmallows, 1 ounce	0
Candy: candy corn	0
Cantaloupe: 1/2 melon	1
Carbonated beverage: all	0
Carrot: raw, 1 cup	trace
Cashew: dry roasted, 1 cup	63

ITEM	GRAMS OF FAT
Catfish: raw, 1 ounce	1
Cauliflower: raw, 1 cup	trace
Celery: raw, 1 cup	trace
Cereal: oatmeal, regular, 1 cup	2
Cereal: corn flakes, 1 ounce	trace
Cereal: 40% Bran Flakes, 1 ounce	trace
Cereal: Grape-Nuts, 1 ounce	trace
Cereal: Raisin Bran, 1 ounce	1
Cereal: Frosted Flakes, 1 ounce	trace
Cereal: Shredded Wheat, 1 ounce	1
Cereal: wheat flakes	trace
Cheese: blue, 1 ounce	8
Cheese: cheddar, 1 ounce	9
Cheese: cottage, creamed, large curd, 1 cup	10
Cheese: cream, 1 ounce	10
Cheese: Feta, 1 ounce	6
Cheese: Mozzarella, whole milk, 1 ounce	6
Cheese: Mozzarella, part skim milk, 1 ounce	5
Cheese: Muenster, 1 ounce	9
Cheese: Parmesan, 1 ounce	9
Cheese: Provolone, 1 ounce	8
Cheese: Ricotta, part skim, 1 cup	19
Cheese: Swiss, 1 ounce	8
Cheese: processed American, 1 ounce	9
Cherries: sour, pitted, 1 cup	trace
Chicken: fried with skin, batter dipped, breast, 4.9 ounces	18
Chicken: fried flour-coated, breast, skinless, 3.5 ounces	9
drumstick, 1.7 ounces	7
Chicken: roasted, breast, 3 ounces	3
drumstick, 1.6 ounces	2
Chicken: liver, cooked, 1 liver	1
Chick peas: (see beans)	
Chocolate: baking, 1 ounce	15
Chocolate: pudding, with nonfat milk	0
Clams: raw, meat only, 3 ounces	1
Cocoa: powder, 1 ounce	trace
Cocoa mix: with nonfat dry milk	1
Cookie: chocolate chip, 4 cookies	9
Cookie: fig bar, 4 cookies	4
Cookie: oatmeal with raisins, 4 cookies	10
Cookie: peanut butter, 4 cookies	14
Cookie: sandwich type, 4 cookies	8

ITEM	GRAMS OF FAT
Cookie: vanilla wafer, 10 cookies	7
Corn: chips, 1 ounce	9
Corn: sweet, 1 ear	1
Corn: canned, 1 cup	1
Corned beef: (see beef)	
Corn starch: 1 tablespoon	0
Cottage cheese: (see cheese)	
Crab: crab meat, canned, 1 cup	3
Crackers: cheese, 10 crackers	3
Crackers: graham, 2 crackers	3
Crackers: melba toast, 1 piece	trace
Crackers: saltines, 4 crackers	1
Crackers: wheat, thin, 4 crackers	1
Cranberry juice: cocktail, 1 cup	trace
Cranberry sauce: 1 cup	trace
Cream: half & half, 1 tablespoon	2
Cream: heavy, 1 tablespoon	6
Cream: our dessert cream, page 250	0
Cream: sour, 1 tablespoon	3
Cream: extra light sour cream, 1 tablespoon	1
Creamer: dry, 1 teaspoon	1
Cucumbers: 8 slices	trace

[D]

ITEM	GRAMS OF FAT
Dates: chopped, 1 cup	1
Dessert topping: whipped cream, 1 tablespoon	1
Doughnut: cake, 1 doughnut	12
Doughnut: yeast, 1 doughnut	13
Duck: roasted, meat only, 1/2 duck	25

[E]

ITEM	GRAMS OF FAT
Egg: fresh, large, whole, 1 egg	6
Egg: whites, large	0
Egg: yolks, large	6
Egg substitute: Egg Beaters®	0
Eggplant: cooked, steamed, 1 cup	1
English muffin: 1 muffin	1

[F]

ITEM	GRAMS OF FAT
Fig: dried, 10 figs	2
Fish: (see flounder, sole, haddock, herring, salmon, sardines, trout, tuna)	
Fish sticks: 1 stick	3
Flounder: baked	1
Flour: white, 1 cup	1

ITEM	GRAMS OF FAT
Flour: whole wheat, 1 cup	2.5
Frankfurter: beef, cooked, 1 frank	13
Frankfurter: Hormel, Light & Lean®, 1 frank	1
Frosting mix: Betty Crocker®, fluffy white, 1 package	0
Fruit cocktail: 1 cup	trace

[G]

Garbanzos: (see beans)	
Gelatin: flavored, 1 package	trace
Gelatin: unflavored, 1 package	trace
Gin: 1 ounce	0
Grapes: 10 grapes	trace
Grapefruit: raw, 1/2 grapefruit	trace
Grapefruit juice: raw, 1 cup	trace
Greens: spinach, mustard, 1 cup	trace

[H]

Haddock: raw, 1 ounce	0.1
Halibut: raw, 1 ounce	0.1
Ham: (see pork)	
Hamburger: (see beef)	
Herring: pickled, 3 ounces	13
Honey: 1 cup	0
Honeydew: 1/10 melon	trace
Horseradish: 1 cup	trace

[I]

Ice cream: regular, 1 cup	14
Ice cream: frozen custard, 1 cup	23
Ice cream: nonfat yogurt	trace
Ice cream: Simple Pleasures®, 4 fluid ounces	less than 1
Ice milk: 1 cup	6
Jelly: 1 tablespoon	trace

[L]

Lamb: chops, cooked, lean only, 1.7 ounces	7
Lamb: leg roasted, lean only, 2.6 ounces	6
Lard: 1 tablespoon	13
Lemon: 1 cup	trace
Lemonade: 1 cup	trace
Lentils: (see beans)	
Lettuce: 1 head	trace
Liquor: (see gin, bourbon, rum, vodka)	
Liver: beef, 3 ounces	3.3

ITEM	GRAMS OF FAT
Lobster: 1 cup	2
Luncheon meat: spiced, canned, 2 slices	13
Luncheon meat: chopped ham, 2 slices	7
Luncheon meat: cooked ham, regular	6

[M]

Macaroni: elbow, enriched, 1 cup	1
Margarine: regular, 1 tablespoon	11
Margarine: soft	11
Margarine: diet "lite"	6
Margarine: Promise® ultra non-fat	0
Milk: whole, 3.3% fat, 1 cup	8
Milk: 2 %, 1 cup	5
Milk: 1 %, 1 cup	3
Milk: canned, condensed, skim milk, 1 cup	1
Milk: canned, condensed, whole milk, 1 cup	19
Milk: dried, nonfat, 1 cup	trace
Molasses: 1 cup	0
Mushrooms: 2 tablespoons	0
Mustard: prepared, 1 teaspoon	trace

[N]

Nectarine: 1 nectarine	1
Noodles: egg noodles, cooked, 1 cup	2
Noodles: chow mein, canned, 1 cup	11

[O]

Oil: corn, 1 tablespoon	14
Oil: olive, 1 tablespoon	14
Oil: peanut, 1 tablespoon	14
Oil: safflower, 1 tablespoon	14
Oil: soybean, 1 tablespoon	14
Okra: 8 pods	trace
Olives: green, 4 medium	2
Olives: ripe, 2 large	2
Onions: raw, 1 cup	trace
Orange: raw, 1 orange	trace
Orange juice: raw, 1 cup	trace
Oysters: raw, meat only, 1 cup	4

[P]

Pancake: buckwheat from mix, egg & milk added, 1 pancake	2
Pancake: plain, home recipe, 1 pancake	2
Peach: raw, 1 peach	trace

ITEM	GRAMS OF FAT
Peanut butter: 1 tablespoon	8
Peanuts: roasted in oil, 1 ounce	14
Pears: 1 pear, raw	trace
Peas: edible pod, cooked, 1 cup	trace
Peas: green, frozen, cooked, 1 cup	trace
Pecans: pieces, 1 tablespoon	5
Pepper: green, 1 pepper	trace
Pickle: dill, 1 pickle	trace
Pickle: sweet, 1 pickle	trace
Pie: apple, 1 piece	18
Pie: creme, 1 piece	23
Pie: pecan, 1 piece	32
Pineapple: raw, 1 cup	trace
Plum: raw, 1 plum	trace
Popcorn: air popped, 1 cup	trace
Pork: fresh, chop, broiled, lean only, 2.5 ounces	8
pan fried	11
Pork: shoulder, braised, lean only, 2.4 ounces	8
Pork: sausage, 3 ounces	22
Potato chips: 10 chips	7
Potatoes: baked, 1 potato	trace
Potatoes: French fried in oil, 10 strips	8
Potatoes: Shake 'n Bake® oven-cooked, 10 strips	1
Pretzels: made with enriched flour, 2 1/4 inch long, 10 pretzels	trace
Pudding mix: with whole milk, 1/2 cup	4
with nonfat milk, 1/2 cup	0
Pumpkin: cooked, 1 cup	trace

[R]

ITEM	GRAMS OF FAT
Raisins: 1 cup	1
Raspberries: raw, 1 cup	1
Rhubarb: cooked, 1 cup	trace
Rice: brown, cooked, 1 cup	1
Rice: white, instant, 1 cup	0
Roll: dinner, commercial, 1 roll	2
Roll: hot dog or hamburger, commercial, 1 roll	2
Rum: 1 ounce	0

[S]

ITEM	GRAMS OF FAT
Salad dressing: commercial,	
Blue cheese, 1 tablespoon	8
French, 1 tablespoon	9
Italian, 1 tablespoon	9

ITEM	GRAMS OF FAT
Salad dressing: fat-free dressings	0
Salad dressing: Mayonnaise, regular, 1 tablespoon	11
Salad dressing: Mayonnaise, fat-free, 1 tablespoon	0
Salami: cooked, 2 ounces	11
Salmon: canned, 3 ounces	5
Salmon: smoked, 3 ounces	8
Salt: 1 cup	0
Sardines: canned in oil, 3 ounces	9
Sauerkraut: canned, 1 cup	trace
Scallops: breaded, fried, 6 scallops	10
steamed, fresh, 1 ounce	1/2
Sherbet: 1 cup	4
Shortening: 1 tablespoon	13
Shrimp: canned, 3 ounces	1
Sole: raw, 1 ounce	.2
Soup: clam chowder, 1 cup	7
Soup: cream of mushroom, 1 cup	14
Soup: chicken noodle, 1 cup	2
Soup: vegetable beef, 1 cup	2
Sour cream: (see cream)	
Soy sauce: 1 tablespoon	0
Soy beans: dry, cooked, drained, 1 cup	10
Soy product: miso, 1 cup	13
Soy product: tofu, piece $2\frac{1}{2}$ by $2\frac{3}{4}$ by 1 inch, 1 piece	5
Spaghetti: no sauce, 1 cup	1
Spaghetti: tomato & cheese sauce, 1 cup	9
Spinach: raw, 1 cup	trace
Squash: raw, 1 cup	1
Steak: (see beef)	
Strawberries: raw, 1 cup	1
Sugar: granulated, brown or powdered, 1 cup	0
Sunflower seeds: hulled, 1 ounce	14
Syrup: cane or maple, 1 tablespoon	0

[T]

ITEM	GRAMS OF FAT
Taco shell: baked, no oil	trace
Tangerine: 1 tangerine	trace
Tapioca: pudding, 5 ounces	5
Tartar sauce: regular, 1 tablespoon	8
Tartar sauce: with fat-free Mayonnaise, 1 Tablespoon	0
Tofu: (see soy product)	
Tomatoes: raw, 1 tomato	trace
Tomato ketchup: 1 cup	trace

ITEM	GRAMS OF FAT
Tomato juice: 1 cup	trace
Tomato sauce: 1 cup	trace
Tortilla: corn, uncooked, 1 tortilla	trace
Tortilla: flour, with shortening, 1 ten-inch	3
Tuna: oil pack, 3 ounces	7
Tuna: water pack, 3 ounces	1
Turkey: ham, 2 ounces	3
Turkey: breast, no skin, 1 ounce	1
Turkey: dark meat, no skin, 1 ounce	1.5
Turnip greens: raw, 1 cup	trace
Turnips: cooked, 1 cup	trace

[V]

ITEM	GRAMS OF FAT
Veal: cutlet, broiled, 3 ounces	9
Veal: rib, roasted, 3 ounces	14
Venison, 1 oz., lean only, broiled	less than 1
Vodka: 1 ounce	0
Vinegar: 1 ounce	0

[W]

ITEM	GRAMS OF FAT
Waffle: home recipe, 1 waffle	13
Waffle: fat-free, 1 waffle	0
Walnuts: English, 1 cup	74
Water chestnuts: canned, 1 cup	trace
Watermelon: 1 cup	less than 1
Whiskey: 1 ounce	0
Wiener: (see frankfurter)	
Wine: all kinds, 1 ounce	0
Worcestershire sauce: 1 tablespoon	0

[Y]

ITEM	GRAMS OF FAT
Yeast: 1 packet	trace
Yogurt: made with whole milk, 8 ounces	7
Yogurt: nonfat	0
Yogurt: low-fat, plain, 8 ounces	4

Source: United States Department of Agriculture and individual manufacturers,label information.

NOTE: For a more complete nutrition analysis order the U.S. Dept. of Agriculture Home and Garden Bulletin number 72 titled "Nutritive Values of Foods."
Send $2.75 to:
U.S. GOVERNMENT BOOK STORE
PUEBLO, COLORADO 81009

INDEX OF RECIPES

I. APPETIZERS

II. SOUPS & SALADS

III. MEAT AND POULTRY

IV. FISH AND SHELLFISH

V. POTATOES, RICE, PASTA & DRIED BEANS

POTATOES

RICE

PASTA

DRIED BEANS

VI. SAUCES

VII. SANDWICHES, TACOS, BURRITOS AND PIZZA

VIII. VEGETABLES

IX. BREAD

X. DESSERTS

COOKIES

FROSTINGS

XI. SPECIAL FOODS

YOUR FAVORITE RECIPES

YOUR FAVORITE RECIPES

ABOUT THE AUTHOR

Some say a rocket scientist? ❀ Norman Rose is a former electronic engineer who worked primarily on the U.S. effort to develop its guided missile program during the 1950s and 1960s. ❀ From 1957 to 1967 he was attached to the U.S. Navy at White Sands Missile Range as a technical representative for the Bendix Corporation. He participated in the research and development of the "Talos" ship-to-air guided missile. As a high school senior he test-fired his own liquid fuel rocket engine. ❀ At the tender age of eleven, Norman found himself in a cook-for-yourself-or-do-without situation. As a child of the great depression he quickly learned to cook and has been doing so ever since. ❀ As an engineer, research, and development specialist, restaurateur, teacher, lecturer, and documentary producer, Norman has now taken on the task of promoting the necessity of fat-free cooking. ❀ His first book, No Fat Please, has been labeled one of America's best-selling underground books, primarily because of word-of-mouth sales from across the country. It has been used as a textbook on fat-free cooking of regular food for regular people. ❀ To inquire about having Norman Rose bring his inspiring and informative message/classes about no-fat cooking to your school, convention, or association, call or write:

WRS SPEAKERS BUREAU
P. O. Box 21207
Waco, TX 76702-1207
Phone: (800) 299-3366
Fax: (817) 757-1454

A MESSAGE FROM THE PUBLISHER

W. R. Spence, M.D.
Publisher

When a sportswriter says a baseball player is a "real hustler," that usually means that the guy can't hit. But when a publisher tells a bookseller that an author is a real hustler, that's the ultimate compliment. Norman Rose is a real hustler who can also communicate. He has taken his message of fun, good-tasting, low-fat food preparation to thousands of people, one on one, and this book enables him to hustle even more by sharing his message with countless readers whom he will never meet personally.

At WRS Publishing, we are only interested in producing books that we can be proud of—books that focus on people and/or issues that enlighten and inspire, books that change lives for the better. **Call us toll-free at 1-800-299-3366 for suggestions or for a free book catalog.**

WATCH FOR THESE OTHER WRS TITLES:

LIFE ISN'T WEIGHED ON THE BATHROOM SCALES Laura Rose contradicts the message that fat women are unworthy and helps them to love the bodies that they have hated for so many years—their own! Offers a message of love and empowerment from a spiritual perspective.

FAMILY FRIENDLY CHILDCARE Choosing childcare is one of the most important decisions a parent ever makes, and trial-and-error methods pose obvious risks. This book is a helpful, sensible, and organized approach from an author with over thirty years' experience in childcare.

LOST AND FOUND A hard-hitting, true story about a strong woman who copes with the death of her husband. Poignantly and beautifully written, this book takes the reader on a journey through grief—a journey we must all take at some time in our lives.

WRS
PUBLISHING
A Division of WRS Group, Inc.
Waco, Texas